HAROLD WILSON

HAROLD WILSON

The Unprincipled Prime Minister?

—REAPPRAISING HAROLD WILSON—

EDITED BY
Andrew S. Crines & Kevin Hickson

Biteback Publishing

First published in Great Britain in 2016 by
Biteback Publishing Ltd
Westminster Tower
3 Albert Embankment
London SE1 7SP
Selection and editorial apparatus copyright © Andrew S. Crines and Kevin Hickson 2016

ISBN 978-1-78590-031-0

10 9 8 7 6 5 4 3 2 1

A CIP catalogue record for this book is available from the British Library.

Set in Bulmer and Gotham by Adrian McLaughlin

Printed and bound in Great Britain by
CPI Group (UK) Ltd, Croydon CR0 4YY

MIX
Paper from
responsible sources
FSC
www.fsc.org   FSC® C020471

CONTENTS

ACKNOWLEDGEMENTS

WE WOULD LIKE to thank, first and foremost, the contributors who generously gave up their time to write for this book. In addition, we are especially grateful to George Howarth MP for hosting its launch in the House of Commons on 23 March 2016.

Our aim was to complete the book in time for the triple anniversaries of Harold Wilson's birth (100 years), his greatest electoral victory (fifty years) and his dramatic retirement as Prime Minister (forty years). This would not have been possible without the enthusiastic support of our publishers, Biteback, and we are extremely grateful to them for all the support we have been given.

This will be the first in what we hope will become a series of books reappraising former Prime Ministers and coinciding with significant anniversaries. The next book, already commissioned, will be a reappraisal of John Major's premiership, due to be published in 2017.

Andrew Crines would also like to thank his mother for being a constant source of inspiration and support up until she passed away in 2012. Her memory continues to inspire. I would like to thank my father for the political discussions, and my brother for the help and support given to me over the years. My thanks go to Richard Hayton and Timothy Heppell for being there to kick me into shape when needed, and also to John Isles and Carl Bowler. Finally, thanks to the people of Huddersfield, birthplace and home to Harold Wilson. It is a town that has touched many, and that will continue to do so over the coming years.

Kevin Hickson would like to thank his family. My dad was a keen supporter of Harold Wilson. When I started reading the biographies of Gaitskellite ministers who had served under Wilson I could not see why he was, as these books were frequently scathing of Wilson both personally and politically. In the course of this project I have come to acquire a new respect for Harold Wilson and to view those more critical voices more sceptically.

NOTES ON CONTRIBUTORS

David Coates holds the Worrell Chair in Anglo-American Studies at Wake Forest University, having previously held chairs at the universities of Leeds and Manchester. He has written a number of books on Labour Party politics, including *Prolonged Labour* (2005).

Andrew S. Crines is lecturer in British politics at the University of Liverpool, having previously taught at the universities of Leeds and Huddersfield. He has published extensively on British politics and specialises in the politics of rhetoric and oratory. He tweets at @AndrewCrines.

Theodore Dalrymple is a retired prison doctor and psychiatrist who now writes for several national newspapers, as well as for *The Spectator* and the *Salisbury Review*. He is the author of several books on British culture.

Peter Dorey is professor of British politics at the University of Cardiff and has specialised in British politics since 1945. His extensive list of publications includes (ed.) *The Labour Governments, 1964–70* (2006) and *The Labour Party and Constitutional Reform: A History of Constitutional Conservatism* (2008).

Mark Garnett is senior lecturer in politics at the University of Lancaster, where he teaches and researches British politics and contemporary political history, especially in relation to the Conservative Party and think tanks.

Kevin Hickson is senior lecturer in British politics at the University of Liverpool, where he has taught since 2003. He specialises in British political ideologies and has published on the political thought of the Conservatives, Labour and the Liberals/Liberal Democrats.

George Howarth is Labour MP for Knowsley, Merseyside, having first been elected to Parliament in 1986. He was previously a Labour councillor and deputy leader of Knowsley Borough Council.

Kevin Jefferys recently retired as professor of contemporary history at Plymouth University and is the author of a dozen books including *Anthony Crosland* (1999) and *Politics and the People* (2007). *Sport and Politics in Modern Britain: The Road to 2012* (2012) was winner of the 2013 Lord Aberdare Book Prize for sports history.

Sir Gerald Kaufman MP is the current Father of the House of Commons, having been first elected in 1970. He was previously a journalist and, from 1965 to 1970, was Harold Wilson's press liaison officer.

Dennis Kavanagh is emeritus professor at the University of Liverpool and a recognised authority on British politics. He has published extensively, including as co-author of every Nuffield study of every general election since February 1974, and on the office of Prime Minister.

Jane Martin is professor of social history of education and head of the department of education and social justice at the University of Birmingham. She has published widely on educational development in Britain and is currently conducting research on Caroline Benn and the campaign for comprehensive education funded by the British Academy/Leverhulme Trust.

Shaun McDaid is a research fellow in the centre for research in social sciences at the University of Huddersfield. He is the author of *Template for Peace: Northern Ireland, 1972–75* (2013).

Catherine McGlynn is senior lecturer in politics at the University of Huddersfield, where she teaches and researches on conflict resolution and identity politics. She has published widely on the politics of Northern Ireland.

Jasper Miles is a PhD student at the University of Liverpool, researching 'the Labour Party and Electoral Reform'. His research interests include the wider debates on constitutional reform in the United Kingdom and political ideologies in Britain. He teaches on both the 'British Politics' and 'Foundations in Politics' modules at the University of Liverpool.

David S. Moon is lecturer in politics at the University of Bath. His publications cover devolution in the UK, the Labour Party, and political ideologies, rhetoric and oratory.

Kenneth O. Morgan is a Labour peer, a Fellow of the British Academy and former vice-chancellor of the University of Wales. His thirty-five books include biographies of David Lloyd George (1974), Keir Hardie (1975), James Callaghan (1997) and Michael Foot (2007); *Labour in Power 1945–51* (1984) and *Labour People* (1987).

Jeremy Nuttall is senior lecturer in modern British history at the University of Kingston. His monograph is *Psychological Socialism: The Labour Party and Qualities of Mind and Character, 1931 to the Present* (2006).

Robert M. Page is reader in democratic socialism and social policy at the University of Birmingham and specialises in British socialism and social policy in historical and contemporary perspectives.

Gillian Peele is fellow and tutor in politics at Lady Margaret Hall and associate professor of politics in the department of politics and international relations at the University of Oxford, where she specialises in comparative UK and US politics. She has published widely, including works such as the *Developments in British Politics* and *Developments in American Politics* series, designed to make politics more accessible to a larger audience.

David (Lord) Steel is a Liberal Democrat peer and former leader of the Liberal Party, first elected to Parliament in 1965. He was also a Member and first presiding officer of the Scottish Parliament. His memoirs were published as *Against Goliath: David Steel's Story* (1989).

Robert Taylor was employment editor for the *Financial Times* and has written extensively on trade unions, including *The Trade Union Question in British Politics: Government and the Unions since 1945* (1993) and *The TUC: From the General Strike to the New Unionism* (2000).

Jim Tomlinson is professor of economic and social history at the University of Glasgow. He has written histories of the economic policies of both the Attlee and 1960s Wilson governments. He is currently writing *Managing the Economy, Managing the People: Narratives of Economic Life in Post-War Britain*.

Rhiannon Vickers is a senior lecturer at the University of Sheffield. She has published widely on the Labour Party's foreign policy, including the two-volume study *The Labour Party and the World* (2004 and 2011) on the Labour Party's foreign policy since its formation.

Tom Watson is deputy leader of the Labour Party and has been the MP for West Bromwich East since 2001. His book *Dial M for Murdoch* on the phone-hacking scandal was published in 2012.

PREFACE

Sir Gerald Kaufman MP

I WORKED FOR HAROLD Wilson at 10 Downing Street for five years. I was part of his innermost circle, spending time with him in his study or the office of his personal secretary, Marcia Williams. It was a lot of time, for he was very demanding. He would expect my presence for long hours every day, and that might be for seven days a week, because he expected those close to him to be available when he needed them.

I travelled with him. I went with him to his Huyton constituency, which he visited frequently, for he was a conscientious MP, holding surgeries at weekends. I stayed with him first at the Adelphi Hotel in Liverpool and then, when he decided he wanted somewhere cheaper (for he watched his pennies, going to sales at Lewis's department store opposite the Adelphi), at the Golden Eagle Hotel in Kirkby.

In Britain he travelled by car or by train, and had a penchant for saving hotel money by travelling in trains' sleeper-cars. I went with him to political events all over Britain. I travelled with him throughout the 1966 general election, which he won by a very large majority.

I went with him abroad. I accompanied him on visits to the United States, where I joined him at the White House for lunch with Lyndon B. Johnson, with chats afterwards in the President's private apartments. I went with him to Africa, to Nigeria and Ethiopia, where we visited Emperor Haile Selassie in his palace in Addis Ababa. I stayed with him in a battleship in Gibraltar harbour on which he conducted talks in an attempt, unsuccessful, to do a deal with Ian Smith to end the illegal secession of Southern Rhodesia.

He was a demanding boss, but he was a very nice person, one of the nicest politicians I have ever known. If you were part of his inner circle, that meant that he shared his leisure time with you, inviting you to eat with him in the No. 10 kitchen, one of his favourite haunts, where he would also hold confidential meetings. He would invite you to accompany him to the theatre (I attended the premiere of *Evita* with him) and the cinema.

He was a very even-tempered man. Only once did I see him fly into a rage, after his defeat in the 1970 election, when, for no discernible reason, he suddenly flew into a momentary rage in sheer frustration at having lost. He could be very funny, both in personal conversation and in speeches. He was by far the funniest orator of all the Prime Ministers I have known and experienced.

He was a wonderful public speaker, way above any other Prime Minister of my political lifetime. He could prepare humorous passages, but he was also an attractive extempore wit. He wrote his own speeches, sitting in a room with his close staff and dictating to a succession of shorthand typists. The drafts would be studied by his close staff, who sat with him and had freedom to interrupt. When a move to oust him was made by Cecil King, boss of the powerful Mirror Group, he was preparing a speech for a Labour Party May-Day rally at the Royal Festival Hall. As he was dictating, he was interrupted by Marcia who, referring to King, said: 'Do you know what's going on?' He retorted, 'I know that I'm going on.' 'Put it in your speech,' I urged. He did, and it brought the house down.

At an election meeting in a 1966 campaign, he addressed a public meeting in a large hall – for he spoke at meetings to which any member of the public could come – and a baby started crying. The mother rose to take the baby out. Harold called out: 'Don't leave. This meeting is about his future.'

He was kind and considerate. Preparing a government reshuffle on one occasion, he was planning to sack a junior minister, Charlie [Charles] Loughlin. Then he heard that Charlie has been bereaved, and that was the end of the sacking. He used to discuss his reshuffles with his close staff, listening to our suggestions. But if he planned to appoint someone who he knew was not to his staff's liking, he kept it from us. He was amenable and sociable, but he was his own man.

He was a masterly tactician and a man of high principle. I was with him when he got a call from President Johnson, demanding that Britain send troops to Vietnam – 'even a band of bagpipers'. He refused, and never got credit for it. When there was a move by some Cabinet ministers, including Denis Healey and George Brown, to end the ban on arms sales to apartheid South Africa, he got me to organise a parliamentary early day motion, drafted by Alex Lyon, MP for York, which was signed by a large number of Labour MPs opposing the lifting of the ban. That was the end of that.

There are no politicians around today who come up to his ankles. One of the greatest privileges of my life was to work for him and to know him well.

FOREWORD

George Howarth MP

I GREW UP IN Huyton during the period that Harold Wilson was not only my local MP but was also the dominant political figure in the UK. I first got to know him as a young Labour Party activist during the two 1974 general elections, in which I acted as a deputy to his agent, Arthur Smith. Later, in the post-prime ministerial phase of his career, I was chair of his Constituency Labour Party and had a little more contact with him in that role.

It is worth pointing out that I do not come to this as an objective commentator. Harold very much dominated the political soundtrack of my early life and, as such, is a political hero. Given that 2016 is the centenary of Harold's birth, it is timely that his role in British politics is re-evaluated. This publication is a valuable contribution to that process.

The contributors to this work examine in some detail the social, political, economic, ideological and personal impact of his political life, together with the climate in the UK during his time as Prime Minister, the way in which these factors affected policy and how he is currently viewed from different critical vantage points on the political spectrum.

Harold's personal qualities are well documented. He had a formidable intellect, which is reflected in the outstanding degree he was awarded in philosophy, politics and economics (PPE) at Oxford. His extraordinary memory was awesome to experience at first hand. For example, during the two 1974 elections, accompanying him on visits to party members and constituents, I was daunted by his recall. He could remember names and details of people's lives with unerring accuracy – a quality not to be underestimated in politics.

Harold's quick wit is the source of many stories about parliamentary exchanges with opponents and dealing with hecklers. One instance occurred at a public meeting locally during the 1970 general election. After an introductory speech from Harold, the meeting was opened up for questions from the audience. The first involved a question about why, having ruled out abolishing grammar schools 'over his dead body' (as he had said in 1966), he was now proposing to do so. Taking a draw on his trademark pipe, Harold responded with the words, 'Friend, you're showing a morbid curiosity with my corpse.' The great amusement of most of those at the meeting was demonstrably not shared by the man concerned who asked the question – he was furious.

The political and economic times of Harold's prime ministerial life were both complicated and unprecedented. His contemporaries in his Labour Cabinets were for the most part political giants, who had, following the Second World War, a mission to create a new economic and social settlement – in terms of health provision, building new homes, setting up a social security safety net and harnessing the 'white heat of technology' to create an efficient and modern economy. It was in many ways the logical extension of the Attlee government's progressive reforming approach.

Denis Healey, Anthony Crosland, Jim Callaghan, Roy Jenkins and Barbara Castle could all lay claim to being a credible party leader and Prime Minister.

Consequently, there were powerful rivalries within the Wilson Cabinets between those who measured their abilities and commitment against each other and Harold Wilson himself. He very much embodied the constitutional principle that the Prime Minister is *primus inter pares* (first among equals) but, having to deal constantly with the visceral political climate that went with such titanic clashes of ego, he always managed, for most of his time as leader, to stay a step ahead.

It was, too, a time of economic instability and change, plagued by inflationary pressures, currency volatility, balance of payments crises and industrial unrest. Harold was to all intents and purposes a Keynesian Social Democrat with a strong belief in modernising an economy emerging from its post-colonial past and struggling to move into an industrial future based on new scientific and techno-logical advances. The post-war settlement, which had established state planning and a mixed economy as a given, was also becoming less a matter of consensus. In January 1970, Ted Heath met with his shadow Cabinet at the Selsdon Park Hotel, during the course of which the outlines of a more aggressive economic approach began to emerge based on more classical market economics. This was a harbinger of the break-up of the consensus that, as the 1970s progressed, devel-oped into a seemingly irreparable breech with the advent of Margaret Thatcher.

Labour's response was not altogether harmonious. Trade unions resented government interference in collective bargaining. Tony Benn and others in the 1970s adopted an 'alternative economic strategy', involving greater industrial intervention, planning and protectionism. At the same time, more moderate forces – led by Roy Jenkins – edged ever-closer to Labour's exit door.

Similarly, the Common Market became an equally divisive issue for the Labour Party. Some, such as Peter Shore, saw it as an unwelcome break with Commonwealth trade and the special relationship with the US. Others, particularly Tony Benn, argued that the founding document of the Com-mon Market, the Treaty of Rome, was an insurmountable barrier to the establishment of a more socialist Britain. Much of the so-called moderate wing of the party, led by Roy Jenkins, were passionately pro-European and saw it in idealistic terms as a future guarantee against the sort of European divisions that had already led to two hugely damaging European wars in the twentieth century. Ted Heath shared their European idealism.

Harold, in holding the ring between the different factions in the Labour Party, and by means of an in–out referendum, managed to keep the party more or less together (a model which David Cameron is at present trying to emulate), but not without cost to his reputation, at least for the short term.

In reputational terms, Harold was accused at the time of manoeuvring for party political advantage and in the service of his own survival by suspending Cabinet collective responsibility for the referendum. However, by carrying out a renegotiation on the British contribution and successfully securing a decisive 'yes' vote in the 1975 referendum, he was able to at least defer an unbridgeable split in the party, which could easily have led to the centre-left splitting altogether, and also have led to an ignominious withdrawal from a project the country had only recently joined. All of which would have had damaging consequences for the country's international standing.

Locally, people who remember Harold, often unprompted, consistently make two points about him that reflect more honourably on his reputation. First, they invariably cite an example of how, as the local MP, he had been helpful in a tangible way to their family or the local community. Second, they express some pride in the fact that, as Prime Minister, he avoided allowing us to be embroiled by America in the war in Vietnam.

Harold knew that to secure reform, Labour had to gain power. He won four elections for Labour. Only two other (Attlee and Blair) of Labour's eleven post-war leaders have won any elections. Ultimately, by means of his prodigious intellect and leadership skills, Harold enabled Labour to make important changes that were needed in Britain. In the mid to late 1960s and early 1970s, he held the Labour Party together, despite potentially catastrophic differences on Europe and economic policy, and maintained some semblance of our country being an important player on the world stage. He deserves much more credit than he has in the past been given for those things alone and much more besides.

INTRODUCTION

Andrew S. Crines and Kevin Hickson

THIS YEAR MARKS the centenary of Harold Wilson's birth, fifty years since he secured his most impressive electoral victory and forty years since his dramatic resignation as Prime Minister. He was one of the leading politicians in the post-war era. In terms of electoral performance, he is the only Labour leader, indeed the only party leader of the twentieth century, to win four general elections.

However, he remains something of an enigmatic and controversial figure. His record as Prime Minister on the first occasion (1964–70) was trounced after Labour left office. The hopes that were built up were too much to meet once the new government realised the extent of the economic crisis facing Britain. His second term (1974–76) is often regarded as an appendix to his career.

To those on the left of the party, Wilson initially gave fresh hope when he took over from their arch-foe, Hugh Gaitskell, following his death in 1963. However, they were later to feel that this hope had been squandered as the government pursued a deflationist economic policy, unemployment rose and nationalisation was, by and large, abandoned. Moreover, Wilson was deemed too close to America, dependent on US financial support and refusing, publicly at least, to condemn the Vietnam War. Following the 1970 general election defeat, the left took greater control of the internal policy-making machinery of the party. After a further retreat from the goals of the left in the 1974–79 government, the party moved decisively leftwards, with the Wilson and Callaghan governments viewed as betraying socialism. The result was the formation of the SDP and the radical manifesto of 1983.

To those on the right, Wilson was viewed with suspicion because of his previous association with the 'leader of the left' Aneurin 'Nye' Bevan. He had resigned from Attlee's government with Nye over the introduction of NHS charges to fund the Korean War. He had challenged Gaitskell for the leadership in 1960 and the deputy leader, George Brown, shortly afterwards. Both Gaitskell and Brown were figures on the 'right' of the party.

Wilson's primary aim on becoming leader in 1963 was to unite the party that had lost the previous three general elections, largely due to internal splits within the party between left and right. This involved a fine balancing act and would result in Wilson being regarded as a somewhat Machiavellian character.

In more recent years there has been an attempt to resuscitate Wilson's reputation and this book is an essential contribution towards achieving this. The passage of time, a greater realisation of the structural constraints under which Wilson operated, and the shift to the right in British politics after 1979 all help to restore a clearer sense of perspective on Wilson.

This was anticipated some time ago by Kenneth O. Morgan when he wrote in 1987 that:

> Since Harold Wilson's stock has plummeted so sharply for so long, one can only suppose that it will some day register an upward movement. It is likely, indeed probable, that historians will take a more charitable and compassionate view of his career and achievements than do commentators who delight in trampling on a man when he is down.[1]

Arguably that time has now come and the chapters that follow offer such an appraisal.

There are arguably five overlapping phases to Harold Wilson's life. The first was in Huddersfield, the town where he was born and began his education, attending the local grammar school before his father lost his job and moved the family to the Wirral. Although Wilson was only a teenager when his family left Huddersfield, he remained fond of the town saying that: 'without being arrogant, we are proud of our town and will be prouder still... Huddersfield will change in the next hundred years. It will rise to still greater heights.'[2] He always remained a supporter of Huddersfield Town Football Club. Upon being elevated to the peerage he took the title of Baron Wilson of Rievaulx after the Cistercian Abbey in North Yorkshire.

The second key phase in Wilson's life was spent in the Merseyside region. He attended school on the Wirral, obtaining a distinguished academic pedigree and a scholarship to Oxford. On entering Parliament in 1945, he represented the constituency of Ormskirk and then Huyton, a particularly poor area that had become Liverpool's overspill area after the bombing of the Second World War. He was to continue to be a representative for that area until 1983 when he finally retired from Parliament. As George Howarth, the current MP for the area, states in his Foreword, local residents old enough to remember him as their MP have fond memories of him as a champion for the constituency.

The third key phase was Wilson's time at Oxford between 1934 and 1937, where he obtained the highest result in his year and distinguished himself as a statistician. He started out as a Liberal, but fell under the influence of G. D. H. Cole, a Fabian socialist who taught Wilson at Oxford, and converted to Labour. He also served as research assistant to the prominent Liberal academic William Beveridge. From 1937 he was a Fellow at the University of Oxford. Although academically distinguished, he never became an 'intellectual' in the sense of some of his fellow Labour colleagues such as Anthony

Crosland, Dick Crossman and Roy Jenkins. He also maintained a passionate sense of the need to widen participation in higher education, including the achievement of which he was most proud – the Open University.

The fourth phase saw Wilson joining the civil service during the war. This would distinguish him from several of his later parliamentary colleagues, such as Crosland, Healey and Jenkins, who enlisted and saw active service. Arguably, Wilson took from his experience a strong sense of the virtues and potential of economic and social planning, for he later became president of the Board of Trade in the post-war Labour administration. His role in the civil service was the start of a long association with Westminster and Whitehall. On entering Parliament in 1945, Wilson was immediately given a ministerial position. He became, eventually, the youngest member of the Cabinet, only serving on the back benches after he retired as Prime Minister in 1976.

The fifth and final phase – Wilson's association with the Isles of Scilly – is significant. This is not only because he had a fondness for the area and holidayed there regularly, but also because it shows something about his character. Despite no doubt becoming a wealthy man, he maintained quite simple tastes. This was something that was frowned upon by his more colourful colleagues in the Labour governments of the 1960s and '70s. His homely image, with raincoat and pipe, resonated with the electorate of the 1960s as he appeared more in touch with ordinary people and modern culture than the aristocratic Tories.

STRUCTURE OF THE BOOK

The book is divided into three main parts:

Part One: Themes – contains a number of contextual chapters. Kevin Hickson begins by setting out the intellectual context within which Wilson operated. There is a more favourable perspective from Jeremy Nuttall, followed by a more critical essay by Dennis Kavanagh. Andrew Crines explores in detail the oratory and rhetoric of Wilson and Mark Garnett then examines how the Conservative Party responded to Wilson.

Part Two: Policies – explores Wilson's impact on public policy, examining the context within which policy was made, the major policy developments, the relative success of those policies and the extent to which they were shaped by Wilson. Obviously the answer to these questions varies, depending on which policy area is examined, but overall a pattern that emerges is that, within the context of the time, Wilson and his governments deserve more praise than has been customarily bestowed upon them.

Part Three: Perspectives – offers perspectives from the left, the right and the centre of politics. Again, what emerges from this discussion is an accord of opinion more sympathetic to Wilson than may have been held in the past. The final chapter explores the way that history judges Wilson.

NOTES AND REFERENCES

1.   K. O. Morgan, *Labour People: Leaders and Lieutenants, Hardie to Kinnock* (Oxford: Oxford University Press, 1992), p. 247
2.   R. Brook, *The Story of Huddersfield* (London: MacGibbon & Kee, 1968), p. i

PART ONE

THEMES

1

WILSON AND
BRITISH SOCIALISM

Kevin Hickson

'Socialism, as I understand it, means applying
a sense of purpose to our national life.'[1]

THIS CHAPTER SEEKS to outline the ideology of Harold Wilson: his position within the ideological spectrum of the Labour Party, his understanding of socialism and criticisms made of it. The task is made difficult by the fact that, unlike a number of his contemporaries, he was not an intellectual, in the sense that he did not theorise about politics, although he was undoubtedly a highly intelligent person.

Above all Wilson was concerned with party management, which, according to his critics, made him appear duplicitous and inconsistent as he frequently positioned with different sides in different policy debates.[2] He feared ministerial plots and frequently sought to reshuffle his ministerial team, either to promote backbench critics (thus ensuring their silence as ministers bound by collective responsibility), or to weaken those in office whom he regarded as a threat. His second term as Prime Minister was more tranquil, but by this time he was already considering retirement and so once again 'ideology' was not deemed a particularly noticeable feature of his latter period as Prime Minister.

Although it can be reasonably argued that his personal beliefs were therefore somewhat masked, this does not mean that ideology was somehow absent. Ideology is taken to mean a set of interconnected beliefs that condition political action and policy formulation.[3] It is argued here that all politicians operate within certain ideological environments, overtly or not. Some political leaders are explicit in their ideology. In Britain since 1945 this was most notably the case with Clement Attlee and Margaret Thatcher. Others operate within certain ideological paradigms – the climate of opinion that conditions political action. Whether through personal choice or structural constraints they are not able to recast that climate of opinion. Ideologies, in this sense, are always present. A non-ideological form of politics is an impossibility, yet ideology is only one factor present in any given political situation. Other factors include the economy, the nature of the parliamentary party, electoral constraints, social change and the media. This chapter is therefore concerned with unravelling Wilson's ideology from these other factors in his politics.

Ideologies, understood as interconnected beliefs, operate as established yet constantly evolving political traditions. There is a recognisable tradition of British socialism. It is also argued that Wilson had a distinctive understanding of British socialism. However, by the end of his two periods in power both left and right of the Labour Party were highly critical of Wilson.

This chapter will, firstly, set out the nature of British socialism. It will then go on to outline Wilson's own personal understanding of socialism. Finally, the chapter will examine the critiques made of Wilson and his governments and evaluate how justified those critiques are.

THE NATURE OF BRITISH SOCIALISM

British socialism is, in essence, an ethical creed based not on Marxian 'scientific' laws of history but on abstract values such as social justice, equality, liberty and democracy. The precise meaning of these values and the priority attached to them often varies but they are at the core of British socialism.[4]

From the outset, the Labour Party – established as the Labour Representation Committee (LRC) in 1900 – rejected the revolutionary route to socialism. Of the constituent parts of the LRC only the Social Democratic Federation was Marxist in its orientation and this was quickly marginalised in favour of the Fabian Society's emphasis on gradualism, based on the ideas of the first significant revisionist critic of Marxism, Eduard Bernstein. The aim of the Labour Party was to persuade people to vote for it in order to gain a parliamentary majority, at which point the state could be 'captured' for the implementation of socialism. Marxism continued to have periodic influence on the Labour Party, such as in response to the two governments of Ramsay MacDonald and the Great Depression of the 1930s, but by 1945 the Fabian ideas had again won through largely owing to the incorporation of 'Keynesian' ideas into the party in the late 1930s. From the mid-twentieth-century perspective this view appeared justified.[5]

The electoral defeat of Attlee's government in 1951 reopened these ideological disputes. For some, notably Hugh Gaitskell and Anthony Crosland, the party needed to undergo a second wave of revisionism taking into account the changes to British society and the economy since 1945.[6] In Crosland's major work, *The Future of Socialism,* post-war revisionism found its fullest expression.[7] According to Crosland the power of the capitalist class had been fundamentally and irreversibly broken as organised labour, the state and a new managerial class now had power. The capacity of democracy to introduce social reform had been demonstrated by the Liberal governments of 1906–14 and the Labour governments of 1945–51. Capitalism had ceased to exist in Britain, at least as understood in Marxist theory. However, Britain was still not a socialist country as there remained too much inequality in income, wealth and social status. The policy of public ownership was relegated in importance to redistribution of wealth and income and comprehensive schooling.

For the left this was insufficient as a form of socialism. The Attlee governments had only nationalised one-fifth of industry and there remained too much power in the hands of corporate managers and shareholders. A future Labour government should therefore seek to extend public ownership, especially into the profit-making sector of the economy so that dividends could be used to fund social improvements. The price mechanism would be further eroded meaning that social need could be prioritised over wealth creation and industrial democracy should be introduced into both the private and public sectors. In addition, the Labour left criticised the foreign policy of Attlee and Ernest Bevin for being Atlanticist, including membership of NATO and support for the Korean War, and the pro-nuclear defence policy. Although the left initially advocated a 'neutral zone' between the Soviet Union and the United States, involving closer European cooperation, they largely opposed the emergence of the European Economic Community (EEC). Although the left had been present during the Attlee governments they were boosted considerably by the resignation of 'Nye' Bevan over rearmament and the Korean War.

WILSON'S SOCIALISM

It was these ideological disputes, as well as the personal rivalry of Bevan and Gaitskell, that split the party after election defeat in 1951. Wilson at first appeared to be on the side of the left by resigning with Bevan and later challenging Gaitskell for the leadership and George Brown for the deputy leadership.

However, he also distanced himself from Bevan in the mid-1950s, replacing his mentor in the shadow Cabinet after Bevan's resignation. By the time he became leader he had adopted many of the right's policy positions. Meanwhile, the right continued to distrust Wilson because he had beaten their preferred candidate George Brown in the 1963 leadership contest, although the latter's personal weaknesses were also a factor, along with the right's vote being split between Brown and James Callaghan. On winning the 1964 general election, Wilson mostly appointed figures from the right of the party to the top Cabinet posts. However, he also maintained close links with those who were associated with the left, notably Barbara Castle and Richard Crossman, who had been allies of Bevan in the 1950s.

Wilson, then, was hard to place as a figure of either the left or the right. It would be better to see him as a centrist. Unlike the left and the right, those in the centre tend to be neglected. One attempt to reconcile this issue was in the book, *The Struggle for Labour's Soul*, in which five ideological positions are identified in the Labour Party since 1945: the old left (Bevanites) and the new left (Bennite), the old right (Gaitskellites) and the new, or 'modernised' right (New Labour), and the centre.[8] The centre consists of those who seek to maintain party unity, balancing the left and right tendencies. This is important in this context since Wilson represents perhaps the paradigmatic centrist in Labour Party terms since 1945.

His primary concern was with party unity. He recognised the damage that was being done to the Labour Party in the 1950s with the left–right splits, as ultimately did Bevan. But he also opposed Gaitskell's attempts to revise Clause 4 of the party constitution, which he regarded – along with others such as Crossman – as creating an unnecessarily divisive split in the party. Gaitskell's style of leadership was too divisive for Wilson. Gaitskell, in contrast, believed that it was necessary, in the more affluent Britain of the 1950s, to show that the Labour Party was not an 'old fashioned' socialist party.

In this he was encouraged by Douglas Jay, but not necessarily by the likes of Crosland on the Clause 4 issue. Equally, Wilson's attempts to balance left and right during his two periods as Prime Minister could be seen as an example of his centrism. His decision to suspend collective responsibility and hold a referendum over continued membership of the EEC was a further example, and his (at least tacit) support for Callaghan as his successor in 1976 over the left-wing Michael Foot and Tony Benn, or the more right-wing figures of Jenkins and Healey, in order to maintain party unity, were further manifestations of his centrism.[9]

Hence, party management was a part of Wilson's socialist ideology, perhaps the key part. It required some considerable manoeuvring as the gulf between right and left at this time was growing. In this context a more divisive leader would have been less likely to win elections and without power no socialist measures could be implemented. But if party unity was an essential feature of Wilson's socialism it should not blind us to other aspects.

In addition to the emphasis on party unity, there were three distinctive elements: constitutionalism, corporatism and patriotism. Each of these three elements requires further examination.

The attachment to constitutionalism may not come as a surprise since the Labour Party had been committed to the gradualist route to socialism from the outset, as stated above. For Wilson, as for many in 'Old Labour', constitutionalism meant acceptance of the existing state. The virtue of the First Past the Post electoral system was that it would allow the Labour Party to govern on its own. Although critics argue that disproportionality is a weakness that requires attention, the justification for it was that it produced 'strong' government. Coalitions would be a rarity, saved for occasions such as wartime. Electoral reform would diminish the chance of governing without the need for coalition. Once a parliamentary majority is secured the existing apparatus of the state can be used to implement socialist policies. Again, this appeared to be proven by the experiences of the Attlee administration, which found the civil service willing to implement the new government's manifesto commitments. As a former civil servant, Wilson assumed the neutrality of the state bureaucracy. The Westminster model also placed emphasis on the idea of parliamentary sovereignty. In the absence of a codified constitution, government Bills could not be struck down as unconstitutional. Moreover, local government was subordinate to central government. All of this implied a system of government that could be used to implement socialism. The problem of the 1950s had been that power had been illusive, not that there would be problems once Labour had finally got back into power.

For these reasons Labour had traditionally opposed constitutional reform. The case for reform would be based on governing efficiency rather than democratic principle and would be limited to ensuring that barriers to the implementation of socialism were reduced. This was the case with the Attlee government, whose main constitutional reform was to reduce the delaying powers of the House of Lords from two years to one in the Parliament Act of 1949. The general absence of constitutional reform was a further criticism the left mounted at that government's record, with no attempt to remove the constitutional remnants of feudalism.

After 1964, the reform agenda was again focused on improving the efficiency of government. The aborted attempts to further reduce the powers of the Lords were undermined by an alliance between those who wanted to abolish it and those who wished to retain it. Administrative reform was put in place with the aim of ensuring that Labour could implement its manifesto commitments, including the separation of powers between the Treasury and a new Department of Economic Affairs (DEA). Even the growing interest in devolution was a pragmatic response to the rise of Scottish and Welsh nationalism and was not based on constitutional principle. According to Labour's traditional understanding of the constitution, devolution would

make governing harder by creating rival centres of power. So, Wilson's belief
in existing constitutional structures was part of mainstream thinking in the
Labour Party at this time.

The second key aspect of Wilson's socialism was his commitment to corporatism. By corporatism what is meant is a belief in the power of the state to
make social and economic improvements through the doctrine of 'planning'.
Arguably, the 1960s were the high point of economic planning in Britain. The
preceding Conservative government had established the National Economic
Development Council (NEDC) with the aim of bringing government, business
and labour together to promote productivity and growth. Harold Macmillan
had advocated planning and partnership between industry, labour and the
government as a 'middle way' between communism and free-market capitalism in the 1930s. But for Wilson, this logic was extended further by his belief
that economic problems could be resolved through the appointment of the
right personnel and the creation of the right governing structures. This was
seen most clearly in his statements on 'national purpose' in the run-up to the
1964 general election. He also thought that the markets responded 'irration-
ally' to the economic measures of 1964–67.[10]

Wilson had been involved in the development of corporatism in the Labour
Party in the late 1950s.[11] Here the aim was to transcend the divisions of left
and right by promoting the idea of planning, which would move beyond the
more pro-market views of the revisionists and the demands for ever more public ownership of the left. Planning would involve an increase in state power
over the economy through largely voluntary methods, aimed at increasing the
rates of productivity through partnerships between the private and public
sectors. In this, Wilson was encouraged by his experiences as a civil servant
and president of the Board of Trade under Attlee and by economic thinking from key advisers such as Thomas Balogh who wanted to see planning
extended beyond the NEDC model.[12]

It reached its fullest expression in Wilson's first speech to the Labour Party conference as leader in 1963, when he articulated the idea of the National Plan, which would use the power of the state to build partnerships with the private sector and the trade unions to promote faster growth. Again, it would be mistaken to see Wilson's attitude towards the unions as lacking vision. He had in mind a more continental model, where unions would play a central role in national policy-making. However, this policy failed as the trade unions in Britain were far more decentralised in their organisation than their continental cousins.[13] State intervention would be necessary if the British economy was to harness the advances of science and technology – the 'white heat' of the new scientific and technological revolution.[14] The National Plan was the expression of Wilson's belief in the politics of corporatism. Its failure in government brings us to the third element of Wilson's socialism.

The reason for the failure of the National Plan was the decision, taken in the first days of the new government, to defend the parity of sterling. One of the reasons for this decision was that the Attlee government had been forced to devalue and Wilson believed that another devaluation would damage the electoral fortunes of the Labour Party. The party would be viewed as the party of devaluation at a time when the strength of sterling was seen as a symbol of British power and prestige. But the consequence was to be three years of deflationary measures culminating in the enforced devaluation of 1967, by which time the National Plan was effectively abandoned.

Another key development at this time, which highlights the nature of Wilson's patriotism, was the Vietnam War. Wilson was determined to keep Britain out, although at the time the lengths to which he went were not known publicly and his governments faced the protests of the anti-war demonstrators.

His attitude towards modernity and multiculturalism were also shaped by his sense of patriotism. He had long been opposed to the death penalty and saw it abolished in 1965. Although he did not seek to stop the implementation of

other 'permissive' measures, such as the legalisation of abortion and homosexuality, measures to make divorce easier and the relaxation on laws of censorship,
he did not appear to share the reformist zeal of the likes of Roy Jenkins.
His governments also implemented measures to improve race relations and
there was clear criticism of the overtly racist campaign of Peter Griffiths in
Smethwick in 1964 and Enoch Powell's 'Rivers of Blood' speech in 1968,
although the Kenyan crisis led to measures to restrict immigration.

Wilson also had a clear sense of lower-middle-class identity and much of
his rhetoric on the 'white heat' was also about ending aristocratic domination
of a large part of British life. He was not unique in winning a scholarship from
grammar school to go to Oxford University, but he was brought face to face
with a student population that was still overwhelmingly drawn from an elite
public school background. He was repelled by this sense of privilege and was
later to use this effectively against both Macmillan and Home, who he claimed
with some justification represented an out-of-touch social elite. His focus was
on modernisation and this meant reducing the power of the old social elites,
as Ben Pimlott explains: 'the attack was not on the abstraction "capitalism",
but on the undiscerning, inefficient, backward-looking better off. Instead of
aristocracy and plutocracy there would be classless meritocracy.'[15] It may also
explain, in part, his feelings towards the Gaitskellites, as many of them, including Gaitskell himself, had come from a privileged background. He instinctively
empathised with the aspirational concerns of working- and lower-middle-class
families and this can be seen most clearly in his education policies, where
he wanted to extend opportunities through comprehensive schools, and the
expansion of higher education generally and the Open University in particular.

So, Wilson held a subtle form of patriotism, which sought to maintain
Britain's position within the world but at a time when her world role was
declining. Indeed, Wilson presided over the further decline of Britain's
military and geopolitical roles. The ultimate enforced devaluation was also

a blow to Britain's prestige. Although Wilson may not have felt instinctively in touch with the new social transformations of the 1960s he did use them to his advantage politically.

REACTIONS

For the right in British politics the Wilson era was one that was very damaging. It was in this era that the New Right emerged.[16] Although free-market thinking was not new in the Conservative Party it had been effectively marginalised by the One Nation Conservatives, who subscribed to the mixed economy and the welfare state, involving a commitment to much of the Attlee government's reforms in so doing. However, by the late 1960s that free market ideology had been revived through think tanks, such as the Institute of Economic Affairs, which found their effective advocate in the person of Enoch Powell. Further economic crises and increased trade union militancy in the 1970s made these ideas seem relevant and ultimately Margaret Thatcher was elected to reverse the drift towards 'socialism' in the post-war era. For neo-liberals such as Friedrich Hayek and Milton Friedman planning was a flawed economic strategy as it could not possibly take account of the infinite relations between producers and consumers in a market economy. Any attempt to 'plan' the economy would be bound to fail and the relative decline of the British economy was the consequence of too much government intervention. Michael Oakeshott went further, arguing that any form of 'rationalism' in politics would necessarily involve the curtailment of individual liberty. The role of the state should be to maintain a framework within which freedom of the individual to make his or her own choices could be secured.

For those of a more authoritarian disposition, the problem with 'socialist' Britain was not that there had been a loss of personal liberty but its excessive abundance, in which traditional morality had declined and where the expansion of welfare provision had created a dependency culture. By the 1970s the result was that the authority of government has been undermined and Britain was in a state of near-anarchy.[17]

For the left, the Wilson era was one of hopes betrayed and there was an inquest as to why that was the case. For some it seemed to be customary practice for Labour leaders to betray the hopes and aspirations of socialist activists. This had been amply demonstrated in 1931 when, at the behest of the King, MacDonald had formed a National Government dominated by the Conservatives and leaving Labour out of power until 1940. Following the 1970 general election defeat, the left took increasing control over the policy-making apparatus of the party, as highlighted with *Labour's Programme 1973*. However, the leadership of the party had never supported the more radical proposals and some were removed from the two manifestos of 1974 or subsequently dropped. The charge of betrayal therefore resonated after the 1979 general election defeat and, with Thatcher moving the Conservatives to the right, Labour moved decisively leftwards, culminating in the general election defeat of 1983.

A dissenting voice from this left-wing critique was journalist and writer Paul Foot, who argued that the left had been wrong to believe that Wilson had been one of their own by the time he became leader in 1963 and that they therefore should not have been surprised that their hopes were dashed. For Foot, Wilson had always been an unprincipled opportunist and the left were naive for believing otherwise.[18]

However, for others on the left the 'betrayal' thesis was overly simplistic. There were other, more fundamental reasons why the Labour Party could not implement socialism. This critique had started to emerge on the extra-parliamentary left from the mid-1950s, when Bevan made his spectacular U-turn on nuclear weapons. It had developed further in the 1960s with the experience of the Wilson governments. Its fullest expression can be found in Ralph

Miliband's *Parliamentary Socialism*, in which he argued that Labour had always been committed to the parliamentary system and that this meant that it could not be a vehicle for socialism.[19] This was because the parliamentary system, especially under existing voting arrangements, meant that there was a need to converge on the centre ground in order to maximise votes. There was little scope to be a radical party when the overwhelming need would be to appear 'respectable' with respectability defined by the norms imposed by socialism's opponents. The hopes of the left would always be frustrated under this system. The leaders of the Labour Party could not be blamed for following the rules of the game. What was needed was to change those rules.

Socialism would require a political realignment and greater use of extra parliamentary activity. The Labour moderates could always claim that internal divisions undermined the party's prospects of being elected to government and that the left would be held responsible. After the inevitable disappointments of Labour governments the left would be resurgent; however, as the electoral cycle moved on the left would be quiet in an attempt to secure future electoral victories. This was the fate of the parliamentary left and hence those who followed Miliband had a more pessimistic view of the prospects of achieving socialism under a future Labour government. Moreover, the forces of capitalism – domestic and international – and the influence of a right-wing press with a concentrated ownership would seek to undermine the 'credibility' of the Labour Party.[20] Hence, Wilson's failure – as the left saw it – was not so much down to his own personal failings, but had deeper structural causes. In the 1970s and early 1980s, the emergence of the 'Bennite' left was influenced by this thesis when calling for elected representatives of the party at both national and local levels to be held more 'accountable' to party activists; for a more profound challenge to the capitalist system; and for the British economy to be protected from the kind of international pressures that had blown every post-war Labour government off course.

Criticism of Wilson from within the Labour Party was not confined to the left, however, with Anthony Crosland providing perhaps the strongest criticism from the revisionist perspective.[21] For Crosland, the socialist case for higher growth, which he had put forward in the 1950s, had been sacrificed at the high altar of protecting the parity of sterling. He rejected the structural analysis of the left, as discussed above, arguing instead that the state had sufficient power to manage the economy through Keynesian techniques and that there was no need for the policies of the emerging Alternative Economic Strategy advocated by the Bennites. Instead, the failure was one of political will: 'Against the dogged resistance to change, we should have pitted a stronger will to change.'[22] Despite the record of success in social and educational reforms, the plans for higher growth had failed. The rate of growth had been greater under the 'thirteen wasted years' of Tory government and unemployment was higher at the end of Wilson's first administration than at the start of it. If inequality had fallen, this could be largely explained by the effects of deflation rather than by positive egalitarian measures. Crosland was also sceptical about the role of planning in microeconomic policy, believing instead that the key to higher rates of economic growth was still in a Keynesian macroeconomic policy. Growth was essential to fund increased social expenditure and to eliminate poverty. He rejected the emerging 'zero-growth' environmentalist lobby, which he regarded as an essentially middle-class concern. The urban environment needed greater protection and improvement than rural areas and for this there was need for further economic growth. Moreover, Crosland believed that the government could still effectively manage the domestic economy: a point he was to make again in government in 1975–76 against cuts in public expenditure as the pound – now floating following the collapse of the Bretton Woods international monetary management system – came under sustained market pressure, culminating in the 1976 International Monetary Fund (IMF) crisis. Any hopes that the problems of sterling had been ended with the collapse of the fixed exchange rate regime were dashed as a result of the IMF crisis.[23]

So, what is the validity of these various arguments?

I think that it is possible to dismiss the arguments of the New Right and the New Left. With the benefit of a longer-term perspective, the record of Wilson's (and Callaghan's) governments compares favourably with what was to come later. The rate of growth – though disappointing at the time – was higher than that achieved by later governments. Though unemployment went up, it was considerably lower than in the 1980s and the social costs of Thatcher's free-market counter-revolution were avoided. Public spending on health and education increased and, although it created new problems, the expansion of public sector housing provision was far greater than under subsequent Labour governments. The New Right and New Labour had not resolved Britain's economic problems and the crash of 2008 showed that the British economy was over-reliant on the banking sector. The 'recovery' under the current Conservative administration has not been felt outside London and the south-east, leading some to argue that we should revisit the regional planning policies of the Wilson era.

Moreover, the New Left critique of parliamentary socialism is difficult to sustain. Firstly, it fails to identify that 'socialism' is a broad term capable of a range of different meanings. Although the parliamentary route may rule out socialism as the Milibandian critique understood that term, there are other forms of socialism (or social democracy) that are best achieved through the parliamentary system. Indeed, it is difficult to see what alternatives there are to the parliamentary route that could deliver more, given the public aversion at critical moments to direct action. Even the case for a change in the electoral system to bring about a realignment of the left is suspect as there would probably not be sufficient public support for a party or coalition of parties further to the left.

This leaves the Croslandite critique. Arguably, Crosland's case for an early devaluation is simplistic and fails to take into account the constraints on the 1964 Labour government's scope for action with a tiny parliamentary majority, a party that was split on the issue, pressure from the US to avoid devaluation fearing it would set off a chain reaction that would culminate in the collapse of the international fixed exchange rate system and the damaging effects it would have on those developing countries that held sterling deposits. By 1966, however, the case for devaluation was stronger with an increased parliamentary majority and continuing economic difficulties that deflation had failed to resolve. A voluntary decision to devalue then would not have looked like defeat and would have allowed the economy to expand by 1970.

Nevertheless, what emerges from this discussion is that Wilson was more principled than he is often portrayed to be (even by his opponents within the party who had particular axes to grind), and that the principles he held can be identified as socialist in that they sought to use the power of the state to create a more just and tranquil society. Wilson's undoubted campaigning and media skills were essential to return Labour to power after a long period of opposition. He knew that the Labour Party was the best, if not the only, vehicle for the advancement of socialism in Britain, and that out of power the party could not advance the socialist cause at all. It is a lesson more recent leaders should learn.

NOTES AND REFERENCES

1.   H. Wilson, *Purpose in Politics* (London: Leagrave, 1964), p. ix
2.   See, for example, D. Healey, *The Time of My Life* (London: Penguin, 1990), p. 331: 'He had no sense of direction and rarely looked more than a few months ahead.'
3.   I have tried to avoid an overly theoretical exposition and those interested in this aspect are directed to M. Freeden, *Ideology and Political Theory: A Conceptual Approach* (Oxford: Oxford University Press, 1998)
4.   Wilson endorsed this understanding of British socialism in *Purpose in Politics*

5.   F. Williams, *Fifty Years' March: The Rise of the Labour Party* (Watford: Odhams Press, 1950)

6.   S. Haseler, *The Gaitskellites* (London: Macmillan, 1969)

7.   C. A. R. Crosland, *The Future of Socialism* (London: Jonathan Cape, 1956)

8.   R. Plant, M. Beech and K. Hickson (eds), *The Struggle for Labour's Soul: Understanding Labour's Political Thought Since 1945* (London: Routledge, 2004)

9.   The other contender was Crosland, but failing to get support he was eliminated in the first round

10. E. Dell, *A Strange Eventful History: Democratic Socialism in Britain* (London: HarperCollins, 2000), pp 334–5

11. I. Favretto, '"Wilsonism" Reconsidered: Labour Party Revisionism 1952–64', *Contemporary British History*, 14, (2000), pp 54–80

12. T. Balogh, 'The Drift Towards Planning', in P. Anderson (ed.), *Towards Socialism* (London: Fontana, 1965)

13. My thinking here owes a lot to discussions with Robert Taylor. See his chapter 'Industrial Relations'

14. H. Wilson, Speech to the Labour Party Conference, Scarborough, 1963, contained in H. Wilson, *Purpose in Politics*, pp 14–28

15. B. Pimlott, *Harold Wilson* (London: HarperCollins, 1993), p. 307

16. See A. Gamble, *The Conservative Nation* (London: Routledge and Kegan Paul, 1974) and *The Free Economy and the Strong State: The Politics of Thatcherism* (Basingstoke: Palgrave, 1988, 1994)

17. For clear statements from this perspective, see P. Worsthorne, *The Socialist Myth* (London: Cassell, 1971) and 'Too Much Freedom', in M. Cowling (ed.), *Conservative Essays* (London: Cassell, 1978)

18. P. Foot, *The Politics of Harold Wilson* (Harmondsworth: Penguin, 1968) and 'Harold Wilson and the Labour Left', *International Socialism*, 33, (summer 1968), pp 18–26, available at: https://www.marxists.org/archive/foot-paul/1968/xx/wilson.htm

19. R. Miliband, *Parliamentary Socialism* (London: Merlin, 1972)

20. D. Coates, *The Labour Party and the Struggle for Socialism* (Cambridge: Cambridge University Press, 1975)

21. C. A. R. Crosland, 'Socialism Now', in D. Leonard (ed.), *Socialism Now and Other Essays* (London: Jonathan Cape, 1975)

22. Ibid., p. 44

23. See K. Hickson, *The IMF Crisis of 1976 and British Politics* (London: I. B. Tauris, 2005)

2

WILSON AND SOCIAL CHANGE

Jeremy Nuttall

THREE PARADOXES

FROM THE STANDPOINT of the mid-1950s, it would have been hard to imagine that Harold Wilson, who stood apart from both the revisionist political outlook of the dominant Gaitskellite Hampstead Set, and its rather glamorous and well-connected social network, would become the central figure of British politics for much of the next two decades. It would have been difficult to predict, too, how far the society over which Wilson would preside, would change from its pre-Suez lingering imperial mentality, and still in some aspects quite Victorian outlook on social and moral matters, to the less deferential, and more liberal, property-owning democracy of the late 1970s. In truth though, if British society had changed considerably by this time, it was change still with certain crucial limits, and Wilson represented the ambiguous mixed feelings of the people as a whole towards change. His vision for, and relationship with British society and its people were full of complexity, contradiction and paradox, as was that society itself. We explore three of these paradoxes below.

SOCIAL MODERNISER OR TRADITIONALIST?

If stability was the defining characteristic of British society in the 1950s, modernity was that of the 1960s, and Harold Wilson was, in important ways, its epitome. A believer in dynamic new technology, he had a faith in expertise, professionalism and planning, and above all a desire to challenge the stuffier, more restrictive side of Britain's class system. He was, thus, one component part, albeit a crucial one, in a bigger motor of modernity in the 1960s, which ranged from the lively, upbeat melodies of the early Beatles, and the irreverence and satire of *That Was The Week That Was*, to the growing popularity of the comprehensive school, and above all the appetite of many ordinary people for loosening restrictions, broadening horizons, moving upwards.

Wilson, of course, helped reshape British society; but as much as this, the society he reshaped needed him, someone to personify in political form, and to lead a pre-existing social appetite for modernisation. His promise to promote the comprehensive school, resulting in Anthony Crosland's *Circular 10/65* in 1965, perhaps exemplified this process most clearly. Though the circular only requested (it did not require) secondary modern and grammar schools to reorganise on comprehensive lines, this was a structural, institutional change that made concrete something that was actually less about structures than a mood, a yearning for the opportunity and social mobility that good education could provide. It was about a belief, as Wilson put it in 1964, that 'unfulfilled and unrealised talents [should] be mobilised'.[1] Moreover, it was a mood that partly preceded the change in national government policy, with some local authorities already going comprehensive in response to parents, not least middle class ones, disgruntled that the eleven plus branded those children who did not pass the exam for entry to grammar school as failures at such an early age.

If the comprehensive school was the policy or institutional change that best captured the new mood of modernisation, the way in which Wilson's personality represented it was just as important. It mattered, symbolically, that he was a young (by the standards of those days), lower-middle-class, grammar-school-educated Yorkshireman, in contrast to his aristocratic Conservative opponent in 1964, Alec Douglas-Home, and indeed, his public-school-educated, upper-middle-class predecessor as Labour leader, Hugh Gaitskell. It mattered, too, that he professed to prefer beer to champagne, wore a Gannex raincoat, smoked a pipe, and watched *Coronation Street*. Not all of this was entirely real. Like Kennedy, he took persona-construction to a higher level. In private he smoked cigars rather than a pipe, and drank spirits, for instance. As his popularity dipped, it fed the claim that he was more style than substance. But most of the image actually reflected the reality, and the sense of a kindly, informal man, with not too many airs and graces, had such purchase because it was largely true. Even his vices were acceptable because they seemed democratic ones, or, like John Lennon's, flaws of the outsider. As Ben Pimlott has observed, people respected the chip Wilson had on his shoulder, because they had one too.[2]

The attachment to modernity was also a useful way for Wilson to move beyond, and in some ways to dodge, controversial divides or choices within the Labour Party and its different visions of socialism. One of Wilson's great political strengths was his chameleon-like ability to appeal to all shades of opinion, and to make people think he was one of them. Early on a semi-detached Bevanite, yet one who would award his crucial Cabinet positions to Gaitskellite or traditional right figures like Jim Callaghan, Roy Jenkins and Denis Healey, Wilson was ultimately neither fully revisionist nor fully Bevanite, but an adept, practical, government-minded politician, and pragmatic reformer. The focus on modernity, on looking to the future, helped distract attention from the question of which wing of the party he was really on, and keep his definition of socialism suitably hazy. It also facilitated a blurring of the issue of whether Wilson and Labour fundamentally stood for a meritocratic society of equality of opportunity, or one of equality of outcome. In the 1990s, with the arrival of Tony Blair and New Labour, there was more political pressure to differentiate between the two. But in the 1960s, with a society where barriers to opportunity were cruder, less subtle, the pledge to *modernise* Britain's social structures, institutions and class system offered the promise of *both* social mobility in the middle, *and* alleviation of poverty at the bottom, without the need to theorise excessively over the nuances of exactly what type of equality would constitute the endpoint. In a way, political ideology then could be painted with a broader brush than is now possible.

The irony was, however, that while Wilson, on important levels, represented Labour's attachment to and accommodation of modernity at its most powerful, he simultaneously exemplified crucial ways in which the party failed to modernise sufficiently, or to keep pace with the social changes of the time. This was even true, in some particulars, of his famed presentational and communicational abilities. This is not to deny his considerable skills as a moderniser in these areas. As early as 1955, the Wilson Report pinpointed the amateurishness of Labour's organisation, 'at the penny-farthing stage in a jet-propelled era', and recommended major reforms, including the use of cars to collect dues.[3] He was a highly adept television performer, taking the medium seriously from an early stage, communicating with, rather than lecturing the viewers, and meeting television's demand for speed with a quick fact or joke. Ever the statistician, he was also willing to embrace opinion polls, much more so than the otherwise modernising Gaitskell.

However, there were also limits to how far Wilson was willing to abandon older ways of doing things. He viewed public relations as 'a most degrading profession', and was sceptical about the use of advertising. His opening rally of the 1964 election campaign, at Wembley, featured the rather familiar and traditional spectacles of a Welsh male voice choir and a colliery brass band. He was also reluctant to allow the communications professionals to shape party broadcasts. Here, then, we witness some of the limits in his similarity to his dazzling American counterpart of the early 1960s. 'I am not a Kennedy', Wilson told reporters, 'I fly by the seat of my pants.'[4]

Perhaps more fundamentally still, for all his ability to fuse the agendas of social equality and social mobility in 1964 and 1966, Wilson, like his party, insufficiently grasped the political significance of the increasingly affluent, aspirational, home-owning, middle-class society emerging by the late 1960s and 1970s. The Labour Party's enduring dilemma of how to speak persuasively for the poor, the secure worker and the socially mobile (at least three distinct groups, not just two) was resolved temporarily in the middle 1960s, but decreasingly convincingly, and to the detriment of the third, and, to some extent, the second of the three, in the ten years thereafter. Stressing, in his speech to the party conference in Blackpool in September 1965, that his 'new Britain will be a Britain of opportunity', Wilson explained that this would involve eroding privileges based on family and school connections as well as enabling the 'keen and thrusting' to advance.[5] But this simultaneous concern for different groups, and different goals, was not always sustained. Ultimately, Wilson simply did not give enough thought to the concerns of those who, while supportive of Labour's belief in a generous welfare state, were worried about the more dogmatic side of egalitarianism, whether in the form of rapidly rising taxes, 'experimental' teaching methods, or an apparent apathy about supporting the desire to own a home or business. The six aims listed in the party's February 1974 manifesto, *Let Us Work Together*, famously included the promise of a 'fundamental and irreversible shift in the balance of power and wealth in favour of working people and their families', and to 'eliminate poverty', but did not make reference to the socially mobile, or those who sat on the cusp between working- and middle-class status.[6]

One can exaggerate this line of argument. Too often, affluence and aspiration are portrayed as characteristics or appetites exclusively of the private sector or the ultra-competitive. In fact, in its promotion of education, its erosion of barriers to equal opportunities, and its support for the values of public service and the careers of public servants, Labour under Wilson did a great deal to further, precisely, *aspiration*. It is also the case that Labour's most severe failure to keep in touch with society's and individuals' developing ambitions came after Wilson left office in 1976, and contributed to the party's defeat in 1979, and for three elections thereafter. Moreover, Wilson was by no means lagging behind his party in his relative inattention to affluence. Indeed, it seems unlikely that any leading Labour figure, including arguably even the ageing, and in some ways quite patrician, revisionist Roy Jenkins, would have been willing to adapt enough to people's rising ambitions, and desire for autonomy and self-sufficiency, by the late 1970s, to avoid some sort of electoral wilderness for the party in the 1980s.

Nevertheless, Wilson's drift and passivity on the issue did lay the foundations of Labour's subsequent disconnect, and as by far the most important political figure of the 1964–79 political era as a whole, he exhibited both the strengths and the limitations of Labour's outlook towards affluence and social mobility. Others, especially on the intellectual right of the party, did see the problem more clearly than he did. Healey was reflecting as early as 1970 on how the party had 'failed to adapt its thinking to the profound social changes it had itself initiated through the Attlee Government'. These included that 'class feeling was receding. Living standards had risen substantially, and most of the British people now felt that they had something to conserve; so self-interest was no longer sufficient by itself to promote greater equality.'[7]

The Mike Leigh play, *Abigail's Party*, first televised in 1977, movingly, humorously, alarmingly, and somewhat mockingly portrayed the insecurities, snobbery and pretentiousness of this newly emerging middle-class world of homeowners, computer-operators and estate agents. Crucially, what was almost entirely missing from the drama was the more laudable side of these people who had striven to rise. They were, in important ways, Wilson's people, and their appearance shortly *after* he had left office demonstrated both that he had helped make them, and that they had now left him behind.

Ultimately, Wilson was, in both personality and political ideology, a fusion of modernity and traditionalism. He exhibited elements of the social progressivism, dynamism and presentational superficiality of modernity, yet also some of the virtues and vices of traditionalism and labourism – loyalty, to ideas and people (he was a reluctant sacker), allied to, at times, an inability to think afresh as society changed. Wilson's attitude to Labour revisionism showcased this double-sidedness. In practical governmental terms, he was, in truth, a revisionist himself. His 1964–70 government's emphasis on a mixed economy, prioritising education and, especially from 1967, sound financial management, was much closer to the vision of Anthony Crosland's *The Future of Socialism* (1956) than Aneurin Bevan's *In Place of Fear* (1952). Yet Wilson was never an explicit revisionist. He had written in 1955 of the 'dangerous nonsense' that Labour should 'break our links with the past and produce a brand new chromium-plated policy based on "new thinking"'.[8] This enduring scepticism reflected the statistician's distrust of too much abstract theorising, as well as a desire not to jettison what he saw as the baby of Labour's principles with the bathwater of outdated ways of applying them. But it also meant that he continued some of the outdated means, and overlooked how some of the principles could become outdated too.

This invites a comparison with Roy Jenkins, the leading exponent of revisionism for most of Wilson's time as leader. Wilson was more realistic than Jenkins about the limits to how far a cerebral, high-minded, liberal social

democracy could be the sole governing philosophy of a sometimes conservative British society and labour movement, which wanted its sectional interests,
and sometimes prejudices, to be soothed, not constantly confronted. That
is one reason why Wilson, not Jenkins, was Prime Minister. Yet Jenkins is
deservedly remembered for standing firm for large social and political causes.
In his liberalisation measures as Home Secretary, his espousal of the European
cause in the 1970s, and his creation of the SDP, when tradition and modernity
seemed in conflict, he strode boldly in favour of the latter, whereas Wilson,
sometimes skilfully, sometimes uneasily, managed the tensions between the
old and the new, and indeed shared them in his own outlook.

RAISING MINDS OR BOOSTING PAY PACKETS?

Depending upon the lens through which one views it, the overall character of the Wilson era in politics, broadly 1964–76, can be seen in two very
contrasting ways. From the first perspective, a long historical view, the most
significant and distinctive feature seems less the fluctuating economic crises
and policies, the desperate attempts to secure growth, stabilise the pound,
or increase real wages – the things that preoccupied Wilson and other senior
politicians so much at the time, and on which historians and commentators
have mainly focused since – and more the underlying social, educational and
moral changes of the time. These were changes that were promoted by a range
of specific government legislation and action, but also reflected a broader
alteration in the climate of opinion. It is certainly strongly arguable that, taken
collectively, no other Prime Minister has presided over such an intense and
wide-ranging programme of reform in these areas.

As well as the promotion of comprehensive schools discussed earlier, educational measures included the expansion of universities and establishment

of polytechnics, and the creation of the Open University in 1969. There were reforms in the sphere of personal or social morality, like the abolition of capital punishment (1965), the legalisation of abortion and male homosexuality (1967), and the relaxation of divorce law (1969). Measures were also taken to assist particular groups facing discrimination or disadvantage, such as the 1965 and 1968 Race Relations Acts, the Equal Pay Act and Sex Discrimination Act for women in, respectively, 1970 and 1975, and the reduction of the voting age from twenty-one to eighteen in 1969. Wilson cannot claim personal credit for all, or even most of this programme, and some of the areas interested him more than others. But he had a strong concern for race relations; the Open University was very much his personal project; and the broad approach of educational expansion was, of course, central to his own. He also deserves credit for appointing the man who was crucial to so many of the reforms, the young Roy Jenkins, to the Home Office in 1965, despite the fact that he was in many ways an obvious political opponent and potential future rival.

Recent historians have been more willing to give credit to the Labour governments of this time for the measures above, and have increasingly weighed these as counter-balances to the period's economic difficulties. Indeed, this has been an important part of the rehabilitation of Wilson's reputation that has occurred since the early 1990s.[9] But this can be taken further, by reconsidering the respective reputations of the Attlee governments of 1945–51 and Wilson's. The former is still widely seen as Labour's finest hour, and as obviously a greater triumph than its successor. For Kevin Jefferys, as for many other historians, as well as Labour supporters, 'Wilson had not managed to emulate Attlee'.[10] Yet there is a case for viewing the two phases, and their achievements, as simply being in fundamentally different spheres. Attlee presided over an agenda focused on material, and indeed physical, improvement: rebuilding the economy and infrastructure after the devastation of war; setting up a National Health Service and other social service protection.

Education policy played a part, but the main legislative change was the Butler Act (1944), which preceded the 1945 government. Wilson's governments did have a significant economic and material agenda, but their greater lasting legacy was an impetus towards more liberal and pluralistic values, social inclusivity, and higher educational ambitions and expectations – fundamentally, the raising of minds. In this, though, as we shall see, not every sense, Wilson's were indeed the first properly 'post-material' governments. Their benefits, being about attitudes and psychologies, were much less tangible than those under Attlee. They were also slower-burning. This has made them seem less significant, but they were not necessarily so.

Indeed, these intangible legacies of the Wilson era are still unfolding, in the enduring battles within society – and within, perhaps, most individuals' minds – between civilised and prejudiced instincts, and between narrowly lived lives, and broader, more ambitious horizons. It is a commonplace assumption – on both the right and the left – that since 1979, the centre-right has shaped the political agenda. In the sense of the preservation and growth of the market side of the economy, this is broadly true. It is much less true, though, of the shifts in attitudes and educational horizons described above (albeit growing steadily more than spectacularly) – many of which had their roots in the Wilson era, almost all of which Margaret Thatcher was unable or unwilling to reverse – which point to liberal and social-democratic outlooks having firmer roots within contemporary British society than is always realised by either their opponents or their advocates.

If the Wilson era was one of higher-than-previous prioritisation of 'post-material' issues of education, culture and attitude, it was also, on balance, one that reaffirmed that the Labour Party was ultimately guided by a moral vision of political and social change more than a belief in class conflict, or of socialism as a largely technocratic exercise in organising resources more efficiently. Wilson's early influences, of Congregationalist religious values, the Boy

Scouts, and his father's unemployment in the early 1930s, instilled in him plain, practical values of hard work, self-improvement and kindly, yet determined, social and political conscience. These led him to see some of the more rigid Marxian-inspired ideas as pretentious and self-indulgent. Famously, at the Labour conference in October 1962, he informed delegates that 'this Party is a moral crusade or it is nothing'.[11] Writing two years later, he explicitly endorsed Morgan Phillips's view that British socialism owed more to Methodism than to Marx.[12] There is a danger in concluding that, because of Wilson's practical, empirical mindset he had little sense of overall moral or strategic vision. He was intelligent, rather than intellectual, in the sense of writing theoretical books. But this intelligence reinforced a relatively clear, consistent and ethically informed strategy and vision for a society of greater equality, opportunity and moral decency to be promoted by government planning and spending.

Linked to this, the fact that Wilson was a politician with both a strong focus on political realities and tactics, and a high concern for his personal political success and position, should not blind us to his moral concern for the national interest. At crucial moments, he displayed this in ways that showed he could stand firmly, bravely behind a principled position, even in the face of powerful sectional interests, and at risk to his own power base. This was certainly evident in his unwavering support, in the face of strong trade union and senior Cabinet opposition, for Barbara Castle's ultimately doomed White Paper, *In Place of Strife*, proposing moderate curbs on trade union strike activity, which appear very far-sighted in the context of the much less balanced approaches to industrial relations, on both sides, over the subsequent two decades. It was also arguably on display in his broadcast denunciation of the 'thugs and bullies' engaged in the Loyalist Ulster Workers' Council strike against the Sunningdale Agreement in Northern Ireland.[13]

Having placed strong emphasis on the educational and moral agenda under Wilson, it is now necessary to qualify this significantly, and suggest our second paradox. For this heightened focus on minds and morals, and, in a sense, on a calm, long-term social vision, co-existed with Wilson's governments being among the twentieth century's most frenetic, centred on short-term, immediate crisis-management, and preoccupied by economic and material concerns. In some respects, this reflected the magnitude of the problems faced – ones that would have bedevilled any government – notably the 'double whammy' of the first really sustained and serious realisation of Britain's relative economic decline in the 1960s, coming virtually alongside the world economic downturn and associated industrial discontent of the 1970s. But the problems were undoubtedly compounded by the over-optimism and political naivety of that multitude of Cabinet ministers with Oxford firsts, who believed, Wilson included, that the excellence of their intelligent, rational, long-termist economic and social planning could override the iron political laws of short-termism and unpredictability in a not always rational world. Almost all governments experience a cycle of excessive hopes followed by – also excessive – disillusionment. But because Labour governments are temperamentally prone to raise higher expectations than Conservative ones, and because the mid-1960s was a time of especially inflated optimism about what experts and central direction could do, the cycle under Wilson was particularly extreme. In this sense, then, as Wilson reflected in his memoirs in 1971, the 1964–70 governments were marked by 'disappointment after disappointment'.[14] The sense of short-term freneti-cism is further captured by his second Chancellor, Roy Jenkins, discussing the urgency of diverting resources from home demand to exports following devaluation in 1967. The normally composed, elegant Jenkins saw his task as one of 'shovelling earth [home demand] out like mad from the moment of my appointment'.[15]

If this recurring preoccupation with short-term economic crises reflected a mixture of bad luck, inexperience (thirteen years out of power was a long time), and raising unrealistic expectations, it does also cast light on some underlying limitations in Wilson's, and Labour's, socialist vision. In its finest expressions, progressive politics aimed to raise minds, to foster a citizenry that was ethically high-minded, educated and thoughtful, and emotionally equipped to enjoy and experience life to the full.[16] This was the way that would lead to the fulfilled individual and also the just, egalitarian-minded society. Changing economic policy, social power structures and educational institutions, as Wilson sought to do, did contribute crucially to this essentially moral or psychological agenda. But these measures were never going to be sufficient, and undoubtedly the economist Wilson, though no more than his party as a whole, significantly over-estimated how far changing economics and structures could go towards achieving a moral transformation. Socialism would be achieved through 'the mobilisation of the economy', Wilson insisted in 1964.[17] Labour's approach would 'put an end to ... personal selfishness', claimed the party's manifesto that same year.[18] Setting the bar this high, all governments would, of course, fail, and one should be wary of sneering at these high ambitions with the hindsight of a more knowing age fifty years on. But there was socialist ideological dogma, too, in this reducing (at times) of moral or educational goals to material, technocratic or statist means. The Wilson years demonstrated that a more active central government could both liberate and stifle; that raising taxes and spending alleviated poverty and promoted social mobility, but often more gradually than hoped, and not for all. Wilson reflected in 1971 that his government's economic disappointments had inhibited the 'social revolution'.[19] In a different sense, though, the reverse was equally true. The greater economic equality and output envisaged rested on changes in education as well as in outlook in the workplace. Certainly, Jim Callaghan had learned by the 1970s that 'it is not enough to enforce changes in the economic structure to ensure the fulfilment of ideals. These require changes also in human attitudes and relationships.'[20]

The comprehensive school was an interesting emblem of this larger issue. On one level, the (fairly gradual) spread of the comprehensive school had relatively straightforward implications: an egalitarian structure would enhance opportunities for those previously attending secondary moderns and labelled as eleven-plus failures. For significant numbers that was true. But the picture was also much more complicated. Inner-city and suburban comprehensive schools often differed significantly in pupil intakes and teachers' expectations. The private schools and the small number of surviving grammar schools remained highly attractive alternatives for many of the more academic or affluent – indeed, Wilson sent his own children to fee-paying schools. Undoubtedly, for some bright working-class (and middle-class) children the demise of the grammar school in their locality deprived them of a ladder of academic opportunity.

Perhaps most fundamentally, the comprehensive school demonstrated that politics under Wilson was still largely that of the broad brush, the grand schematic change. There was relatively little government interest at that time in what went on inside these schools, in the actual quality of learning and teaching, the micro-educational agenda that has gained attention since the late 1980s. Yet real educational opportunity rested as much on this – on the teaching in the classroom, the books in the home, the loving attention from parents – as on the school structure. Anthony Crosland had seen, perceptively, even in 1962, that the desired change in educational expectations would be a long, generational one in which 'parents, having been properly educated themselves, will stimulate the faculties of their children'.[21]

Historians have often seen Wilson's years as the last flowering and then decay of a social-democratic or progressive political era. Viewed from this educational perspective, however, the Wilson era was more about beginnings than endings. As Wilson pointed out in 1966, his government was engaging in merely 'the first stages' of 'releasing the talents and energies of millions of our people'.[22] The 'post-material' age, then, where educational goals would rank higher than pay packets or economic policies, had really only begun to be hinted at under Wilson. Symbolically, when Callaghan asked Wilson for the Education portfolio following his resignation in 1967 over devaluation – it being a post that he had long found alluring – Wilson regarded it as too minor for someone of Callaghan's status.[23] It is an interesting illustration of priorities, Wilson's, but also those of British politics, and indeed the people, whose educational expectations were considerably less than they are today. The raising of minds and the boosting of pay packets were not incompatible goals, but they did point to two very different horizons, both of which characterised Wilson and the society he led.

WILSON, THE PEOPLE AND THE PACE OF CHANGE

Harold Wilson was, in some respects, an intriguing combination of Stanley Baldwin and Tony Blair. It is perhaps unsurprising, on closer inspection, that the politics of the 1960s and 1970s, and of Wilson, its leading figure, should reflect elements of these earlier and later political generations, both in replicating the yearning for social stability, unity and peace and quiet of the 1930s, and in anticipating the dynamic, forward-looking agenda of social change in the 1990s. It is tempting to see this as a distinction between the younger and older Wilson, the youthful agent of change in 1964 giving way to the unifier and stabiliser of 1974, in more troubled and turbulent times. There is truth in that, but ultimately both these sides of Wilson were always there. Even the 1964 party manifesto, for all its emphasis on rapid change – Labour would 'revitalise and modernise the whole economy', there would be 'a revolution in our educational system' – hinted at an awareness of constraints that might lead to a more gradualist tempo of reform. There was 'no easy solution' to national problems, it warned; improvements in welfare services would 'not be achieved all at once'. [24] Wilson had been clear even then that his socialism was 'evolutionary'.[25] The two Wilsons remained evident in the mid-1970s. The party's formal programme was in many ways more left wing than it had been a decade earlier, yet Wilson was also increasingly explicit about his principal role being to soothe the divisions within party and country. His successor reflected perceptively on Wilson's offer of both 'stability' and 'dynamic action'.[26] Here, then, was the third apparent contradiction or paradox.

Yet it was this very range and adaptability, as well as internal contradiction, that gave Wilson both his weakness and his strength. There *was* something in the critique, shared by both revisionists and the left, that Wilson fudged too much, manoeuvred too much, thought insufficiently of the long term. For former deputy leader George Brown, on the right, reflecting in 1971, the 1964 government 'didn't offer enough idealism'.[27] To Barbara Castle, on the left, Wilson failed to develop a cohesive plan.[28] But this is also a critique that must be extended to the British people as a whole. Whether on 'the Troubles' in Northern Ireland, industrial or race relations, Women's Liberation or student protest, Britain was an unsettled, uncertain society at this time. It was probably never quite as unstable or divided as it sometimes appeared, but if people often focus on the failings of politicians, it is necessary to remind ourselves of the headaches that the people themselves offered up to their leaders. It is difficult to think of any other leading political figure of the period who matched Wilson's skill, patience and tolerance in healing and soothing divisions. In difficult times such as these, that achievement should not be overlooked. In important ways, Tony Greenwood (Secretary of State of the Colonies 1964–65) was right to praise Wilson's skilful maintenance of party unity, and to lament that his 'appreciation that a changing situation requires flexibility is sneered at as opportunism'.[29] Wilson's failure to look sufficiently to the long term was one that most ordinary people often felt suited them, as they preoccupied themselves with their own day-to-day dilemmas and amusements.

Wilson, then, was a contradiction and paradox, who could lead the British people in the 1960s and 1970s precisely because they too were paradoxes. This was not, in the end, a society in which most people were ever on the brink of revolution, or even socialism, as if people could even agree what that meant. It was a society in which people were often a mix of collectivist and individualist impulses, social democracy and conservatism, hungry for change, yet fearful of it. People liked the avant-garde, surrealist humour of *Monty Python*, yet also the comforting, gentle, nostalgic humour of *Dad's Army*. The conservative Mary Whitehouse and Enoch Powell symbolised something of the age, as well as the rebellious John Lennon and Tony Benn, yet many considered all four to take things too far. The balancer, Wilson, was probably closer than any of the above four figures to capturing the core mood of his times, to mirroring both its advances and its failings. He only really *began* to address the fundamental problems of society's untapped potential, the under-performing economy, and the ability of vested interests in both the unions and business to flaunt their power over others. At times, indeed, he indulged and sustained these problems. But, ultimately, he moved Britain steadily in the right direction: more liberal, inclusive, socially protective and socially mobile, not reaching the highest summits, but laying some crucial foundations, in a careful, kindly and decent way.

NOTES AND REFERENCES

1.   H. Wilson, Guildhall Speech, 16 November 1964, in H. Wilson, *Purpose in Power* (London: Houghton Mifflin, 1966), p. 18
2.   B. Pimlott, *Wilson*, pp 266–7
3.   L. Black, *The Political Culture of the Left in Affluent Britain, 1951–64* (Basingstoke: Palgrave Macmillan, 2003), pp 10, 42
4.   Ibid., pp 185–6
5.   H. Wilson, Speech at the Labour Party conference, 28 September 1965, in H. Wilson, *Purpose in Power*, pp 134, 150
6.   *Let Us Work Together*, Labour Party general election manifesto, 1974

7.   D. Healey, *The Time of My Life* (London: Methuen Publishing Ltd, 1990), p. 346

8.   H. Wilson, *News Chronicle*, October 1955, in Harold Wilson Papers, MS Wilson, col. 1723, Bodleian Library, Oxford

9.   See, notably, G. O'Hara and H. Parr, 'Introduction: The Fall and Rise of a Reputation', *Contemporary British History*, 20/3, (2006), p. 300; and B. Pimlott, *Wilson*, pp 560–67

10.   K. Jefferys, *The Labour Party Since 1945* (Basingstoke: Macmillan, 1993), p. 77

11.   H. Wilson, Speech to the Labour Party conference, 1 October 1962

12.   H. Wilson, *The Relevance of British Socialism* (London: Weidenfeld & Nicolson, 1964), p. 1

13.   B. Pimlott, *Wilson*, pp 544, 633–4

14.   H. Wilson, *The Labour Government, 1964–70* (Middlesex: Michael Joseph Ltd, 1974), p. 18

15.   R. Jenkins, *A Life at the Center* (New York: Politico's Publishing Ltd, 1991), p. 211

16.   On these themes, see J. Nuttall, *Psychological Socialism: The Labour Party and Qualities of Mind and Character, 1931 to the Present* (Manchester: Manchester University Press, 2006)

17.   H. Wilson, *The Relevance of British Socialism*, p. 101

18.   *The New Britain*, Labour Party general election manifesto, 1964

19.   H. Wilson, *Labour Government*, p. 18

20.   J. Callaghan, *Time and Chance* (London: Politico's Publishing Ltd, 1987), p. 396

21.   C. A. R. Crosland, *The Conservative Enemy* (London: Schocken Books, 1962), pp 172–3

22.   H. Wilson, *Purpose in Power*, p. xi

23.   J. Callaghan, *Time and Chance*, p. 222; and K. O. Morgan, *Callaghan: A Life* (Oxford: Oxford University Press, 1997), p. 277

24.   *The New Britain*, Labour Party general election manifesto, 1964

25.   H. Wilson, *The Relevance of British Socialism*, p. 2

26.   J. Callaghan, *Time and Chance*, pp 150, 161

27.   G. Brown, *In My Way: The Political Memoirs of Lord George Brown* (London: Gollancz, 1972), p. 265

28.   B. Castle, *Fighting All the Way* (London: Macmillan, 1993), pp 335, 352

29.   T. Greenwood, *Express and News*, 30 July 1971, in T. Greenwood Papers, MS Eng., cols 6359/ 95, Bodleian Library, Oxford

3

1966: AN OPPORTUNITY SQUANDERED

Dennis Kavanagh

I FEAR THAT AN exercise in reputation retrieval for Harold Wilson is still something of a losing battle. To lead four Labour governments was a remarkable achievement, perhaps even more remarkable in view of the party's poor electoral record after his departure. He loved to quote statistics, particularly when they showed him in a favourable light. Some of his favourites were that he had been Prime Minister four times, a feat not achieved since the time of Gladstone, that he was the only post-war PM, apart from Churchill, to lose an election and later be returned to 10 Downing Street, and was the first in the twentieth century to increase his majority at consecutive general elections. But his reputation has suffered in part because they have been perhaps the most diarised and memoirised elections of modern times. The picture that emerges from the recollections of his colleagues is unfavourable; the collective and seemingly indelible portrait is of a Prime Minister associated with tactical manoeuvres, lack of strategy and short-termism.

REPUTATIONS

Political reputations vary over time as perspectives develop and changing circumstances shape judgement. Attlee's and Thatcher's remain high, those of Chamberlain and Eden low. When he retired as Prime Minister in 1976, Wilson's reputation was also at a low point and in the forty years since, it has not risen. In 1990, Roy Jenkins wrote that if he was a dealer in Prime Minsters' shares, he would buy Wilson's but, woundingly, added 'of course ... there is room for a very sharp recovery in Wilson's before they begin to approach par'.[1] In 2016, that judgement still holds.

Labour's reluctance to praise its leaders has been matched by its refusal to dump them, even when they were clearly not up to the job or were an electoral handicap. For much of its history, the party has been uneasy about the idea of personal leadership, starting out not with a leader but a chairman of the Parliamentary Labour Party (PLP). Operating in a party with many checks and balances, in the form of an elected National Executive Committee (NEC), election of the shadow Cabinet by MPs, and the authority vested in the annual party conference, the leader has often had to be a skilled coalition builder. Keeping different interests and factions on board has suited the conciliator more than the pathfinder.

Wilson has not suffered the vilification visited on Ramsay MacDonald, Labour's only figure of national standing in the interwar years, or on Tony Blair, its greatest election winner. Instead, he has suffered neglect, his governments seen as wasted opportunities. An obituarist commented at the time of his death in 1995 that he had been 'almost air-brushed out of the Labour Party history'.[2] Although a key figure, he now seems to have been more a passive than an active participant in it all. He is a transitional Labour leader, standing between the 1945 government, with its belief in planning and state intervention, and Blair, who donned the mantle of Labour as the party of modernity, speaking of 'New Labour' and a 'new Britain'.

This chapter assesses Wilson's leadership of the government he formed in 1966. The brief spells in 1964, and February and October 1974, are hardly fair tests, given the party's lack of a workable majority in the Commons and the expectation that they would soon be followed by a fresh election in search of a more authoritative mandate. Both governments were dominated from the outset by an inherited economic crisis, the balance of payments deficit in 1964, and rampant inflation, quadrupling of Arab oil prices and industrial relations strife in 1974. Moreover, from 1974 onwards, he was often in poor health and at times distracted. His policy adviser Bernard Donoughue quotes him as saying in 1976: 'I have been round this racetrack so often that I cannot generate any more enthusiasm for jumping any more hurdles.'[3] The mobilising leader of 1964 compared himself ten years later, on his return to 10 Downing Street, to a family doctor and hoped to achieve 'peace and quiet for the country'.[4] The 1966 government provides a fair test, free of the above extenuating circumstances. It was the only time between 1950 and 1997 that the party had a workable majority in Parliament. However, in August 1965, *The Economist* had already sounded a discordant note when it compared Wilson to 'Mr Micawber waiting for something to turn up'.

Wilson was perhaps the dominant figure in British politics in the 1960s and 1970s. But these are years associated with decline – of Britain, of Britain's economic standing, of the Labour Party, of Keynesian economics and, more broadly, of the post-war political consensus. A collection of *The Guardian*'s Peter Jenkins's press columns for the period is aptly entitled 'Anatomy of Decline'. Few politicians have emerged with credit from the period. The decades have gained a bad press, not least from internal critics of the Labour and Conservative governments. Edmund Dell's verdict on the 1966 government was 'it had promised a great deal, but delivered very little'.[5] In his *Diaries*, the Cabinet minister Richard Crossman commented that, after the July 1966 measures, Wilson just wanted to remain in office. Following the 1967 devaluation, he was more cutting, saying that Wilson 'has failed more abysmally than any Government since 1931'.[6] Anthony Crosland, a member of the Cabinet, dismissed the government's record on economic growth as 'lamentable'. The Nuffield 1970 general election study stated that Wilson's 1966 government had 'an unenviable record of disaster'.[7]

Edward Heath's government (1970–74) was regarded with similar disdain by the Thatcherites. Governments of the 1960s and 1970s had proved the failure of the post-war consensus, particularly the reliance on incomes policies, commitment to full employment and Keynesianism. Talk of the failure of the market was replaced by talk of the failure of the state and the limits of government. In his *The Prime Minister in a Shrinking World*, Richard Rose emphasises the constraints of the modern Prime Minister outside the Westminster village, a case of Glendower's 'I can call spirits from the very deep' being trumped by Hotspur's 'But will they come when you do talk to them?'[8]

LABOUR'S ELECTORAL RECORD

It is worth recalling just how bad Labour's electoral record was during this period. In the thirty-eight years between 1951 and 1979, it was in office for just eleven and only for four did it have a clear parliamentary majority. The pendulum between the parties swung unevenly and it was a Tory-dominated two-party system. In the forty-six years (and thirteen general elections) from 1951 to 1997, Wilson was Labour's only successful election winner. The 1959 election defeat was Labour's third in succession and its vote share the lowest since 1935. The gradual decline in the working class and of manufacturing industry and the growth of a more affluent society seemed to point to continued decline. The survey *Must Labour Lose?* (1960) by Mark

Abrams and Richard Rose argued that the party was losing touch with younger voters and that its image among supporters and non-supporters 'is one which is increasingly obsolete in terms of contemporary Britain', too old-fashioned and too tied to the working class.[9] Wilson took the lessons on board.

During the twentieth century, the party achieved working majorities only in three general elections: Attlee's in 1945, Wilson's in 1966 and Blair's in 1997. It took twenty-one years after 1945 for Labour to win again with a working majority and a further thirty-one to win another. But, whereas the Attlee and Blair governments could point to achievements (and in Blair's case three election victories), historians have not made similar claims for the 1966 government.

INTO GOVERNMENT

Expectations had understandably been placed on hold after Labour's narrow election victory in 1964, a majority of four seats. There was relief and gratitude that at last the party had ended a thirteen-year spell in the wilderness. But after the triumph in the general election of March 1966 expectations were high. The new government was now backed by 47.9 per cent of the electorate and a majority of ninety-eight seats. Labour had many advantages over continental socialist parties. The absence of PR, and concomitant coalitions, meant that a single-party majority could use office as a battering ram of change. Labour leaders approved of the concentration of power in the executive allowed by the British constitution. Social class was the main divide in the electorate and the growth of the working class was making Labour the natural majority party. It was also supported by a united trade union movement; one not fragmented on grounds of ideology or religion, as in France or Italy. Plus there was still a widespread belief in the efficacy of the parliamentary road to transforming society, contrary to Ralph Miliband's rubbishing of such a hope in his *Parliamentary Socialism.*

The portents seemed so favourable for Wilson and Labour from the time he became leader in 1963. There was a general belief in the beneficence of active government, a view shared by many Conservatives. After all, Conservative governments had tried income policies (with a National Incomes Commission), regional policies, economic planning (with the National Economic Development Council) and expanding public services. Commentators could point to the success of economic planning in France and there was widespread admiration for the achievements of the command economy in the USSR. Arguments for markets and monetarism got short shrift. Active government was the way to go, summed up in the election slogan 'Let's Go with Labour'. In September 1965, the Labour government unveiled its National Plan, including sector-by-sector growth targets, the steps necessary to boost productivity and achieve overall growth of 25 per cent over the six years 1964 to 1970, and a voluntary incomes policy.

This was also the heyday of Keynesian economics, around which Labour's left and right could unite. It supplied the tools for economic management and a pragmatic case for state intervention and spending. The 1945 achievements of full employment and a welfare state were now taken for granted. The Labour historian Eric Shaw notes that Keynesianism supplied an answer to what Labour should do after its loss of office in 1951 and avoided answering the question of whether 1945 was just the first step on the road to the socialist commonwealth, or should be regarded as a base with achievements that should be consolidated.[10] Crosland argued that the changes relegated the importance of public ownership as the ark of the socialist covenant. Business had been tamed and economic growth could be taken for granted. Socialism should therefore be about promoting equality via progressive taxation. Labour governments could spend the fruits of economic growth to advance social justice. Economic growth would also make accept-able redistribution via taxation and public spending from the well-off to the less advantaged.

As the opposition and alternative government Labour could ride the wave of dissatisfaction. International league tables showed that Britain was near the bottom of the class, failing to keep up with other west European states, and several books and pamphlets fed the mood of 'What's Wrong with Brit-ain'. The party seized the *zeitgeist* of change and modernisation, promising to end 'thirteen wasted years'. It was summed up in the 1966 election slo-gan 'You know Labour government works'; the statement said little about the political direction.

It was also a time in which there was a call for new men to take up posi-tions of political leadership as well as posts in industry. In Britain the youthful (taken to mean dynamic) Wilson, aged forty-eight, would displace the aged Harold Macmillan and then his successor Alec Douglas-Home, the 14th Earl of Home; they were redolent of the grouse moor, an 'old boy network' and the products of the public schools (like both Attlee and Gaitskell, how-ever). Instead, the grammar-school-educated Wilson represented 'change, dynamism, science, skill, professionalism and upward mobility'.[11] (In 1965, Conservatives followed the grammar-school path by electing Ted Heath as leader.) The new Labour leader encouraged comparisons with the youth-ful President Kennedy and mentioned that he had read T. H. White's *The Making of the President 1960*. In an election broadcast in July 1964, he said he would 'emulate Kennedy by offering a hundred days of dynamic action'. Wilson would make 10 Downing Street 'a powerhouse' and establish new departments like a ministry of technology and a Department of Economic Affairs to help 'forge' a new Britain.

The period saw some rethinking, largely among the revisionists, about what a future Labour government should do. Roy Jenkins, Anthony Crosland,

Douglas Jay and Denis Healey all wrote eloquently on the subject. Wilson was not among them. When Wilson challenged Gaitskell for the leadership in 1961, it was not on grounds of ideology but that Gaitskell was needlessly divisive over Clause 4 and defence. Wilson likened Gaitskell's decision to change Clause 4 of the party constitution to 'taking Genesis out of the Bible'. Dismissing what he termed 'theology', he thought it was an argument over words that did not matter much.

Finally, Labour was more united than it had been for many years; the deaths of Bevan and Gaitskell helped to moderate the bitter left–right divisions of the 1950s. The leader, Hugh Gaitskell, had fought and lost his battle after the 1959 general election defeat to rewrite Clause 4 and its commitment to public ownership. In 1960, he lost again when the conference voted for unilateral disarmament. He refused to accept it and managed the following year to overturn that resolution, and in the process shattered the belief in the authority of conference.

As the new leader, Wilson brilliantly exploited this opportunity to park the divisions between the left and right over defence and public ownership with his invocation of the scientific and technological revolution. Different groups could unite on science, putting their own interpretations on what it meant for policy. He was not alone in latching on to science, for under Gaitskell the party policy document *Labour in the Sixties* contained a section on 'the scientific revolution'. In his party conference speech in 1963, Wilson claimed he was harnessing science to socialism and socialism to science, something that both left and right could unite on. He linked science to his vision of the 'modern' and more meritocratic Britain. Rarely using the word socialism, he was offering to make capitalism work better and produce a fairer society. In Wilson's hands the term was ideology-free: 'Socialism, as I understand it, means applying a sense of purpose to our national life: economic purpose, social purpose and moral purpose. Purpose means technical skill.'

CHASTENED IN OFFICE

What is remarkable is how soon Wilson's aim of economic modernisation was put to one side and the government became embroiled with staving off economic threats, whether of balance of payments deficits, weakening sterling or increasing inflation. It was crisis management as these threats demanded immediate action from ministers. But the plans for economic modernisation, about creating new institutions and changing the culture in the workplace and among managers, were essentially long-term. The confidence of financial markets would not wait. A week in politics was a long time. By 1970, Wilson had found a new reason for being in government.

Both Keynes and Beveridge, architects of much post-war economic and welfare policy, were aware of the potential inflationary consequences of free collective bargaining with relatively full employment. Neither man, however, envisaged an unemployment figure as low as the normal 3 per cent or less during the 1950s and 1960s. They expected the trade-off for full employment to be moderation on wage settlements by employers and unions. Wilson, like his immediate predecessors, found his governments increasingly drawn into formulating incomes policies, partly to combat inflation but also to reassure overseas holders of sterling. In addition, he found that his broadly similar policies worked no more effectively.

Many commentators regard Wilson's decision to rule out devaluation at the start of his government in 1964 as the decisive first step in the failure of his economic policy. It ended with the government being forced to devalue three years later, having sacrificed in vain its mandate to end the 'stop–go' cycles of economic management. After being confronted with the unwelcome news that the new government was inheriting a balance of payments deficit of £800 million, he could have pinned the blame for a decision to devalue on the outgoing Conservative government. But, politically, he did not want Labour to be castigated as the party of devaluation – he had been a member of the Cabinet that had devalued in 1949 – and he correctly warned that devaluation was not an easy option. Despite much retrospective wisdom his view was broadly supported at the time, not least in Whitehall. But the immediate increase of old age benefits and some other welfare benefits, together with ending prescription charges, did not reassure the markets that the government was serious about the alternative to devaluation, namely deflation. Subsequent measures were too hesitant and incremental to convince.

The election success in March 1966 presented another opportunity to devalue and hold the Conservatives responsible, although with less credibility than would have been the case eighteen months earlier. The new government soon faced more pressure on sterling, bad trade figures and a damaging strike in May and June by the National Union of Seamen. The government, 'blown off course', brought in the savage 'July 1966' package of deflationary measures, including a wage freeze for six months followed by a period of 'severe restraint': cuts in spending and increased duties on petrol and alcohol. This was the classic 'stop' response of Conservative governments that Wilson said he would not repeat, and all to reassure the financial markets. In effect, the much-lauded National Plan, unveiled a year earlier, was aborted. The battle to avoid deflation was given priority over growth. Indeed, the DEA had long argued that the growth targets were unachievable as long as the pound was valued at $2.80. But the trade figures improved and actually moved into a surplus – for a while.

But the tide had not turned. In September 1967, there was a damaging dock strike, sterling again came under pressure and, in November, Wilson finally admitted defeat. The pound was devalued by 14 per cent against the dollar to $2.40. The following January, the new Chancellor, Roy Jenkins, brought in a package of further cuts, including the important symbolic restoration of prescription charges and postponement of the school leaving age.

All the economic sacrifices and the abandonment of Labour's ambitious initial plans to improve the country's public services had been in vain.

Over the lifetime of the 1964–70 governments, there were five different incomes polices, either voluntary, compulsory or statutory. A voluntary policy was introduced in 1964 as well as a National Board for Prices and Incomes. With a comfortable majority in 1966, the government imposed a wage freeze, and that was followed by three years of statutory incomes policy. This was the government's answer to curbing inflation. But there were huge costs. The policies alienated the unions, who saw their members' living standards being squeezed, and added to the difficulties of running the party, as conference voted down the policies.

Incomes policies became caught up with the reform of industrial relations or, more specifically, the trade union question. Ministers were concerned not only about inflationary wage settlements but also about increasingly restrictive practices and unofficial strikes. They were convinced that reform of industrial relations was an essential step in improving the country's economic performance. In 1965 the government had set up the Donovan Commission to report on industrial relations and it was disappointed when, three years later, the commission proposed only a tidying up of the existing, largely voluntary system. This was too complacent for Employment Secretary Barbara Castle, and Wilson. Ministers had grown concerned over the growth of unofficial strikes since the commission had been set up. They also wanted to move away from the unpopular incomes policies. But, believing that something would have to replace the policies, Wilson thought that action on industrial relations would reassure overseas holders of sterling. Mrs Castle opted for a radical overhaul. Her White Paper, *In Place of Strife*, offered a legal framework in which there would be a balance of rights and responsibilities in industrial relations. The proposals included a 28-day pause for unofficial strikes, pre-strike ballots and sanctions.

Most of the PLP were horrified. Wilson was launching this project and taking on the party and the unions when his own and the government's standing in the country were so low. In the event he could not carry his Cabinet and the Chief Whip told him a majority of Labour MPs would not support it. An isolated and humiliated Prime Minister backed down and had to settle for the TUC's offer of a 'solemn and binding' declaration that it would use its good offices to curb unofficial strikes. It was window dressing. As the main study of the episode concluded: 'The power of the Prime Minister was thus sufficient for him to remain in office, but insufficient for him to remain in office *and* have his way.'[12]

What is extraordinary is that Wilson's successors in No. 10 were caught in the same minefield and saw their governments virtually collapse.

WILSON'S STYLE

Many colleagues and commentators complained that Wilson's leadership of the 1966 government was marked by fudge, verbal ambiguities and a lack of a consistent purpose, apart from keeping Labour and himself in office. This view strengthened as he reversed so many positions in opposition after 1970. Critics (notably Roy Jenkins) suspected he did not have a resignation in him. Some of this Vicar of Bray style was shaped by his determination to keep the party united, even if it saw him enduring personal humiliations or, in his own words, 'wading through shit'. The U-turns over devaluation and the reform of industrial relations were damaging but he carried on regardless and he kept the party together.

More defensible was his unheroic acceptance of a referendum on Britain's membership of the EEC, having earlier ruled it out. He recognised not only his loss of political capital, but also the changed mood of the party and the difficulty of asking the party to support what were now the Conservative terms of membership. By relaxing collective responsibility he kept a divided Cabinet and party together, helped to win popular consent for membership in the referendum in 1975, and stopped the party from repudiating membership. He may not have had much choice, but his handling of the issue was a good illustration of what he called his 'politics of pragmatism' – messy and indirect but still effective – and not lost on David Cameron in 2016.

Yet he did take bold positions. Ruling out devaluation from the start in 1964 and hanging on for three years was very much his decision, even after Brown and Callaghan had decided it was no longer possible, politically or economically, to hold the parity. He also took a risk in backing a legal framework for industrial relations, despite the opposition of the unions and many MPs.

There was never much in his record to sustain Wilson's reputation as a man of the left, although the detestation of many of the Gaitskellites encouraged the perception. He was a loner. His association with the left dated from his unexpected resignation (with Bevan and John Freeman) in 1951 over the introduction of prescription charges; less noted was that he soon joined the shadow Cabinet but Bevan did not. It was a politically advantageous resignation from an exhausted government, which was soon to be ejected from office.

The leftist image was reinforced when Wilson challenged Gaitskell for the leadership in 1960. Although not a unilateralist or an advocate of public ownership, as were many of Gaitskell's critics, he objected to Gaitskell's style of leadership, which he found divisive. Being at least to the left of his rivals was an important basis of his position. And MPs on the left would back him when the alternative was a candidate of the right. He was the best they had. He won the leadership election in 1963 in part because George Brown and James Callaghan divided the votes of right-wing MPs. And he remained leader because his right-wing rivals could not settle on one of them to support.

Giles Radice's book, *Friends and Rivals: Crosland, Jenkins and Healey*, has brilliantly explored the rivalries and jealousies between the three and how they worked to sustain Wilson in office, however weak his authority.[13] But Wilson was always aware of the loyalty many MPs retained to the late Hugh Gaitskell and it fed his sense of insecurity. One such MP admitted to David Butler (the leading analyst of elections) that he regarded Wilson as somebody like 'the usurper of my mother' (Hugh Gaitskell)![14]

He ran a broad church as party manager. When he first formed a shadow Cabinet in 1963 and a Cabinet in 1964, he knew that the majority had not voted for him. Forming his Cabinet again in March 1974, he gave high office to many pro-European and right-wing MPs who had defied him on the vote to enter the EEC.

More than anything else Wilson wanted, in his own words, to establish Labour as the natural party of government. The ambition increased over time, as he failed on so many policy fronts, not least on the economy. The majority in 1966 was only the second time this had been achieved in the party's history. It was so often out of office that he suspected it had developed an opposition-minded mentality. He believed that the party had been damaged by perceptions of its historic weakness on managing the economy – witness the memories of 1931 and 1949 (hence the refusal to devalue for so long). By 1970, he believed he had achieved this objective and confidently expected to win the general election in that year. The Nuffield study of the election noted that in his speeches and in the handouts of his statements the main theme was 'responsibility' and the word 'socialism' occurred once.[15]

After the surprise general election defeat in 1970, the government had few defenders, even among former Cabinet ministers. In the election campaign, Wilson did not appear to have much new to offer beyond continuing with 'strong' government. The party's election manifesto for the campaign effectively asked for a 'doctor's mandate', giving the good Dr Wilson the freedom of action to finish the job he had started. Wilson privately blamed defeat on what he called the 'scar tissue' from the tough measures that had been taken. The party had over a million fewer votes than in 1966. His memoir of the government was remarkably free of self-criticism, even self-awareness, and celebrated the surplus on the balance of payments as the supreme achievement. The book was of a piece with the author, failing to convey a sense of strategy or a set of priorities.[16]

When Labour was in opposition again, there was a sharp swing to the left, particularly in the party outside Parliament. Labour ended up repudiating much of what it had done in government – pledging withdrawal from the EEC; adopting widespread nationalisation and planning agreements with leading companies; supporting public spending and taxation; and repealing the Conservative government's Industrial Relations Act 1971. Having to repudiate so much of what he had espoused in government caused his reputation to sink even further.

CONCLUSION

The 1966 Labour government failed in its central mission to achieve high economic growth and to end stop–go cycles of economic management. By 1970, it had achieved lower economic growth, higher inflation and higher unemployment than its Conservative predecessor. The failure was not just about taking measures it had not intended to take, but that so often the measures were the opposite of what had been intended. Devaluation is the outstanding one and no amount of Wilson saying that 'the pound in your pocket' had not lost value could disguise this. Avoiding devaluation had been a highly personal Wilson project and so much was sacrificed in its defence. For Wilson, it was never glad morning again.

In its defence, the government could point to Crosland's expansion of comprehensive education; the creation of the Open University; transport minister Barbara Castle's introduction of breathalyser tests and seat belts in new cars; the liberalising measures on capital punishment, abortion and divorce, and decriminalising homosexuality. Above all, for Wilson, there was the eventual surplus on the balance of payments, the reward for the travails and damage to living standards brought about by devaluation and deflation.

But on the other side of the ledger, apart from the economy, Britain's application to join the EEC was vetoed by De Gaulle in 1967. The veto was not unexpected (not much had changed since De Gaulle had rebuffed Macmillan's original application in 1963). Wilson's commitment to keep troops east of Suez was abandoned, although he had regarded their presence as a symbol of Britain's status as a global power. Despite three years of fitful negotiations he failed to persuade Ian Smith to revoke the unilateral declaration of Rhodesian independence. Trade union reform was started and then abandoned. The National Plan was virtually stillborn because of the over-riding commitment to defend the pound at $2.80.

The struggles with a series of economic crises gave rise to Wilson's scapegoating rhetoric about 'gnomes of Zurich', 'speculators' who were 'selling Britain short at home or abroad', and 'politically motivated' strikers, all of which 'blew [the government] off course'. But the governments of Heath, Callaghan, Major and Brown faced similar economic storms without resorting to such rhetoric.

Any fair assessment of Wilson's premiership has to take account of a bigger picture. His government was dominated by attempts to curb inflation with incomes policies (five in all), which worked for a while but eventually collapsed, and to reform industrial relations, with or without the cooperation of the unions. His successors, Edward Heath and Jim Callaghan, found that their administrations were preoccupied with similar challenges and, like him, they failed. British domestic politics in these years was inseparable from battles over incomes policies and reforming industrial relations, and continued relative economic decline. That Wilson was not alone in failing suggests that the problems went beyond inadequacies of political leadership, party ideology or Keynesian social democracy. The British political class was trying and failing to combine the commitment to full employment with free collective bargaining and low inflation. Callaghan acknowledged the dilemma of maintaining the post-war consensus in his much-quoted speech to the party conference in 1976, which warned that the old Keynesian pump-priming policies of spending the country out of recession no longer existed. He said: 'We used to think that you could just spend your way out of a recession and increase employment by cutting taxes and boosting government spending.' He added that that option only worked by injecting inflation into the economy, 'and each time that happened the average level of unemployment has risen. Higher inflation, followed by higher unemployment. That is the history of the last twenty years.'

Having witnessed the policy and electoral failures of the Wilson, Heath and Callaghan governments, it was left to Mrs Thatcher to draw the conclusion that the government could not – and should not – promise to deliver on that set of commitments. In 1979, she set off on a different course.

NOTES AND REFERENCES

1.   R. Jenkins, *Portraits and Miniatures* (London: Macmillan, 1993), p. 322
2.   Obituary, *The Times*, 24 May 1995
3.   B. Donoughue, *Prime Minister: The Conduct of Policy under Harold Wilson and James Callaghan* (London: Jonathan Cape, 1987), p. 14
4.   D. Butler and D. Kavanagh, *The British General Election of October 1974* (London: Macmillan, 1975), p. 291
5.   E. Dell, *A Strange and Eventful History: Democratic Socialism in Britain* (London: HarperCollins, 2000), p. 39
6.   R. H. S. Crossman, *The Diaries of a Cabinet Minister, Vol. 1* (London: Jonathan Cape, 1975), p. 581
7.   D. Butler and M. Pinto-Duschinsky, *The British General Election of 1970* (London: Macmillan, 1971), p. 45

8.   R. Rose, *The Prime Minister in a Shrinking World* (Cambridge: Polity Press, 2001)

9.   M. Abrams and R. Rose, *Must Labour Lose?* (London: Penguin, 1960)

10.   E. Shaw, *The Labour Party Since 1945* (Oxford: Blackwell, 1996), p. 58

11.   D. Marquand, *Britain Since 1918* (London: Weidenfeld & Nicholson, 2008), p. 93

12.   P. Jenkins, *The Battle of Downing Street* (London: Charles Knight and Co., 1970)

13.   G. Radice, *Friends and Rivals,* (London: Little, Brown, 2002)

14.   D. Butler, interview file, Nuffield College, Oxford

15.   D. Butler and M. Pinto-Duschinsky, *The British General Election of 1970*

16.   H. Wilson, *The Labour Government, 1964–70* (London: Weidenfeld & Nicolson, 1971)

4

WILSON AS ORATOR

Andrew S. Crines

B EFORE BECOMING LEADER of the Labour Party, Harold Wilson
enjoyed an impressive political career. In his early years, he pitched
his ideological tent with the moderate left, yet it is important to note
that as the years passed, it became increasingly 'impossible to find out what
Harold Wilson really believed'.[1] In terms of his ideological beliefs, Wilson
was essentially a pragmatist. His pragmatism enabled him to speak to the
movement as a whole, who in turn responded with both support and heck-
ling. Wilson was not afraid to confront his hecklers with a witty line, but
mostly would strive to convince his audiences that his arguments were the
sole route to Labour's future prosperity.

During the early years of his leadership, this benefited his rhetorical strategies by enabling him to advance a new vision for the future of Labourism.
Indeed, he articulated 'scientific socialism' as some great new venture, predicated upon his rhetorical *ethos* (character) which would put the divisions

of the 1950s to one side. The divisions within the party during the preceding decade had gifted him a highly fractious party who were questioning whether they would see office again.

But in 1964, Wilson returned Labour to power with a vision to implement his ideas of a futuristic form of socialism. This was a new socialism and, as Prime Minister, he used his oratorical skills to great avail in managing the divisions within the party, particularly when his credibility was being undermined by economic events. The economic difficulties began coming to a head after July 1966, when he argued strongly (and publicly) against the advice of economists by resisting devaluation. For him to rhetorically navigate this political minefield presented Wilson with a significant oratorical challenge, yet it was one which he attempted. Into the 1970s, the party was ideologically divided on a range of issues, such as economic strategy and how to defend Britain *vis-à-vis* nuclear defence. Yet it was the Common Market that provided Wilson with the most immediate party-management issue. As leader, Wilson was required to manage the party and to present a coherent message on the subject, which he sought to do in July 1971 to a special Labour conference.

The following elements have been selected for their importance to Wilson's leadership of the party: in terms of renewal ('white heat'); economic management (devaluation); and party management (Common Market). In selecting these key moments, some reflections of Wilson's oratorical and rhetorical strategies will emerge, although rhetorical and oratorical theory will be avoided. It would be inappropriate to engage in extensive justifications of oratorical analyses here. Nevertheless, this chapter will loosely embrace the three modes of persuasion identified by Aristotle. These are *ethos* (character/credibility); *pathos* (use of emotion); and *logos* (use of empirical arguments). These have been selected because they provide useful insights into deconstructing political speech.

LABOUR'S PLAN FOR SCIENCE –
THE WHITE HEAT OF TECHNOLOGY

The 'white heat' speech, delivered in 1963 to the Labour Party conference, represented a major challenge to the basic tenets of how Labour saw itself. Wilson's speech put to one side the old divisions and assumptions about the Labour Party, and instead argued that the party had to prepare for the modern age. As Matthew Francis argued: 'Wilson did indeed seek to project an image of the Labour Party as a dynamic and modernising force.'[2] As well as arguing for a new concept of socialism, Wilson also presented a warning to those who refused to renew. '[Wilson's] message was underpinned with a warning that economic decline and national irrelevance would be the inevitable consequence of a failure to adapt to technological change.'[3] His use of *pathos* was designed to compel the audience to accept his argument or face potential irrelevance to the social and economic needs of the nation. Indeed, 'there was thus an undercurrent of fear and foreboding in a speech that was otherwise characterised by its hopefulness and optimism'.[4] Succinctly, Wilson's strategy was to trigger a debate within the Labour Party about the realities of modern Britain and how the tenets that underscore socialism can and should respond to them.

This strategy unsettled many within the conference chamber. Indeed, while Wilson appeared to be arguing that Labour should embrace the realities of an increasingly interconnected world, some had spent their careers striving to protect British workers from the very things he was arguing Labour should now accept. Yet the rhetorical character of the speech was one of renewal. It was this renewal that Wilson believed was vital – 'there is no room for Luddites in the Labour Party'.[5] Needless to say, opponents questioned the value of this route, asking what benefits would fall to the working classes by embracing new technologies? In response, Wilson looked to the international stage, where the kinds of changes to working practices he was advocating were already under way. He told the conference that 'already in the engineering and automobile industries in the United States they have reached a point where a programme-controlled machine tool line can produce an entire motorcar – and I mean an American motorcar, with all the gimmicks on it – without the application of human skill or effort'. Wilson was warning delegates that the traditional working practices were simply inadequate to compete with the realities of a changing global economy. Put simply, those who looked back to a romanticised history were failing to respond to the immediate changes already impacting upon industries; Britain had to respond by modernising. Importantly, for Wilson these challenges did not represent the end of social-ism as a concept; rather 'these facts, these inescapable facts, put the whole argument about industry and economics and socialism into a new perspec-tive'. For him, this was a new standpoint, which Labour had to embrace in order to remain relevant. Despite this use of *pathos* to instil a sense of fear in his audience, Wilson was keen that they saw it as an opportunity to keep socialism relevant in the modern world, and that by embracing its newness Labour would be better positioned to present a programme for government that would appeal to the electorate.

As part of that, socialism would need to go beyond heavy industry and into the spheres where the modern world was being constructed. He argued that 'we must harness socialism to science, and science to socialism'. By doing so, socialism would be renewed and remain relevant to modern Britain. One of the most important areas for 'scientific socialism' would be within edu-cation. In order to meet the requirements of the new economy, the inequalities in education would need to be reformed, moving towards a comprehensive system where the talents of the nation could be given an equal opportunity to succeed. To advance this argument, he again looked at Britain's competitors, arguing that 'we simply cannot as a nation afford to neglect the educational development of a single boy or girl. We cannot afford to cut off three-quarters or more of our children from virtually any chance of higher education. The Russians do not, the Germans do not, the Americans do not, the Japanese do not, and we cannot afford to either'. His was a progressive, social-democratic vision for science and education in a new British economy. The only alternative, he argued, was 'the Conservatives solution of mass depopulation of Britain's industrial areas'. Thus, for Wilson, the labour movement had no option but to embrace his vision of renewal in order to avoid irrelevance and, ultimately, economic disintegration in Labour's historic heartlands.

Wilson set out a loose plan for how his vision could be implemented and also how successful the new industries would be. For example, he argued that although 'the automative revolution here will be later and slower', because the British economy was entering the race late, '[it would] be ready to create ten million new jobs in Britain by, say, the mid-1970s'. This was a *logos*-driven message of hope that the new economy would produce clear benefits within a decade. This would occur alongside the decline of the old industries, such as coal. He continued setting out his vision for how the economy would be transformed using scientific principles: 'First, we must produce more scientists. Secondly, having produced them we must be a great deal more successful in keeping them in this country. Thirdly, having trained them and kept them here, we must make more intelligent use of them when they are trained than we do with those we have got. Fourthly, we must organise British industry so that it applies the results of scientific research more purposively to our national production effort.' This strategy was designed to provide renewed ideological impetus for Labour. As the realities of the changing world around Britain impacted upon the traditional industries, so Britain must – for Wilson – transform with it. Succinctly, socialism had to embrace, not run from, the modern world and that to do this 'we are going to need a revolution in our attitude to education, not only higher education but at every level'.

Wilson's vision for a renewed Labourism put internal divisions to one side in the hope and expectation that the promise of a future role for socialism in a changing world would help unify those divisions. The future drove his argument, yet it would be facile to say that this vision coloured his time as leader. This was one moment in Wilson's leadership and to overstate its impact would be to misjudge the political realities that he faced as leader – the small majority; the internal divisions; the economic problems. However, despite these, it is undeniable that Wilson's speech captured a vision of socialism that looked to the future. He wanted his audience to believe that socialism had a future, which could be realised through Labour's capacity to ideologically renew, rather than simply looking backwards to battles long since lost. This, for Wilson, would be to miss the opportunities offered by change.

'THE POUND IN YOUR POCKET' – DEVALUATION

Given Labour's economic inheritance from the Conservatives, and its own programme of investment after assuming office, the second Wilson administration was unable to influence the economy in the way that Wilson had intended. Because Labour had devalued the pound in 1949, Wilson was keen to avoid the label that Labour was simply the party of devaluation, fearing this would be an electoral gift to the Conservatives.[6] This was particularly problematic given the pound was under considerable pressure on the international markets. In an attempt to deal with the problem without devaluation, a programme of deflationary measures was introduced in 1966. These included cuts to public spending and higher taxes.[7] Wilson's was a defiant strategy, which he summarised to the nation in a broadcast saying 'we are under attack, this is your and our country, we must work for it'.[8] It was an attempt to rhetorically tap into the British sense of resilience and fight, reminiscent of Churchill's defiance against Hitler and the Nazis. Indeed, historian and writer Dominic Sandbrook argues that Wilson was trying to capture the image of 'plucky little Britain' – a defiant nation against the international markets. Wilson's defiant strategy carried a clear message: devaluation was off the agenda.[9]

By constructing his defiance in this manner, Wilson left himself little or no room for manoeuvre with the electorate, who were broadly convinced of his argument.[10] But the success of Wilson's early defiance would be the strategic 'Achilles heel' that would undermine his rhetorical *ethos* sixteen months later when he justified devaluation to the nation. The timing of his broadcast was key. At 21.30 on Saturday 18 November 1967, the pound was devalued by 14.3 per cent. The move was made the day before he explained the decision to the nation. By making the announcement at this time, he was able to avoid damaging coverage in the Sunday morning papers. Indeed, *The Observer* even ran a story stating that there was no devaluation because the Cabinet was divided on the issue.[11] Furthermore, the timing of Wilson's speech to the nation was intended to ensure that he got his message across to the electorate with as little distortion as possible.

His subsequent address to the nation took place on the Sunday evening, thereby ensuring he was able to garner the clearest opportunity to explain and defend his decision to go back on his long-standing position not to devalue sterling. The opening line of the broadcast sought to contextualise the *logos* of the decision by arguing that it was collective: 'the Cabinet last Thursday took the unanimous decision to devalue sterling'.[12] This immediately set the scene for his argument, thereby ensuring that he was able to carry his Cabinet with him on the decision; it was also a partial attempt to avoid personal blame for the reversal of fiscal policy. He went on to further contextualise the decision by saying that it was subject to considerable secrecy, owing to the international money markets. His argument sought to draw out the distinction between international and domestic economic strategy as he told the nation that the alternative to devaluation was 'borrowing from central banks and governments abroad'. Here, he was hoping to demonstrate that he was defending Britain's economic interests by finding a UK-based solution that would protect the British economy in the longer term. Despite this, he 'paid tribute to them for their help and cooperation these past years', thereby continuing to contextualise the decision as a collective necessity, hoping to avoid the perception that it was his humiliating climb down.

To ensure that the decision appeared authoritative, Wilson argued that 'in our view it would have been irresponsible to continue dealing with these successive waves of speculation', thereby striving to appear certain that the outcomes of the decision to devalue would be preferable to the risk of damaging future speculation on the markets. He further stated that he wanted to 'tackle the root cause of this speculation', thereby appearing to be in control of the strategy. Indeed, 'we could not accept restrictions on our national growth, industrial expansion, and our determination to achieve and maintain full employment'. The construction of his argument was clear: the alternative to devaluation was continuing economic uncertainty, threats to the British economy, and higher unemployment. By highlighting these elements, Wilson was striving to justify the decision as a defence of the working people, casting himself as a sound economic strategist and the decision to devalue as a sound economic strategy.

Wilson stated that Britain was being artificially constrained by the value of sterling, and that devaluing it would show 'we are determined to break out of the straitjacket that has restricted us and successive governments now for fifteen years'. By claiming that devaluation would be essentially liberating for Britain and its economy, Wilson was suggesting that the high value of sterling had been a constraint upon British prosperity. He went on to point out that the size of the Budget deficit was the result of previous governments' failures to deal with this restriction, and that by devaluing the pound, he would be able to deal with the deficit in a way that he and his predecessors had been unable to. He continued, 'for three years we have fought, and it is our duty to fight, to overcome that deficit', thereby positioning the decision to devalue within that fight. Indeed, 'by our policy, by the efforts of our people, we reduced that deficit last year to less than a quarter'. Here he was informing his audience that he and his Cabinet had enjoyed a catalogue of previous success, and on this foundation he had constructed the *ethos* of the decision to devalue.

As Wilson continued, he reasoned, 'tonight is not the time to attribute blame to the last government or this government'. By adopting this position, Wilson aimed to shift the focus away from government actions. Indeed, 'time was needed to modernise and restructure our industries, to build up our trade ... time was needed to cut down our overseas defence commitments, but that time was denied us.' Again, Wilson sought to defend the action of his administration by suggesting that they strove to act positively in the face of negative external pressures. He described those pressures as 'whenever Britain ran into short-term difficulties, there were some who sold sterling in a panic, and there were others who gambled against us in the hope of a quick gain'. This argument related back to the point he had made earlier in the speech concerning the dangers of speculators, and the dangers of not taking action to build a stable economy. He suggested that 'our position was steadily improving', thereby framing the devaluation as a necessity against the backdrop of Britain's exposure to international risks over which the British government had little or no control. Indeed, 'we had to take the measures of July 1966' in order to produce a more stable environment, which he was striving to build upon.

As he continued addressing the nation, he went on arguing that:

> [t]he problem is this. We, Britain, are a major trading country. Like any business firm, our financial position depends on how much we sell to others. But because we also need a national bank, because sterling

is an international currency, it is subject to speculative attacks for short
run reasons which have nothing to do with Britain's trading position.

These speculative attacks became a consistent theme of Wilson's argument. Put
simply, his justification for devaluation was predicated upon defending Britain
and its economy from external forces that sought to use sterling for their own
profit. These external forces were the source of Britain's economic problems, and
Wilson argued that 'our decision to devalue attacks our problems at the root'.

His rhetorical strategy was to sound convincing, certain, and decisive in
defending the decision to devalue. As his argument moved towards conclusion, he began to set out what the decision meant for his immediate audience.
He first restated that the value of the pound abroad was worth less than it had
been. Anticipating the uncertainty this may have caused to his audience, he
went on to reassure them 'that doesn't mean, of course, that the pound here in
Britain, or in your pocket, or your purse, or in your bank has been devalued.
But it does mean we will now be able to sell more goods abroad on a competitive basis.' Here Wilson was striving to convey the message that everyday
domestic economic circumstances remained unchanged. However, he did
note that 'the goods we buy from abroad will be dearer', but in an attempt to
turn this into a positive argument, he suggested that 'for many of these goods
it would be cheaper to buy British', thereby striving to improve the domestic
economy and addressing the problem of cheaper imports.

In summation, the rhetorical difficulty with the speech was *ethos*. Given
Wilson's previous positions had been clearly opposed to devaluation, he risked
appearing disingenuous in his new position. Indeed, the extent to which he
justified and portrayed it as a positive attracted criticism from both Barbara
Castle and, less surprisingly, Edward Heath. Furthermore, the phrase 'pound
in your pocket' became symbolic of the electorate's growing distrust of Wilson,
confirming a suspicion that he was both untrustworthy and Machiavellian.

This persona became problematic for Wilson during the remainder of his second term as Prime Minister, perhaps leading to electoral consequences in 1970.

A COMMON MARKET?

Britain's relationship with the Common Market has always been a contentious one, not least for the Labour Party. A keynote speech, in which Harold Wilson outlined his position on the Common Market, was made on 17 July 1971 to the Labour Party conference. He began by 'reminding conference of the policy we have followed as a party over these past years. Our 1966 manifesto said, "Labour believes that Britain in consultation with her EFTA partners, should be ready to enter the European Community provided essential British and Commonwealth interests are safeguarded." On this basis, in May 1967, the Labour Cabinet decided to apply for entry.'[13] By reminding the conference of Labour's earlier position, he was able to argue that Labour had, for the most part, settled on a positive position to join the Common Market, provided specific interests were protected. To outline the main areas for protection the '1969 conference carried a resolution calling for adequate safeguards for Britain's balance of payments, cost of living, National Health and social security systems and power of independent decision in economic planning and foreign policy'.

His case for joining the Common Market was dependent upon these safeguards being met. Indeed, Wilson's argument continued by laying the foundations for a set of circumstances in which joining the Common Market would be unwise. These were:

> If, when the decision is to be taken, the disadvantages for Britain appear
> excessive in relation to the benefits which would flow from British entry,

> the Government clearly would not propose to Parliament we should enter
> the Communities … Britain's strength means we shall be able to meet the
> challenges and realise the opportunities of joining an enlarged Community.
> But it means, too, that if satisfactory terms cannot be secured in the negoti-
> ations, Britain will be able to stand on her own feet outside the Community.

The significance of Wilson's position was to outline the importance of securing a favourable deal for Britain as a condition of joining the Common Market.
His terms did not simply mean securing access to the Market for its own sake,
rather they sought to protect Britain as a distinctive sovereign state with clear
social policies. Wilson stated, 'the position of this Party has remained consistent over this whole period', which was to secure 'the necessary safeguards'
prior to joining.

By outlining his case for how Labour would embrace membership, he
was able to construct his argument against the Conservative government and
the hasty terms that they had secured. He argued that Heath had failed to
safeguard Britain's traditional relationship with the Commonwealth, saying:

> There is the certain damage to some of our large, traditional export markets
> which will be affected by our being required to adopt the Community's
> rules. This damage will be the greater in Commonwealth markets, because
> the Commonwealth preference from which we now benefit will go, and dis-
> crimination against the Commonwealth can limit their ability to buy from us.

His warning that Heath had failed to secure the necessary protections for
Britain's traditional markets was aimed to construct the argument that the
Prime Minister had been imprudent over the terms of entry. Furthermore,
using *logos*, Wilson criticised Heath for failing to outline the costs of membership of the Community. He asked, 'Why has the government denied to

the British people the information they need in forming their view of the advantages and the costs of entry into the Market?' By making this argument, Wilson intended to imply a degree of fiscal secrecy on the part of the government, bordering on the duplicitous. He went on to argue 'I have seen estimates of £500 million–£600 million a year, indeed more' to underline the initial costs of Britain's membership on the terms Heath had agreed. Alongside these concerns, Wilson also argued that trade with New Zealand had been forfeited by Heath's terms, as had protection for sugar imports. When Wilson had pressed Heath for reassurances in these areas, he reflected that 'to these and other questions there was no reply'.

For the key part of his speech, Wilson turned his attention more directly towards the party politics of Britain's membership of the Common Market. He set out his position:

> In my view, the Conservative government, in the rush to obtain terms – any terms – sold the New Zealand interests short, and for that matter British interests short … It means an unnecessary tax on cheap, efficiently produced food, for one purpose only, for the purpose of subsidising dear, inefficiently produced food.

As is discussed widely elsewhere, his argument was that Heath was too keen for Britain to join the Common Market, and by achieving entry had committed Britain to an unfavourable relationship with the six members. Wilson speculated that Heath's determination was driven by a desire to appear to be a 'good European'. He criticised this desire, saying:

> I cannot accept, and never have accepted, that the test of being a good European is one's willingness at great cost to subsidise inefficiency, nor that the very desirable objective of greater political unity in Europe, for which

so many of us have worked, cannot be realised except at the cost of a
burden of some £500 million subsidy to French agriculture.

His argument was turned towards the arbitrary borders within which the
Common Market appeared to believe solidarity and trade existed exclusively. This argument was made to remind the conference that the principles
of trade and togetherness should not be restricted to a small area. 'So far as
our party is concerned, I hope the readiness to take into account the views
of our fellow Socialist parties does not stop short with Western Europe.' For
Wilson, Labour's solidarity with non-Common Market countries and other
sister parties was threatened by 'obsessive rigidities, which over the years
have come more and more to dominate the Common Market bureaucracy'.

Alongside these threats to solidarity with others, Wilson also warned of
Heath's longer-term strategy for ever closer union with the Common Market.
Indeed, he suggested that the economic integration of six countries was the
start of a larger project. Wilson attacked this vision, saying Heath's 'is a vision
which goes far beyond economic integration and political co-operation. Even
if he is muting this for political reasons now, he has repeatedly made it clear
that his vision is of a Europe involving a degree of defence integration none
of us in this Party would accept.' For Wilson, there was little to indicate that
the electorate was being given all the details over the nature of Britain's membership of the Common Market. Indeed, Wilson accused Heath of deceiving
the electorate at the 1970 general election, saying the Conservative manifesto
merely promised 'to negotiate; no more, no less'. Rather than sticking to this
election promise, instead 'he has done a deal. He is ready to sign on the dot-
ted line, and he is ready to do so because he says that otherwise Britain is
finished.' For Wilson, Heath was 'using the tactic to railroad the people of this
country into making their decision in a mood of panic and hysteria, instead
of with a level-headed approach which such a decision requires'.

Fundamentally, Wilson's argument was that Heath had secured membership of the Common Market on terms that Labour would have rejected. Heath had failed to safeguard vital areas of British interest in order to secure entry at any price. Given this imprudence, Wilson criticised the Conservatives for failing to recognise Britain's global position, and by doing so discarding important relationships with the Commonwealth and others. Later, however, Wilson promised a referendum on Britain's membership of the Common Market for reasons of party management, in which he returned with renegotiated terms.

CONCLUSION

Needless to say there are countless other speeches, such as the 'I'm Going On' speech that Wilson delivered in 1969, that cannot be evaluated here in a single chapter. Indeed, analyses of Wilson's speeches and his political impact could fill volumes. He was a skilled orator and rhetorician who successfully guided Labour through its various internal divisions by using carefully chosen language. Unlike Douglas-Home, he was not afraid to use the new broadcast media to communicate directly to the public. Rhetorically, Wilson's main issue concerned his *ethos*. Over the course of his leadership, he gained a reputation for deception, which was evident in the response to his devaluation speech. This contrasts with the more positive reception he garnered for the 'white heat' speech. However, the reputation was virtually confirmed following the conference speech concerning the Common Market. Despite this, as a child of Huddersfield, Wilson's oratory was textured with a Yorkshire accent that gave his arguments an authentic feel. He also represented a Liverpool seat, rooting his political *ethos* firmly in the north. This texture provided gravitas and a sense of reliability that compelled his audiences to trust him, be they conference, media or public audiences.

Of the three keynote speeches considered here, it is clear that Wilson was a master of the art of political manipulation. His pragmatism kept him out of major ideological battles, yet his position as leader meant he had to manage the party divisions in a way that would enable him to push his political agenda. Thus, the 'white heat' speech went beyond the Gaitskellite/Bevanite axis of the 1950s to call for unity; the devaluation speech sought to justify a position he had eschewed in the preceding months and years; his Common Market speech sought to present a pro-Common Market criticism of both it and Heath. These three speeches show Wilson at his most strategic, yet also his most effective. He was able to establish the precedence of Labour renewal in 1963; justify the unjustifiable in 1967; and criticise Heath for achieving what he had failed to do as Prime Minister in 1971. Without a doubt these were moments of political triumph, but they were also points of manipulation for which Wilson's less than favourable reputation is likely deserved.

NOTES AND REFERENCES

1.   C. Ponting, *Breach of Promise: Labour in Power 1964–70* (London: Penguin, 1989), p. 402
2.   M. Francis, 'Getting Hotter', *Modern Contemporary*, 1 July 2013, available at: http://moderncontemporarybham.wordpress.com/tag/white-heat-of-technology/
3.   Ibid.
4.   Ibid.
5.   H. Wilson, 'Labour's Plan for Science', speech to the annual conference of the Labour Party, Scarborough, 1 October 1963
6.   E. Dell, *A Strange and Eventful History*, pp 321–2
7.   N. Woodward, 'Labour's Economic Performance 1964–70', in R. Coopey, S. Fielding and N. Tiratsoo (eds), *The Wilson Governments 1964–70* (London: Pinter, 1997), pp 72–101
8.   H. Wilson, 'Pound in Your Pocket' speech, 19 November 1967
9.   D. Sandbrook, *Never Had it So Good: A History of Britain from Suez to the Beatles* (London: Abacus, 2008)
10.   Ibid.
11.   BBC, Harold Wilson Night, 14 February 2015
12.   H. Wilson, 'Pound in your Pocket' speech, 19 November 1967
13.   H. Wilson, Speech to the Labour Party conference, 17 July 1971

5

WILSON AND THE
CONSERVATIVES

Mark Garnett

O N 27 JULY 1966, the House of Commons debated a Conservative motion censuring the Labour government's economic management. Closing the opposition's case, the shadow Chancellor Iain Macleod identified three 'guilty men': his opposite number, James Callaghan, the First Secretary of State, George Brown, and the Prime Minister, Harold Wilson. Of the latter, Macleod declared that 'as long as he sits in this House, on whichever side he sits, my Hon. and Right Hon. Friends do not feel that we will ever be able to trust him again.'[1]

Macleod liked this line enough to repeat it verbatim in his speech to the 1966 Conservative Party conference. However, the most arresting feature of Macleod's attack was its relative restraint. The wording implied that Wilson had only forfeited the trust of Conservative MPs since the general election of March 1966. In reality, most Conservatives had regarded him as deeply untrustworthy even before he succeeded Hugh Gaitskell as Labour leader in February 1963 – and there were plenty of Labour MPs who felt the same misgivings.

Macleod's comment, indeed, can be regarded as an example of a more general uncertainty in the Conservative Party's dealings with Wilson between 1963 and 1970. Wilson would have generated an unusual degree of ill-feeling among his opponents if he had been elected Labour leader at any time. However, his emergence in the early months of 1963 presented a particularly potent threat to the Conservatives. The argument of this chapter is that they never solved the 'Wilson problem', partly owing to factors which few politicians (not even Wilson himself) fully comprehended, but also thanks to their own mistakes and misadventures. For convenience, the discussion concentrates on Wilson's dealings with his first three Conservative counterparts – Macmillan, Home and Heath.

WILSON VS MACMILLAN, 1963

As two well-informed contemporary observers reflected, in the early days of Wilson's leadership, 'he took the offensive on every issue … He seemed to go out of his way to provoke his political opponents.' After Wilson had been in his new position for just a month, the former Conservative Party chairman Lord Hailsham identified 'a new and far more destructive and irresponsible mood' within the Labour Party, which Wilson was abetting.[2]

Wilson's pugnacious approach obviously reflected his temperament, but no opposition leader could have resisted the temptation to take the offensive against a governing party that bore the battle scars from more than a decade in office. In July 1962 the Prime Minister, Harold Macmillan, had tried to respond to the impression of staleness by culling seven Cabinet colleagues in the so-called 'Night of the Long Knives'. This attempt to refresh government personnel might have borne fruit if a new sense of purpose had been injected at the same time; but Macmillan's attempt to negotiate British entry into the European Economic Community (EEC) ended in humiliating failure on 29 January 1963 – less than a fortnight after the death of Hugh Gaitskell created the vacancy that Wilson filled.

It would be a mistake to exaggerate the immediate political impact of General de Gaulle's veto; after all, Macmillan had been careful to minimise the importance of his initiative, and Wilson's personal ambivalence towards 'Europe' (combined with the serious divisions within his party) made it difficult for him to exploit the issue. Nevertheless, the impact of the veto on Macmillan and his colleagues ensured that Wilson enjoyed a psychological edge from the first day of his leadership – and this was not an advantage that he was inclined to relinquish.

Macmillan was no stranger to international setbacks, having taken office in 1957 as a result of the Suez crisis; and he had overcome that devastating blow to British prestige by leading his party to a remarkable victory in the 1959 general election. However, although Wilson himself attacked Macmillan for his conduct during the Suez crisis the main responsibility clearly lay with Anthony Eden. The blame for the EEC fiasco could not be deflected.

Macmillan and the Conservatives also faced deeper-rooted challenges. Labour's defeat in 1959 had provoked speculation about its chances of ever returning to office now that its working-class support was being eroded by 'affluence'.[3] However, an upwardly mobile electorate was also likely to be less predictable. Far from automatically favouring the Conservatives, the rise of a rootless 'bourgeoisie' could benefit any party that could project a 'modern' image and embrace social change. The 'Night of the Long Knives' can be seen as Macmillan's dramatic acknowledgement that Conservative support could no longer be taken for granted.

There was as yet no clear sign that an electorate undergoing a process of social transition had changed its attitude to party leaders. The researches of Butler and Stokes later confirmed that in 1964 voters still tended to like the leader of 'their' party, rather than supporting a party because they liked a particular leader.[4] However, the growing importance of television as a medium for political communication was beginning to raise questions on this score, since it had already shown a propensity to showcase leaders at the expense of senior colleagues (and, indeed, of policy). Reflecting on Wilson's victory over George Brown in the 1963 leadership election, Macmillan acknowledged in his diary that 'Wilson is an able man – far more able than Brown. He is good in the House and in the country – and, I am told, on T.V.'[5] These character-istic ruminations – implying that the 'unflappable' Macmillan could never be unsettled by something as superficial as a television programme – were reprinted in his memoirs. The relevant passage of Macmillan's diary contin-ues: 'But he is a fundamentally dishonest – even 'crooked' man – almost of the "Three Card Trick" kind'.[6] On the surface Macmillan seemed intrigued by the prospect, but his remarks betray an undercurrent of fear.

Macmillan was exposed to Wilson's parliamentary skills in their first clash at the newly reformed Prime Minister's question time. When Macmillan stumbled in response to a question about nuclear weapons, Wilson jeered that 'the Right Hon. Gentleman has read the wrong supplementary answer to the supplementary question, could I remind him what the question was?'[7] Wilson could not have hoped for a better opportunity to develop his portrait of Macmillan as the semi-senile leader of an outmoded party.

Unwittingly, the Prime Minister himself added substance to this narrative through his response to the scandal surrounding the Minister for War, John Profumo – another problem that (unknown to the public) had taken a more serious turn in the days before Wilson's rise to the Labour leadership. In the key parliamentary debate of 17 June 1963, Macmillan attempted to show that he and his senior colleagues had acted properly. Whether or not they had undertaken their enquiries with sufficient seriousness, Macmillan's frank account was an inadequate answer to the arguments that Wilson had used in his own speech. This had begun with a justification of his own response to the affair, in which he implied that he had been guided throughout by an over-scrupulous adherence to the national interest. After this sanctimonious and misleading preamble, Wilson launched into a highly partisan attack on the government, which broadened into an assault on the 'small and unrepresentative section of society' that the Conservatives sought to defend, and of which Profumo was 'a corrupted and poisoned excrescence'.[8] In the Labour Party, thankfully, the British people enjoyed an antidote that could be administered at the next election.

As D. R. Thorpe has written, 'Macmillan felt none of the personal animosity towards Wilson that he had for Gaitskell'; indeed, they established something like a 'mutual admiration society', often sharing a drink even after 'heated exchanges' in the Commons.[9] Wilson might be 'fundamentally dishonest', but he provided stimulating company – especially for someone like Macmillan, who regarded party conflict as a regrettable distraction from serious politics. He might also have been flattered by Wilson's obvious desire to derive profitable lessons from his own example, displaying in particular an equal aptitude for gaining positive publicity from trips to Washington (to see Kennedy) or Moscow (Khrushchev).

Whether or not Wilson felt a genuine liking for Macmillan, by the autumn of 1963 it seemed likely that he would soon be facing a new sparring partner. Macmillan's mishandling of the Profumo affair encouraged Conservative backbenchers to speculate about his position, and although the Prime Minister's spirits had revived by September it was difficult to see him as anything other than an electoral liability. Wilson's instincts – rather than anything he had learned from Macmillan – inspired him to set aside his previous pugilism in his party conference speech, and to conjure a much more positive vision of a Britain that could be suffused with the 'white heat' of a scientific revolution.

To ensure Labour's identification with this beneficent scenario, Wilson made no direct allusion either to Macmillan or the Conservatives; he contented himself with a glancing reference to 'the dangers of the old boy network'.[10]

Before the Conservatives assembled for their own 1963 conference, Macmillan had suffered a health scare and decided to step down. Amid the ensuing leadership battle – which was partly conducted in public, even if the crucial decisions were made with 'customary' secrecy – it was easy for the Conservatives to imagine that they monopolised the full attention of the British public. However, while Wilson could not claim the credit for toppling Macmillan – indeed, he would have preferred his weakened rival to stay on until the next election – his energetic opposition had transformed the political landscape in little more than seven months. Even members of his own party, who disliked him on personal and/or principled grounds, would have found it hard to dissent from his boast on the eve of the 1963 Labour conference, that his party was 'united in our attack on the Conservatives in Parliament and in the country'.[11]

WILSON VS HOME, 1963–65

Whether or not Macmillan's maladroit response to the Profumo scandal arose from his inability to fathom the mores of modern life, as his critics alleged, his conduct during the leadership crisis of 1963 suggests a curious detachment from the new political realities. Even if Macmillan did not preside over a deliberate plot to block 'Rab' Butler and ensure the succession of the former Foreign Secretary, Lord Home, it seems that his calculations (and those of his collaborators) were unaffected by the Wilson factor. Apart from his ill-concealed animosity towards Butler – who, in all honesty, was ill-equipped to deal with Wilson – he readily abandoned his championship of another peer,

Quintin Hogg, when the latter took his own brand of 'showmanship' a little too far for establishment tastes.

Ultimately, Home prevailed because very few of the key Conservative players regarded him with outright antipathy (which is telling enough in itself, suggesting that the party was prepared to forgive his enthusiastic support for Neville Chamberlain and appeasement). If Home's appeal to the wider public was considered at all, his aristocratic background was probably seen as an advantage since he could be expected to command a degree of 'deference' from confirmed Conservative supporters. This attitude was evident in a memorandum that Macmillan composed for the Queen, emphasising that from a certain (socially exclusive) perspective Home might be regarded as an estimable character, while unwittingly suggesting that he was almost laughably inappropriate as a candidate for the political leadership of a modern democracy.[12] If the same principles had governed the 1963 Labour leadership contest, Harold Wilson would probably have decided not to offer himself as a candidate.

Macmillan and his allies were right in so far as residual social deference was still strong enough to gain acceptance for Home as Conservative Party leader (to the frustration of outspoken critics like Iain Macleod). However, while Macmillan could regard Wilson as an entertaining drinking companion, many grassroots Conservatives had quickly developed a genuine loathing for the latter, thanks largely to the characteristics that the cynical ex-premier had found so amusing. Activists could be forgiven for hoping to be led into the forthcoming election by an individual who would do more than simply keep Labour out; preferably the leader would be capable of trading verbal blows with Wilson, and maybe of even wiping away his self-satisfied smile. In this context it is difficult to decide which was more damaging – Home's aversion to television studios, or his lacklustre debating style, which had not improved during an absence of almost two decades from the House of Commons.

Even before Home had disclaimed his peerage and returned to the Commons via a convenient by-election, Wilson had pounced on an old quotation in which the new Prime Minister had confessed to using matches as mathematical aids. At least Home could fend off Wilson's jibe that a '14th Earl' was an inappropriate leader for a democratic country, by quipping that 'Mr Wilson, when you come to think of it, is the 14th Mr Wilson'; he also denounced his adversary as 'a slick salesman of synthetic science'.[13] It is fair to say that Wilson was not at his best during his duels with Home, as if (like a football team whose opponents are reduced to ten men) he lost concentration when the odds suddenly shifted in his favour. For example, in the debate on the Queen's Speech in November 1963 he borrowed one of Home's favoured sporting analogies and insisted that 'we intend to play the ball and not the man'. However, this did not prevent him from interrupting Home's speech to correct a very trivial slip in the Prime Minister's arithmetic.[14] There was a danger that voters might respond to this unequal contest perversely, by regarding the privileged Home as a plucky underdog. Wilson would have been better advised to sit back and let Home make his own (inevitable) blunders, rather than resorting to bullying tactics.

Nevertheless, in the months before the 1964 general election Conservative strategists had to recognise that the leadership issue was unlikely to bring them many dividends. According to the Nuffield study of the campaign, the party's approach to 'the Wilson problem' went through four stages. Initially, there were hopes that he could be discredited through his links to Labour's left-wing Bevanites, but after becoming leader not even Home (who habitually referred to Labour as 'the Socialists' and spotted 'Reds' under every bed) could portray him as doctrinaire. The next stratagem was to depict Labour as a 'one man band', in an attempt to persuade wavering voters who were impressed by Wilson that they would be sadly disappointed by the rest of his team if they should ever be entrusted with office. This ploy was particularly interesting, since it suggested that the professionals at Conservative Central Office (if not the politicians who had foisted Home on the party) were alive to the new electoral salience of leadership. For the same reason, however, it was an unpromising approach, since it suggested an admission that Wilson was better equipped for the premiership than Home; it also overlooked the fact that Wilson's front-bench team was unusually gifted by post-war standards.

Once these (relatively) inventive approaches had proved unavailing, the Conservatives resorted to negative tactics. However, by March 1964 strategists had concluded that personal attacks on Wilson were helping rather than harming him. This led to the fourth and final approach – to mention Wilson as rarely as possible, in the hope that this would reduce the salience of the leadership issue.[15] This was probably the best of all the unpromising options, but the Tory strategists defeated their own object by including dangerous venues in Home's election itinerary. In particular, at Birmingham's Bull Ring on 8 October the Conservative leader was prevented from speaking by hecklers. By contrast, Wilson enjoyed a trouble-free campaign, prompting some commentators to complain of a lack of dramatic interest.[16]

In the event, Labour secured an overall majority of just four seats; compared to 1959, its vote-share had barely increased. A wafer-thin defeat, after thirteen years of Conservative rule, produced a critical reaction in Home's favour. As Kenneth Young put it: 'His essential sincerity and decency had got through to the public at a moment when no other qualities would have done.'[17] For D. R. Thorpe, Home had exercised considerable appeal among 'people for whom decency, patriotism, integrity and restraint were accepted and expected standards of behaviour'.[18] These sympathetic rationalisations of the 1964 result imply that the public regarded the contest as a referendum on the respective leaders, and that voters had been too savvy to fall for Wilson's superficial attractions; as we have seen, such agent-centred interpretations of the 1964 result seem inappropriate. From a different perspective, Wilson's biographer Ben Pimlott accepted that Labour might have won in 1964 if Gaitskell had survived, but judged that 'Wilson exploited every chance to the full, scarcely made an error, and had the edge as a popular vote-gatherer'.[19]

WILSON VS HEATH, 1965–66

Once installed in Downing Street Wilson continued to attack the Conservatives, especially (and with considerable justice) in relation to the economic situation they had bequeathed to him. Home was ill-equipped to defend his party's record, or to launch effective counter-offensives against the new government. His unequal struggle against Wilson continued until July 1965, when he was persuaded to stand down by a combination of poor opinion-poll ratings and evidence of growing disquiet within the parliamentary party. Since the inconclusive election, Wilson had been the effective arbiter of Home's fate. The expectation that the new Prime Minister would call another poll at the first promising opportunity made it difficult for the Conservatives to contemplate a change at the top; but once Wilson had ruled out a 1965 election the opposition could look forward to using its newly devised formula for choosing a leader.

Wilson had undoubtedly influenced the schedule for Home's departure, and he was a key factor in the ensuing Conservative leadership contest. Of the two main contenders, Reginald Maudling was widely regarded as gifted but insufficiently combative; in addition, having served as Chancellor for the last two years of the Conservative government he had left an incipient economic crisis for Wilson to gorge upon. Edward Heath was also associated with policy failure (in this case, the ill-fated EEC application), but through no fault of his own. In addition, although he had been an emollient Chief Whip under Sir Anthony Eden and Macmillan, Heath had emerged as an effective and abrasive debater since the 1964 election – most recently in the key field of economic policy. Conservative MPs could be forgiven for thinking that he would provide effective opposition to Wilson.

These considerations made Heath the 'rational' choice in 1965, but his margin of victory (150–133 votes) in the leadership election suggested residual doubts (as well as considerable admiration for the allegedly indolent Maudling). Some of these misgivings probably arose from the feeling that Heath's personality had changed 'in the period when he was aspiring to the leadership'. He now seemed aloof and aggressive, even to his closest Conservative allies.[20] In part at least, this transformation probably reflects Heath's insecurity, as the first leader of his party to have risen without significant social advantages.[21] Yet Heath was also conscious that if he became opposition leader he would never be able to compete against Wilson on the latter's terms. Rather, he would have to emphasise that serious politicians should eschew the kind of tactical gambits, clever quips and downright flippancy that epitomised the Prime Minister.

The contest between Wilson and Heath, which lasted for almost exactly a decade, is particularly interesting since in ideological terms the two men had much in common. They both could have found a home within Lloyd George's Liberal Party, if that option had been available as a viable vehicle for ambitious young politicians at the time when both men were deciding on their future allegiance. In those circumstances, they might even have formed a constructive partnership. As it was, the demands of tribal conflict accentuated their personal differences to the point of caricature. On the human level, the contrasts ostensibly favoured Heath, who could boast of notable achievements outside politics (in music and yachting), while Wilson seemed to find his sole source of relaxation in pipe-smoking. However, if voters had been asked to choose between the rival leaders as drinking companions, Wilson would almost invariably be preferred, even by Conservative voters.

Conservative MPs who thought that Heath would provide a parliamentary antidote to Wilson were disabused by their new champion's first outing. Introducing a motion of censure against the Labour government, Heath obeyed 'the courtesies which are traditional between the two Front Benches' by 'thanking the Prime Minister for the welcome which he extended to me in my new position last Thursday'. These remarks would have seemed innocuous enough, were it not for the fact that Heath was speaking to a motion which included an explicit condemnation of Wilson's personal role in the mismanagement of national affairs, and he barely paused for breath before plunging into his indictment.[22] Wilson himself might have been dexterous enough to shift by gradual stages from friendly formalities to point-scoring partisanship, but nimble footwork of that kind had never been Heath's forte. It was not surprising that 'Heath's speech failed altogether to rise to the occasion'.[23]

Even at this early stage, many Conservative MPs began to wonder whether they had made the wrong choice when they preferred Heath to Maudling. They were asking themselves the wrong question: if they had wanted to maximise the chance of stopping Wilson, they should have roused themselves for an effective rebellion against the coup that landed them with Home in 1963, and insisted on a more agile and robust successor to Macmillan. Hailsham would have been a more appropriate candidate for that role than Heath, and even if he had not managed to prevent a Labour victory in 1964 he would have ensured that the Conservatives returned to opposition in a fighting mood.

As it was, by the time that Home was forced to face facts, Labour's slender advantage in the House of Commons bore no relation to the extent of Wilson's dominance of the British political scene. As a result, the Conservatives were almost certain to lose the next election; the only question was one of timing. Having chosen the wrong man to replace Macmillan, the Conservatives had a chance in 1965 to contain the damage by electing a 'caretaker', who would sacrifice himself so that the next generation at least had the chance

of starting from scratch. However, for various reasons no such figure contested the leadership in 1965; and in any case the party was hankering after
a speedy return to office rather than a protracted period of renewal. Ever
since the 1964 defeat, Heath had acted both as master-builder and demoli-
tion expert, by heading his party's Advisory Committee on Policy as well as
emerging (as one journalist put it) as 'the hatchet man of the opposition'.[24]
Thus Heath's elevation to the Conservative Party leadership in 1965 was not
simply an example of miscasting by the over-excited parliamentary electorate;
while he had been hired in the expectation that he could do an impossible
job, his activities in 1964–65 had been designed to demonstrate that he was
ready and willing to give it a try.

When Wilson finally called the election for 31 March 1966 he could at
least feel assured that the 'leadership factor' would be helpful to Labour.
As in 1964, the Conservatives had decided that personal attacks on Wilson
during the election campaign would prove worse than fruitless, especially
if delivered by Heath himself; shadow ministers should take the lead in any
'negative campaigning'. Unfortunately for the Conservatives (and especially
for Heath) this sensible approach could not erase impressions that had been
created in the pre-election period. On all the key indicators – even including
the question of 'trust' – the opinion polls showed a marked preference for the
Prime Minister over Heath.[25]

WILSON VS HEATH, 1966–75

After the election – which produced an overall Labour majority of ninety-
seven – it was remarkable how quickly senior Conservatives ditched the 'quick
comeback' line and grasped the alternative 'long-term' narrative. As one insider
put it: 'We thought we probably couldn't win this time, but we were going

to make sure we were in a position to win next time.'[26] Other contemporary observers found it difficult to discern the lineaments of a Conservative comeback in what had been a predictable and conclusive defeat; as Butler and King put it: 'In the aftermath of victory it seemed possible that Labour ... might be about to enter into a long hegemony.'[27]

Heath himself seemed unperturbed by the result, maintaining his previous posture as a leader who spurned political gimmickry of any kind. In the long run, Wilson's brilliance would be no match for Heath's diligence. As one critic put it just before the 1970 general election: 'Heath radiates a kind of seriousness which is almost insupportable'. Robert Rhodes James attributed this unappealing public persona to an over-reaction to his main rival, 'to the point when he went to considerable lengths to be as different from Wilson as possible'. Heath could thus be accused of 'cultivating difference for the sake of difference', largely owing to 'the antipathy not only of the leadership but most of the party towards Wilson personally'.[28]

When the Conservatives won the 1970 election, Heath was not alone in hailing the result as a personal vindication. The voters, he assumed, had broken Wilson's spell and seen him as a shallow showman. Yet the opinion polls told a different story: Wilson was still far more popular than Heath. To senior Conservatives, such findings were inexplicable. If Macleod had been right in his claim that the Prime Minister was unworthy of trust in July 1966, he had done little to restore his reputation in subsequent years; the 'Pound in your Pocket' broadcast after the 1967 devaluation of sterling, and his manoeuvrings over industrial relations in 1969, lent support to Ferdinand Mount's reflection that 'the qualities required of a Prime Minister are distinct from, perhaps even opposite to, those required in a Leader of the Opposition'.[29] On this view, Wilson's acknowledged superiority to Heath in the arts of opposition would seem spurious when the latter had proved his aptitude for the job that really mattered.

Unfortunately for Heath, by February 1974 critics could argue that he had proved inadequate to any senior leadership role; and between the Conservative defeat of that month and the contest in October he had augmented his record for inept opposition. However, Heath's fall from office owed little to Wilson, whose 'white hot' vision for Britain's future had subsided into a desire to keep his party united.

This is not to say, though, that Wilson no longer exercised influence over the Conservative Party; indeed, he can be identified as a crucial catalyst for future developments. Back in January 1970, he had personified the emerging Conservative policy programme in the shape of 'Selsdon Man', implying that the party wanted to take Britain back to the 1930s (if not to the Stone Age). As a characterisation of Heath and (most of) his colleagues, this was ridiculous; but in hindsight right-wing Conservatives rather liked the idea that their party had won the 1970 general election on a reactionary programme which Heath had subsequently betrayed. Wilson's second favour to Heath's 'Thatcherite' opponents was his failure to challenge the marked shift to the left that followed Labour's 1970 defeat. This added considerable force and apparent urgency to the anti-Heathite canard that since 1945 the Conservatives had forgotten their alleged historic adherence to free-market principles and had tried to woo the electorate with a watered-down version of 'socialism'. There was just enough truth in this distorted charge to spread alarm among unreflective Conservatives, once Wilson had allowed his party to endorse a programme that really *did* include some socialist elements.

CONCLUSION

Harold Wilson and Edward Heath dominated British politics for a decade after July 1965, but by March 1976 both of them seemed to be 'Yesterday's

Men'. From an ideological perspective their departures (one involuntary, the other apparently by choice) seemingly epitomise the failure of a pragmatic approach to British politics, bringing closure to 'an age of consensus'.

Alternatively, it could be argued that Wilson and Heath were like men bound together on a sinking ship. They began their careers in an era of relative electoral stability, underpinned by the alignment of the middle and working classes to their respective parties. Of the two, Wilson was better set up to master a new demographic context, being ideally equipped to muster support from a more volatile electorate. Having said this, taking context into account it would be difficult to argue that he was a better Prime Minister than Heath. Both men failed to deliver on their key promises. However, Wilson and (particularly) Heath can be absolved from personal blame given the onerous and numerous challenges that Britain faced in those years.

Moving from individuals to institutions, one could argue that Labour was exceptionally lucky, in that an unexpected leadership vacancy arose at the time when this factor was beginning to grow in importance (at least in the eyes of the media) and a suitable candidate was available. Once Wilson had proved his mettle, in unequal contests against a weakened Macmillan, the Conservatives could have sought a worthy champion to enter the lists. At the time, their acceptance of Home – a lacklustre performer who nevertheless enjoyed respect within the party – was just about defensible if one accepted that leaders made no difference in general elections. This view seemed to be vindicated by the 1964 result, which would have been a bloodbath for the Conservatives if it had been a purely 'presidential' contest.

However, by the summer of 1965 Conservative MPs could no longer tolerate a leader who was so obviously out of sympathy with the modern world. In their panic, they persuaded themselves that finding the right leader was essential, rather than optional, and they used their new 'democratic' procedures to elevate an individual who, for all his positive qualities, was certainly not the effective antidote to Wilson that they had now decided that they needed. In reality, if the Conservatives had wanted someone who could measure up to Wilson at the appropriate time, they would have chosen either Hailsham or Macleod in 1963; but having missed the bus in disastrous fashion when Macmillan stood aside, they kept on bungling their decision. Although Margaret Thatcher is widely regarded as the saviour of the Conservative Party, arguably that institution would be in better shape even today if it had been more adroit in its choice of her predecessors.

NOTES AND REFERENCES

1. Hansard, HC Debs, Vol. 732, col. 1846, 27 July 1966
2. A. Howard and R. West, *The Making of the Prime Minister* (London: Jonathan Cape, 1965), p. 39
3. M. Abrams and R. Rose, *Must Labour Lose?*
4. D. Butler and D. Stokes, *Political Change in Britain: The Evolution of Electoral Choice* (London: Macmillan, 1974), pp 362–8
5. H. Macmillan, *At the End of the Day: 1961–63* (London: Macmillan, 1973), p. 396
6. P. Catterall (ed.), *The Macmillan Diaries: Vol. II, Prime Minister and After, 1957–66*, (London: Macmillan, 2011), p. 541
7. Hansard, HC Debs, Vol. 672, cols 1080–81, 26 February 1963
8. B. Pimlott, *Wilson*, pp 294–6
9. D. R. Thorpe, *The Life of Harold Macmillan* (London: Pimlico, 2011), p. 538; A. Horne, *Macmillan, 1957–86* (London: Macmillan, 1989), p. 157
10. H. Wilson, *Purpose in Politics*, p. 14
11. Ibid., p. 3
12. D. R. Thorpe, *Alec Douglas-Home* (London: Sinclair-Stevenson, 1996), pp 300–301
13. K. Young, *Sir Alec Douglas-Home* (London: Dent & Sons, 1970), pp 174, 176
14. Hansard, HC Debs, Vol. 684, cols 20 and 39, 12 November 1963
15. D. Butler and A. King, *The British General Election of 1964* (London: Macmillan, 1965), p. 195
16. D. Denver and M. Garnett, *British General Elections since 1964* (Oxford: Oxford University Press, 2014), pp 22–3
17. K. Young, *Sir Alec Douglas-Home*, p. 218
18. D. Thorpe, *Alec Douglas-Home*, p. 375
19. B. Pimlott, *Harold Wilson*, p. 319
20. R. Rhodes-James, *Ambitions and Realities: British Politics 1964–70* (London: Weidenfeld & Nicolson, 1972), pp 110–11
21. M. Garnett, 'Edward Heath', in C. Clarke *et al.* (eds), *British Conservative Leaders* (London: Biteback Publishing, 2015), p. 304
22. Hansard, HC Debs, Vol. 717, col. 1070, 2 August 1965

23.   J. Campbell, *Edward Heath: A Biography* (London: Jonathan Cape, 1993), p. 191
24.   Ibid., p. 168
25.   D. Butler and A. King, *The British General Election of 1966* (London: Macmillan, 1966), pp 71–2
26.   Ibid., pp 183–4
27.   Ibid., p. 269
28.   Rhodes-James, *Ambitions and Realities*, pp 118, 143
29.   T. Stacey and R. St Oswald (eds), *Here Come the Tories* (London: Tom Stacey, 1970), p. 18

PART TWO

POLICIES

6

ECONOMIC POLICY

Jim Tomlinson

AROLD WILSON IS the only professional economist ever to have become Prime Minister. He is most aptly described as an 'economic statistician' rather than a theorist, but he did have a broadly consistent approach to economic issues, which is evident throughout most of his time as a key figure in Labour's economic policy-making.[1]

Before outlining this approach and how it relates to Labour's policies in government after 1964, we need to step back and look at the larger narratives about the post-war British economy that have shaped understandings of the economic policies of Wilson-led governments, especially the 1964–70 period.

POLITICAL NARRATIVES OF ECONOMIC EVENTS

To read accounts of economic policy-making in the 1960s by participants or historians is to encounter tales of perpetual crisis and, in most accounts,

ultimate failure. This is fully explicable. Setting itself the target of 4 per cent
annual growth and the avoidance of both devaluation and 'stop–go' macroeconomic policies, the government was constantly buffeted by balance of
payments and exchange rate crises. Ultimately, it was forced into devaluation
in 1967 after having sought to prevent this by sharply deflationary policies.
Along the way, the growth target was abandoned and, with it, the 1965 National
Plan, which had been at the centre of Labour's strategy.

This sense of failure has been hugely reinforced by the narratives of economic policy that have developed since the 1970s. Most important is the
Thatcherite narrative. At the core of Thatcherite claims about Britain was
that the country's economy had been in continual decline since at least the
Second World War, and that the problems of the 1970s were not the result
of immediate causes such as the break-up of Bretton Woods or the rise in oil
prices associated with the formation of the OPEC cartel, OPEC 1, but the
culmination of fundamentally mistaken policies throughout the 1950s and
'60s. Thus, Thatcherism drew on 'declinist' narratives that were widespread
in Britain from the late 1950s, but gave them a radical, neo-liberal flavour to
underpin an agenda aimed at undermining the whole 'post-war consensus'
and instituting a new regime of 'rolling back the state'. [2]

Such a narrative clearly placed the Wilson governments of the 1960s and
'70s in a storyline of unmitigated failure. But this narrative was then reinforced
by New Labour. New Labour's central claim, that a radical departure from
traditional Labour policies was required, was based on endorsing criticism
of Labour in the 1960s and '70s. Characteristically, Tony Blair's speech to the
2005 Labour Party conference castigated Labour's leaders back to the 1960s
for not understanding the challenges they faced:

> They were great people. But we were not ready then to see change was com-
> ing, accept it and then shape it to progressive ends. United we should have

been the advocates of economic and industrial change in the changing world.

And if we had been, how many fewer lives would have been destroyed?[3]

Powerful as these narratives have been, they are, of course, intensely politically motivated, and the task of the historian is, with the benefit of hindsight, to subject them to critical scrutiny. How far, fifty or sixty years after the events they portray, do narratives of failure adequately reflect economic developments and policies in the 1960s and early 1970s?

THE ECONOMY IN HINDSIGHT

In making these judgements, we can usefully look at the major economic policy goals in turn: employment, inflation, the balance of payments and the exchange rate, and growth.

It has long been recognised that, in terms of employment, the post-war period down to the late 1960s was a 'golden age', with unemployment averaging under 2 per cent. This contrasts with both the preceding and succeeding decades, with not only sharp cycles leading to millions in unemployment (1930s, 1980s, 1990s, 2008–12), but chronic persistent levels of joblessness. This pattern has underpinned high levels of poverty among the unemployed, while the weakening of Labour's bargaining power that has resulted was crucial to the step-change upwards in inequality from the 1980s.

Critics of post-war policies have argued that this success in employment was bought at too high a price in terms of inflation and fiscal expansion. This view was most famously expressed in public by Jim Callaghan at the 1976 Labour Party conference, when he said:

We used to think that we could spend our way out of recessions, but I have to tell you that this option no longer exists, and that in so far as it ever did exist it only worked on each occasion since the war by injecting bigger doses of inflation into the economy.[4]

What is not often noted about this famous speech is that its central claim is untrue. There is no upward trend in British inflation in the 1950s and '60s, with the figure fluctuating around 2 to 3 per cent. Only right at the end of the 1960s does inflation go up sharply, in the wake of the 1967 devaluation.

It is also worth noting that the macroeconomic policies that Callaghan castigated were not characterised by fiscal extravagance: throughout the 1950s and '60s Britain on average ran current account fiscal *surpluses* not deficits; the unsurprising result of economic buoyancy.[5]

Undoubtedly the Wilson governments of the 1960s were obsessed with the balance of payments, yet measuring performance in this area is especially fraught with difficulties. First of all, this obsession only arose due to the fixed exchange rate regime that endured into the early 1970s; today, with flexible exchange rates, much larger deficits relative to GDP are hardly mentioned in public debate. Second, it is important in assessing balance of payments performance to distinguish those elements that result from government activity (overseas military and other spending) from the commercial accounts, which, in broad terms, register the competitiveness of the economy. In the 1950s and '60s, the underlying deficit arose largely from the first of these, while the commercial accounts were usually in surplus.[6] So, if there was 'failure' here, it was a failure of policy decisions about, for example, military spending 'east of Suez' rather than something that can helpfully be labelled a failure of *economic* performance.

In the 1960s, Labour's problems with the balance of payments were exacerbated by the growth of capital exports, both long-term and short-term. From Attlee and Cripps onwards, post-war governments had encouraged the export of long-term capital, especially to the Commonwealth, but by the 1960s there were growing worries that the impact of this on the balance of payments, at least in the short run, was adverse.[7]

Unlike long-term capital movements, most policy-makers in the 1940s had regarded tight controls of short-term capital flows as desirable in order to prevent the 'hot money' flows of the inter-war years with their highly disruptive effects. As Keynes put it at the time of Bretton Woods, '[t]he whole management of the domestic economy depends on being free to have the appropriate rate of interest without reference to the rate prevailing elsewhere in the world. Capital control is a corollary to this.'[8] Unfortunately, this lesson from the 1930s had been 'unlearned' in the late 1950s, when the Conservative government, encouraged by the City, allowed the growth of the 'Euromarket' in dollars in London, underpinning a big revival of short-term capital movements. By the time Labour came to power in the 1960s, this pass had been irrevocably sold, so Labour was faced with 'hot money' flows that exacerbated the payments position and the sense of perennial crisis.

The final performance measure is that of economic growth. Condemnation of Labour's economic policies draws heavily on long-standing condemnation of the slower rate of growth in Britain than in much of Western Europe, evident from the 1950s. Recognition of this gap was the 'rational kernel' in the otherwise absurdly panic-stricken declinist frenzy of the early 1960s.[9] But, as has subsequently been shown, around 80 per cent of this slower growth can be accounted for by the fact that, at the beginning of the 1950s, Britain's GDP per head was the highest of any major country in Europe, and over the succeeding decades these countries proceeded to catch up, as would be expected in the 1950s and 1960s world of easy international movement of capital, management and production processes and knowledge.[10]

This relatively 'slow' growth still left Britons enjoying the most sustained (and equally shared) rise in their living standards ever. It is also of note that the rate of productivity growth, usually identified as a key element of relative decline, rose through the 1950s and '60s, from 2 per cent per annum in 1951–55 to 2.8 per cent per annum in 1964–68, while the relative position (compared with West Germany) also improved, a gap of 0.82 per cent per annum in 1951–64, narrowing to 0.34 per cent in 1964–73.[11] Whether this owed much to the policy regime is returned to below, but the important point here is that, far from Britain's performance weakening compared with major competitors, the gap was progressively narrowing as these countries exhausted some of the early impetus of 'catch-up'.

This convergence and catch-up aspect of Britain's post-war economic performance is a powerful corrective to much of the declinist literature. It also helps us understand the balance of payments position. As noted above, while this was not primarily driven by deterioration on the commercial account, i.e. worsening competitiveness, insofar as this was occurring we can see it as a necessary manifestation of other countries catching up with Britain. In an open world economy, other countries' faster growth and faster growing productivity, combined with fixed exchange rates, was bound to show itself in a weaker British trade performance.

Distance may not lend enchantment to the economic experience of the 1950s and '60s, but it does bring a powerful dose of perspective and correction to 'crisis and failure' narratives. This does not mean, of course, that we can simply reverse the usual message and exempt governments of this era, including that of Wilson, from all criticism. Rather, having set out some of the longer-term circumstances within which they operated, we can proceed to a more nuanced assessment of their approaches, achievements and failures.

'WILSONISM' AND THE ECONOMY

Wilson's approach to the economy was strongly influenced by his experience as a minister in the Attlee government, when, after a junior post, he was appointed president of the Board of Trade in 1947 (at the age of thirty-one, he was the youngest Cabinet minister for almost 150 years). Much of what he learned in this role was distilled in a paper he wrote in 1950 called 'The State and Private Industry'. This diagnosed 'almost a vacuum in socialist thought' about this relationship, and went to argue for a long-term policy of close links between the two. While not rejecting the contemporary Labour Party assumption that in the long run most (large) companies would come into public ownership, he urged 'that for perhaps a quarter of a century or more we should be operating a mixed economy, with the private sector of crucial importance in many matters affecting full employment, exports, productivity and the standard of living'.[12]

The contents of this paper reinforce Ilaria Favretto's view that, in the years before he became Prime Minister, Wilson helped to develop what she calls a distinctive 'centre-left technocratic' position within the Labour Party, along with figures such as Richard Crossman, Peter Shore and Thomas Balogh. This position focused attention on issues of efficiency and growth, and assumed that these goals would be achieved by economic 'planning', where this ambiguous term would not mean Soviet-style *dirigisme*, but rather outcome-focused state interventionism, with a wide array of sticks and carrots deployed with the aim of improving the performance of the private sector.[13]

This 'supply-side socialism', with its enthusiasm for new methods and new technologies, was very strong under the Attlee governments, epitomised above all by the policies of Stafford Cripps, but has been relatively neglected in accounts of Labour in the 1950s owing to the focus on the battles between Bevanism and Crosland/Gaitskell-style 'revisionism'. In interesting ways, such a focus brought Wilson closer to the mainstream of elite thinking in Britain at this time, which, contrary to many of the absurdities of C. P. Snow's claims about the dominance of 'literary culture', was actually characterised

by huge enthusiasm for scientific and technological advance, an enthusiasm that was reflected in Britain's enormous investments in scientific and
technological research.[14] This cast of mind is nicely suggested by Prime
Minister Anthony Eden's words in the preface to the 1956 White Paper
on 'Technical Education':

> The prizes will not go to the countries with the largest population.
> Those with the best systems of education will win ... our scientists are
> doing brilliant work. But if we are to make full use of what we are learning,
> we shall need many more scientists, engineers and technicians.[15]

Concerns with growth and efficiency re-emerged as central to political debate
as the 'declinist' surge gained momentum from the late 1950s. Much of this
critical material initially came from the centre-left, forming the key element in
attacks on the Conservative government, and suggested that Britain's economic
failings were part of a wider social sclerosis, characterised by governmental amateurism, underpinned by an elitist, old-fashioned education system
orientated to past imperial glories rather than contemporary technological,
industrial and economic realities.[16] As the target of this criticism, the government responded with an ambitious 'modernisation' strategy, involving
many of the same themes as the centre-left technocrats in the Labour Party.
The need for higher productive investment, better training, more spending
on scientific research, encouragement of labour mobility and reallocation
were all common ground. The Conservatives even committed themselves to
'planning', albeit in even more collaborative and consensual language than
the Labour technocrats.

In the run-up to the 1964 election, Wilson acknowledged this shift in the
Conservative Party, arguing (inaccurately) that it was a case of the Tories taking up Labour's modernising agenda, suggesting their election theme should

be 'Little Sir Echo', and that the core election issue was 'Can the Conservatives or Labour best galvanise our sluggish, fitful economy?'[17]

Wilson's most famous speech in the run-up to the 1964 election was at
the Labour Party conference of 1963. This was the 'white heat of technology' speech, two features of which stand out. First, contrary to the claims
of later New Labour critics, Labour leaders such as Wilson recognised
and embraced change. A characteristic passage has Wilson claiming that
'[t]he period of seventy-five years from the last time we were in Scarborough, in 1900, to the middle of the 1970s will embrace a period of technical
change, particularly in industrial methods, greater than in the whole industrial revolution of the last 250 years'. Second, he then went on to talk about
automation, as a *deus ex machina* to which the party had to respond, in terms
that exactly parallel the way in which New Labour ideologues would later
talk about 'globalisation':

> It is no good trying to comfort ourselves with the thought that automation
> need not happen here; that it is going to create so many problems that we
> should perhaps put our heads in the sand and let it pass us by … If we try
> to abstract from the automative age, the only result will be that Britain will
> become a stagnant backwater…[18]

Of course, these claims were highly politicised; aimed at persuading party
members that this agenda should supersede the sterile internal battling
between Bevanites and revisionists. They were also aimed at the electorate, seeking to persuade them that Labour was a forward-looking party of
all producers, keen to lead a modernisation that would reverse 'decline'
and deliver a more efficient but also fairer Britain, free from the encum-
brances of the 'old gang' of amateurish dilettantes who (it was alleged) had
previously ruled Britain.

LABOUR IN POWER IN THE 1960S

Within a short period of taking office in October 1964, the new government set out its modernising agenda. But, before any of that could happen, it was faced with an immediate crisis surrounding the balance of payments, with a current-account deficit twice as large as previously known, leading to large-scale sales of sterling and downward pressure on the pound. In retrospect, many have seen the failure to devalue in this initial phase in office as the crucial, defining error of the whole of the Labour government's period in power. Yet the arguments against such a move were (and are) compelling. First and foremost, devaluation would have to have been followed by the kind of deflation that actually occurred after 1967 if resources were to be released for exports. Such a policy might have improved the trade balance, as it did (eventually) after devaluation took place, but the political cost was high, as the general election of 1970 was to show. This loss of political support was not only because the value of the currency had been made a national virility symbol (though the Labour government foolishly reinforced that view), but also because of the substantial blow to working-class living standards devaluation brings. Cuts in the external value of the currency have their first effect in shifting resources from wages to profits, working mainly through raising the price of consumption goods. This was hardly a policy to commend itself to a centre-left government with a tiny majority.

Some have seen Labour's defence of the pound's parity as another instance of an elected British government subordinating itself to the interests of the City. Certainly the City did generally support this defence, although the move had already begun to detach City activity from the pound by 'going global'; this was the long-term significance of the rise of the 'Eurodollar' market in London from the late 1950s. It is also true that the City, for whom the Governor of the Bank of England, Cromer, acted as an unabashed spokesman, was wholly unscrupulous in trying to get its way against the desires of the elected government, especially on government spending. But all that said, the Labour government was not the cat's paw of the City.

Labour faced the dilemma that (for good reason) it supported a regime of fixed exchange rates, but this regime was increasingly under threat. Part of the problem for Britain was the overhang of the sterling balances (held in London by foreign owners), with outstanding debts far greater than Britain's non-sterling reserves. Although, in retrospect, we know that these balances were more secure than they seemed at the time, their existence formed a constant source of concern in the markets and made sustaining 'confidence' very much harder. Second, as noted above, Britain was a major capital exporter. Labour in the '60s showed scepticism about the presumed benefits of this role, and controls on long-term capital flows to destinations inside the sterling area were introduced for the first time. But action on short-term capital flows was much more difficult, given the entrenchment of dealings in foreign currencies in London, underpinned by the influx of foreign banks. More broadly, control of such flows in a world of growing trade was becoming more and more complex, as the opportunities of exploiting 'leads and lags' in trade settlements to move funds internationally expanded.

If there was a foundational flaw in Labour's approach to the economy when it took office, it was the absence of developed policies to deal with the balance of payments situation it faced. After all, balance of payments problems had been a recurrent feature of the post-war British experience, and policies to try to deal with such problems do not seem to have been as sophisticated as the situation required. But such criticism must be qualified by recognition that successful policies of this kind would have been very hard to find, given the context of liberalising capital markets and Britain's especial external vulnerability as still the owner of a major reserve currency.

Labour was, of course, fully aware of the recurrence of balance of payments problems; but much of the party's policy response was shaped by a 'productionist' mentality, which suggested that the key way to avoid such problems was to expand the production of exports. This was reminiscent of the 'export or die' approach of the 1940s, which reflected the problems of *that* era; but Britain's problem in the 1960s, unlike that earlier decade, was not a failure to make enough exports to fund its imports. While expanding exports could no doubt help in the long run, the immediate problems were more to do with monetary and capital flows (and overseas government expenditure), which required a different set of responses, with different political connotations.

Labour was serious about expanding output. The National Plan of 1965 famously embodied the ambition to raise the rate of growth to 4 per cent per annum. In the face of the deflationary response to the balance of payments position, this was not achieved – although, in a world of catch-up and convergence, growth was still respectable at 2.4 per cent per annum (1965–70).

How was this accelerated growth rate supposed to be achieved? Part of the answer was the application of the 'white heat of technology'. Few critics of the Labour government have resisted ridiculing this rhetoric, suggesting it was empty bombast on Wilson's part. However, Wilson undoubtedly took the issue seriously. In the 1950s, at Gaitskell's behest, he had been drawn into extended discussions on science and technology policy, notably with the Nobel-Prize-winning physicist Patrick Blackett, and this had pushed his existing 'supply-side socialism' in an even more technocratic direction.[19] This interest was translated into important policy measures in the 1960s, especially (but not only) under the aegis of the Ministry of Technology or 'MinTech'.

MinTech figures less in most accounts of the Labour government than the other major new Ministry, the Department of Economic Affairs (DEA). The creation of the DEA owed something to the need to find a suitably high-profile job for the mercurial talents of George Brown. But it also owed much to Wilson's long-standing and heartfelt hostility to the Treasury. One of Wilson's boasts in his memoirs is that he was 'one of the very few PMs who had never come under the control of the Treasury. I had fought them to a standstill all my political life.'[20] This hostility was in part grounded on a traditional leftish view about the Treasury as a constraint on public spending, but also as an institution allegedly uninterested in the 'real' economy. Even if these criticisms had some force, it was not the best way to deal with this by creating a new body that suggested an implausible institutional separation of supply-side/long-term and macroeconomic/short-term policies. There was an exaggerated belief in Balogh's characterisation of Treasury and other civil servants as the 'apotheosis of the dilettante', part of the characteristic hyperbole of the 'declinist' mindset of the times.

While the creation of the DEA tells us much about the attitudes of Wilson and the centre-left technocrats, its substantive achievements were limited. It generated a National Plan and, while this document does not deserve the derision often heaped upon it (it contained serious analysis of many supply-side issues), the notions of indicative planning contained within encapsulated an optimism about the capacity to expand the economy without regard to macroeconomic considerations, which was one of the major problems in Labour's approach to economic policy in the 1960s.

MinTech was both more interesting and more substantial in its achievements.[21] Its name suggests its origins in the technocratic milieu in which Wilson existed while Labour was in opposition. It expanded to eventually become a 'super-ministry' of industry, focused especially on raising the technological level of British industry by diverting research resources (money and people) from military and prestige products into commercially viable production. It was by no means entirely successful in this endeavour – hugely wasteful expenditure on nuclear energy, weapons and Concorde continued. But there was some diversion away from other aerospace and military work, in part because (eventually) Britain's 'world role' was slimmed down. The ministry also increasingly discovered that Britain's technological weaknesses lay less in the misallocation of research resources and more in the corporate organisations and structures within which these resources were deployed. Such problems were not amenable to any short-run policy 'fix', but the ministry arguably did nudge companies in such areas as computing in the right direction. A similarly positive, if relatively marginal, role was played by the Industrial Reorganisation Corporation, with its remit to encourage mergers in sectors where enhanced scale would have positive effects on efficiency.

Because it does not fit with any of the major narratives, another important contribution to improved efficiency supported by the 1960s' government policies has been largely neglected. This is the policy of what we may call 'humane restructuring'. The numbers employed in major nationalised industries fell enormously under Labour – coalmining by 208,000, railways by 128,000 between 1964 and 1969. In the private sector, this was also a period of rapid structural change, encouraged by the 'shake-out' linked to the government's Selective Employment Tax. The paradox of all this is that we now know that rather than seeing the expansion of the overall industrial labour force, this continued the decline that had begun in the 1950s, and that spread to manufacturing in the 1960s. But if the government (like everyone else) did not see that the future was to be one of de-industrialisation, what it did do was facilitate structural change without putting most of the burden on the workers displaced. Income-related unemployment benefit and redundancy payments cushioned the impact of change for most workers, and while unemployment (especially among older men) edged up after 1967, most 'displaced' workers soon found alternative employment in what was still fundamentally a fully employed economy.[22]

While 'stop–go' was not abolished and devaluation was followed by a severe 'stop', some aspects of the 'supply side' of the economy had improved.

Despite the allegations of many critics, Labour was far from ignoring supply-side problems, nor did it seek to preserve the pattern of employment. It is not unreasonable to believe that some of the buoyancy of productivity in the period was aided, if not directly caused, by the government's various policies.

POLICY, 1974–76

Wilson's second period as Prime Minister before his resignation in spring 1976 is largely an epilogue to his career as well as a prologue to many of the key developments of the 1970s. He did, however, play an important role in shaping Labour's approach to power in 1974 and its early responses to the crisis that soon engulfed it.

In February 1974, Labour under Wilson unexpectedly returned to government, inheriting an appalling legacy from the previous government, enormously added to by the stagflationary impact of OPEC 1. In opposition between 1970 and 1974, Wilson had faced a marked leftward shift in Labour's dominant ideas – ideas seriously out of kilter with his own views.

The issue that propelled Labour into power was, of course, that of government–trade union relations. Across the Western world, the 1960s had seen the worsening of industrial relations, and while Britain saw no general strike (like Belgium or France) or 'Hot autumn' as in Italy, the 1960s saw greater militancy among British unions, which propelled them into clashes with the Labour government. Wilson had never been a 'union man' like many leading Labour figures, but had always sought to maintain close and cordial relations with union leaders. This relationship had come closest to breaking down with the proposed changes to industrial relations law in *In Place of Strife* in 1969, but after these were not implemented in the face of union opposition, Wilson focused on maintaining good relationships. Out of this came the 'Social

Contract' of 1972–73, which sought to secure a 'deal' between the unions and a future Labour government. This would give the unions an important role in Labour policy-making, and rule out statutory intervention in collective bargaining ('incomes policy'), in return for recognition by the unions of the need for wage restraint.[23]

Whether such a model could have survived in 'normal' times was never tested, as the contract came to be pursued in a period of much faster inflation and much higher unemployment than its architects ever envisaged. While Wilson remained premier, the contract did not deliver significant restraint on wage-bargaining; only after the unions 'stared into the abyss' of hyper-inflation in 1976 did it have an impact on their bargaining stance.

In the face of stagflation, Labour under Wilson was forced to retreat from its traditional, social-democratic stance, most notably with the beginnings of fiscal tightening announced in Healey's 1975 Budget, which Wilson fully supported. However, the 'centre-left technocrat' agenda was not given up. While the National Enterprise Board was put forward by the left in the party as a vehicle for major expansion of public ownership, this was successfully resisted by Wilson, and its role as an instrument of intervention, albeit largely aimed at rescuing 'lame ducks', fitted with a Wilsonian view about the need for an active state role in industry.

CONCLUSIONS

A proper assessment of Wilson's impact on economic policy requires both a recognition of the highly politicised narrative frames commonly applied to this period and an understanding of the particular milieu within which Wilson's approach to policy emerged. The aim here has been, within the tight limits of space, to do those two things.

The most important conclusion is that the 'declinist' narrative has distorted our understanding of much of post-war British economic history and policy, and a recognition of that fact helps to offer a perspective on these years that at least may rescue Wilson from some of the more tendentious versions of the condescension of posterity.

The primary purpose of this essay has not been to award Wilson 'marks out of ten', but some tentative conclusions can be offered about how far his role shaped the successes and failures of Labour's economic policies.

Wilson sought to find a 'third way' policy agenda between a left that continued to prioritise public ownership as the defining feature of socialism and a right that sought to redefine that ideology in ways that most members of the Labour party rejected. 'Technocratic socialism' was a combination of a number of ideas common in the 1950s and '60s about growth, about science and technology and about the role of the state in the economy. Like all political projects, when applied, it fell short of its supporters' hopes. It did, however, aid the modernisation of Britain's industrial economy in the 1960s, and did so in ways that did not make most of the costs of change fall on the workers. As well as maintaining close to full employment (though the labour market deteriorated after 1966), Labour was able to achieve a significant improvement of both the absolute and relative position of those at the bottom end of the income distribution.[24]

In responding to Britain's pressing balance of payments problems, technocratic socialism was inhibited by its 'productionist' approach. It took the crisis around devaluation for Wilson to seriously address the need to cut back on Britain's overseas commitments, and, ironically perhaps, it was a Chancellor drawn from the right of the party, Roy Jenkins, who was most willing to be radical not only in largely ending the 'east of Suez' role, but even questioning that most sacred of sacred cows, the 'independent nuclear deterrent'. Similarly, Wilson was seemingly slow to recognise the need to grasp the nettle of ending sterling's role as a reserve currency; again, it took the devaluation crisis to force agreement on this change, essentially sealed by the Basel Agreement of 1968. There was less inhibition in questioning the benefits of Britain's role as an exporter of capital, perhaps because this fitted with the 'productionist' priority attached to raising domestic investment.

Overall, while the long-term impact of the frequent economic 'crises' of the 1960s is often exaggerated in terms of the economic welfare of the mass of the population, they could have been less damaging (not least to the Labour Party's reputation for competence in economic management) if some of the measures adopted in response to the balance of payments crisis surrounding devaluation had been adopted earlier. The reasons this was not done were multiple. As already suggested, the 'productionist' approach of Wilson's technocratic socialism was an obstacle to focusing on the elements of the balance of payments most urgently in need of reform. Addressing the problems of the international role of sterling and overseas government spending was bound to be constrained by the political complexity surrounding any solutions, which had defeated previous post-war governments. It is in retrospect wholly unsurprising that it took a major crisis for these constraints to be overcome.

NOTES AND REFERENCES

1.   This statistical expertise was recognised in his election as president of the Royal Statistical Society in 1972/73

2.   D. Cannadine, 'Apocalypse when? British Politicians and British "Decline" in the Twentieth Century', in P. Clarke and C. Trebilcock (eds), *Understanding Decline: Perceptions and Realities of Britain's Economic Performance* (Cambridge: Cambridge University Press, 1997), pp 263–9; and J. Tomlinson, 'Thrice Denied: "Declinism" as a Recurrent Theme in British History in the Long Twentieth Century', *Twentieth Century British History*, 20, (2009), pp 227–51

3.   T. Blair, Speech to Labour Party conference, 27 September 2005; and see G. O'Hara and H. Parr, 'Conclusions: Harold Wilson's 1964–70 Governments and the Heritage of "New" Labour', *Contemporary British History*, 20, (2006), pp 477–89

4.   J. Callaghan, Speech to Labour Party conference, 28 September 1976

5. The overall fiscal balance (Public Sector Borrowing Requirement) averaged around 2 per cent, far less than in succeeding decades

6. W. Manser, *Britain in Balance: The Myth of Failure* (London: Penguin, 1971), pp 18–27

7. W. Reddaway, *Effects of UK Direct Investment Overseas* (Cambridge: Cambridge University Press, 1967)

8. J. M. Keynes, *Collected Writings: The Clearing Union, Vol. 25* (London: Palgrave Macmillan, 1971), pp 148–9

9. J. Tomlinson, 'Inventing "Decline": The Falling Behind of the British Economy in the Post-War Years', *Economic History Review*, 49, (1996), pp 734–60

10. N. Crafts, 'The Golden Age of Economic Growth in Western Europe, 1950–73', *Economic History Review*, 48, (1995), pp 429–47

11. R. Matthews, C. Feinstein and J. Odling-Smee, *British Economic Growth 1856–1973* (Oxford: Oxford University Press, 1982), p. 25; and S. Broadberry and N. Crafts, 'UK Productivity Performance from 1950 to 1979: A Restatement of the Broadberry–Crafts view', *Economic History Review*, 56, (2003), p. 723. A recent survey by two pro-market economic historians has described the performance of manufacturing, usually the most maligned sector, as 'reasonable between 1951 and 1973': S. Broadberry and T. Leunig, *The Impact of Government Policies on UK Manufacturing since 1945* (London: LSE, 2013), p. 4

12. The National Archives [hereafter TNA] PREM 8/1183, 'The State and Private Industry', 4 May 1950, covering note by Harold Wilson

13. I. Favretto, '"Wilsonism" Reconsidered: Labour Party Revisionism 1952–64', *Contemporary British History*, 14, (2000), pp 54–80

14. D. Edgerton, *Warfare State: Britain, 1920–70* (Cambridge: Cambridge University Press, 2006)

15. Parliamentary Papers, 1955/56, Cmnd 9703, Vol. xxxvi

16. M. Shanks, *The Stagnant Society: A Warning* (Harmondsworth: Penguin, 1961)

17. H. Wilson, Speech at Swansea, 25 January 1964, in H. Wilson, *The New Britain: Labour's Plan: Selected Speeches* (Harmondsworth: Penguin, 1964)

18. H. Wilson, Speech at Scarborough conference, 1 October 1963, in H. Wilson, *Purpose in Politics*, pp 15–16

19. H. Wilson, *Memoirs: The Making of a Prime Minister* (London: Weidenfeld & Nicolson, 1986), p. 194

20. Ibid., p. 1

21. D. Edgerton, 'The "White Heat" Revisited: The British Government and Technology in the 1960s', *Twentieth Century British History*, 7, (1996), pp 53–82; and R. Coopey, 'Industrial Policy in the White Heat of the Scientific Revolution', in R. Coopey, S. Fielding and N. Tiratsoo (eds), *The Wilson Governments, 1964–70* (London: Continuum International Publishing, 1993), pp 102–22

22. J. Tomlinson, *The Labour Governments, 1964–70: Vol. 3, Economic Policy* (Manchester: Manchester University Press, 2004), pp 123–34, 220–21

23. P. Ziegler, *Wilson: The Authorised Life of Lord Wilson of Rievaulx* (London: Weidenfeld & Nicolson, 1993), pp 392–3

24. A. Atkinson, 'The Distribution of Income in the UK and OECD Countries in the Twentieth Century', *Oxford Review of Economic Policy*, 15, (1999), p. 60

7

INDUSTRIAL RELATIONS

Robert Taylor

THROUGHOUT HIS SEVEN and a half years as Prime Minister, Harold Wilson faced the challenge posed by Britain's troubling industrial relations in a relatively stagnant or low-growth economy. However, he was determined to take the offensive and not simply respond to the course of events. Often rightly seen as essentially a man of compromise and consensus, and above all as an arch-pragmatist, Wilson was keen to encourage a modernisation of the trade unions. He saw their reform as central to his grand design of achieving economic growth, material prosperity and social justice. Wilson held a surprisingly idealistic vision of how the trade unions could become essential partners with his government in the creation of a social-democratic state in Britain. The scale of his ambitions for Labour in government was set out in his launch of the party's 1964 general election campaign at the annual meeting of the Trades Union Congress. Wilson invited the trade unions to participate in what he called a 'great adventure' with a Labour government, to transform the country and end the years of stop–go economics that he believed had encouraged caution and defensive attitudes and deterred 'inventiveness, innovation and enterprise'.[1]

Wilson had just returned from a trip to Sweden and was enthused by the ability of that country's trade unions to work in tandem with the state and employer organisations in accepting and welcoming necessary change. 'We shall consult, not present you with a diktat,' Wilson assured the enthusiastic delegates.[2] He promised legislation to protect the trade unions from legal attack in the holding of strikes and enthused about new technology and science and the need to boost regional planning, training and industrial restructuring. In return, he wanted the trade unions to embrace a voluntary national prices and incomes policy and make a reality of the 'planned expansion of incomes related to the country's rising productivity'.[3] He ruled out pay restraint by the state or a wage freeze. However, Wilson said he did expect the trade unions to cooperate in the technological revolution and abandon restrictive labour practices. Wilson spoke warmly of creating a tripartite partnership to bring about long-overdue change through cooperation.

As newly elected Prime Minister in October 1964, Wilson was keen to build on the goodwill of the trade unions. He brought Frank Cousins, the left-wing leader of the Transport and General Workers' Union, into his Cabinet as Minister of Technology and made Ray Gunter, a former white-collar transport union official, Minister of Labour. He held regular meetings with the TUC to try to secure their trust and support. The famous era of beer and sandwiches at 10 Downing Street had truly begun. Wilson appointed a Royal Commission on industrial relations under Lord Donovan and even made George Woodcock, the TUC's General Secretary, a member of it. In his TUC speech, he had dismissed the idea of a Royal Commission because it would 'take minutes and waste years'.[4]

Over the next four years, Wilson sought to win the TUC's support in carrying through an effective incomes policy. But, from the early decision of his Cabinet not to devalue sterling, the emphasis was inevitably not on wage growth but on the necessity for wage restraint for all. The government's economic inheritance was dire, with a huge balance of payments deficit, and the money markets needed reassurance. Wilson sought and gained the active participation of the TUC in supervising a voluntary restraint on pay rises. But, by the time of the seamen's strike in the early summer of 1966, Wilson was losing patience with the trade unions as wage rises soared far above any improvement in labour productivity. However, it was his public attack on the executive of the Seamen's Union for containing what he called 'a tightly knit group of politically motivated men' that angered the wider trade union movement. A resort to a crude 'reds in the bed' scare by the Prime Minister brought widespread criticism. Jack Jones, in the Transport and General Workers' Union, believed it revealed Wilson's ignorance of industrial relations and soured government/trade union relations.

From the summer of 1966, after his landslide election victory, Wilson was compelled by adverse economic pressures to enforce a compulsory prices and incomes policy, with the reluctant acquiescence of the TUC. His government's electoral popularity plummeted and the devaluation of sterling in November 1967 did little to immediately improve the economy. By the summer of 1968, the interminable efforts to administer a statutory prices and incomes policy seemed to have run their course, with no tangible upturn in the country's economic fortunes. At the same time, the trade unions as institutions were being blamed for an upsurge in worker militancy through a rash of unofficial strikes, mainly in the car and engineering industries.

That June (1968), the Donovan Royal Commission reported after over three years of deliberation. Its conclusions were hardly radical, with a firm commitment to the so-called voluntary system of industrial relations and advocacy of slow, piecemeal change. It read too much like an academic publication and seemed to fall far short of what Wilson believed the dire circumstances of the times required.

IN PLACE OF STRIFE

The Donovan Report disappointed the Prime Minister, who now sought a more dynamic approach to the reform of industrial relations. He decided to replace Gunter at the Ministry of Labour with his close political ally Barbara Castle in a new super Department of Employment and Productivity. Her arrival at St James's Square suggested Wilson was in the mood to find a more active role for the state in industrial relations and was no longer willing to allow the trade unions to modernise at what he saw as their own languid pace. Castle's resulting *In Place of Strife* White Paper seemed dynamic and ambitious compared with the caution and timidity of Donovan. The overwhelming preoccupation of the White Paper was with the need to improve and strengthen collective bargaining, through limited state intervention. Wilson was delighted with its contents. He thought what it proposed would outwit Conservative Party leader Edward Heath's anti-trade union plans and win back lost popularity. Castle had believed Donovan suffered from having George Woodcock's fingerprints all over it. She, just like Donovan, wanted to strengthen and not weaken the trade unions and favoured raising their status and improving their legal rights. But she and Wilson agreed that this would not be enough and believed the trade unions, in return for support, must accept greater responsibilities in preventing the needless disruption of the country's economic life.

Almost all of the White Paper's proposals met with widespread approval in the labour movement. Even James Callaghan, the Home Secretary and its most serious critic, said he agreed with 90 per cent of the document. But, the problem for its opponents lay with the proposals it contained to deal with inter-union disputes and, above all, unofficial strikes through so-called penal sanctions by fining workers who rejected conciliation. 'Harold was already showing signs of being more hawkish than I was,' admitted Castle. 'Strikes were an issue on which he felt vulnerable.'[5] It was the way in which Wilson dealt with the White Paper that plunged the government into a prolonged and needless crisis that turned into arguably one of the most serious in the Labour Party's history. 'The government wasted six months on a hopeless fight, which caused permanent damage to relations with the trade unions without making them any less necessary to our survival,' mused Defence Secretary Denis Healey in his memoirs. '*In Place of Strife* did for Wilson what the hopeless attempt to delete Clause 4 from the party constitution had done for Hugh Gaitskell.'[6]

What particularly puzzled the Prime Minister's critics, and even his friends, was the uncharacteristic manner in which he dealt with the issue. He seemed to grow more reckless and provocative, not cautious and pragmatic, as was his usual style of government. Often he seemed to come close to the end of his tether. 'Harold could easily have extricated himself but he entered into the spirit of the battle enthusiastically,' wrote Castle in her own memoirs. 'I got the impression that the idea of resigning over an issue like this positively appealed to him. Whatever others did we were not prepared to budge.'[7] No doubt, Castle's aggressive style of behaviour upset the trade union leaders. They disliked her stridency and impatience and often her inability to discuss her proposals with colleagues in a calm and understanding manner. But, until the end of the crisis, she continued to enjoy Wilson's whole-hearted support. It is possible that a real settlement might have been possible if Wilson and Castle had decided to legislate on the whole of the trade union reform package in the next parliamentary session and not try to rush through the so-called penal clauses over unofficial strikes in a short, sharp Bill. But, by the spring of 1969, Wilson and his Chancellor Roy Jenkins had mistakenly come to the conclusion that the proposed limited action on dealing with inter-union and unofficial strikes should become a substitute for a more rigorous prices and incomes policy as a means to reassure overseas financial confidence in the post-devaluation economy.

Most of the Cabinet appeared increasingly to disagree with them. Ministers were bewildered with what seemed like an unnecessary challenge to the trade unions over unofficial disputes. The most unyielding opposition in the Cabinet came from James Callaghan, the Home Secretary, once described by the journalist Peter Jenkins as 'the keeper of the cloth cap': 'We have got ourselves into unnecessary difficulties through the way in which this whole matter has been handled,' he complained in an *aide mémoire* at the time. 'The passion for instant government and instant response is one of the besetting faults of the Prime Minister.'[8]

However, from the start, Wilson did not want to impose change on the trade unions by state compulsion. He sought to win the active cooperation of the TUC in turning the White Paper into legislation and advised Castle to confide in the TUC's inner core – the Finance and General Purposes Committee – before presenting her plans to the Cabinet. But the trade union leaders listened to her proposals in sullen silence and proceeded to leak them to the press. The opposition to the so-called penal measures aroused formidable resistance across the labour movement from the very beginning. Despite Woodcock's studied ambivalence (Castle said he privately backed her), the TUC General Council lined up against them. So did the majority of Labour's National Executive Committee. The trade union group of Labour MPs was also opposed, as was much of the rest of the PLP. A series of annual summer trade union conferences threw out the proposals to deal with unofficial strikes with overwhelming majorities, although Wilson and Castle noted that rank-and-file trade union opinion was more favourable.

The wearisome and interminable round of talks between Wilson, Castle and senior TUC figures over the proposed short, sharp Bill dragged on into the early summer of 1969 with no signs of a settlement. But efforts to reach some kind of deal grew more intense after Woodcock's retirement on 1 March. His successor was Vic Feather, the gregarious, jolly fixer at Congress

House, who was a consummate believer in conciliation. From his first days as TUC General Secretary, Feather was determined to prevent a showdown that could have destroyed the government and to strengthen the TUC. Over endless informal sessions in No. 10, replenished with brandies and cigars, Wilson and Feather sought to find common ground. These meetings failed to provide a breakthrough. Feather wanted Wilson to sack Castle but he refused to do so. Efforts to pin the blame for the crisis on her alone failed as the Prime Minister dug in his heels.

Feather then made it clear to Wilson that he was prepared for the TUC to work out an alternative way forward and not rely on negative opposition from the trade unions to defeat the so-called penal clauses of the Bill. In early May, Wilson sensed a strong desire on the part of the trade unions to avert a split in the movement. The TUC agreed it would discipline trade unions that refused to accept its recommendations to settle inter-union disputes and unofficial strikes. A programme for action was drawn up by the TUC and endorsed unanimously at a special one-day conference. It seemed Feather had ridden to the rescue with the support of the two newly elected militant trade union leaders: Jack Jones and Hugh Scanlon. However, they could not settle their differences with Wilson over how to deal with unofficial strikes. 'Wilson and Castle were basically academics and it was difficult to persuade them to see things from a shop-floor angle,' complained Jones.[9] Wilson's resolve was starting to crack under pressure. He was unnerved by Scanlon's warning that fining unofficial strikers would prove unworkable because workers would organise a whip-round to pay any fines or start more strikes. 'I knew the militants of Merseyside well enough that this would be extremely likely there and no legislation could deal with it,' admitted Wilson.[10]

He now wanted what he called 'a solemn and binding' commitment from the TUC to strengthen its own procedures and rule book so it could discipline recalcitrant affiliate trade unions that defied a TUC ruling over an unofficial dispute. Wilson was trying to seek a way back from an exposed salient and even suggested the government's penalties on unofficial strikers should be held in abeyance. This offer did not meet with the approval of Jones and Scanlon, who wanted Wilson to abandon any further move to deal with unconstitutional strikes by the use of legal sanctions. The Prime Minister was furious at such intransigence. He told Jones and Scanlon that what they were demanding would make his government a lame duck and turn the TUC into a state within the state, putting itself above a democratically elected government. The two trade union leaders were not intimidated by Wilson's arguments. For his part, he thought the two men had overreached themselves in presenting him with what he saw as an ultimatum. He even believed the TUC's tough attitude would alienate Labour MPs. Wilson convinced himself that the TUC would give grudging, reluctant acquiescence to a Bill that would put the unofficial strike plans into cold storage.

By 17 June, however, it was clear that the Cabinet wanted an end to the drama. The majority recognised the TUC had gone a long way to meet Wilson and Castle on how to handle future unofficial disputes, believing the differences between the two sides to now be marginal. The stress on Wilson was considerable as ministers backed away from further confrontation with the TUC. The Prime Minister lost his temper and lashed out verbally against his colleagues. Jenkins likened him to King Lear raging against the elements; others thought he had become petty and vindictive. But, on the following day, agreement was finally reached with the TUC – to widespread relief. It left Wilson not triumphant but deflated and he warned of a future Cabinet reshuffle in which he would exact his revenge on the faint hearts. 'Everyone is relieved but they have a very cool appreciation of Harold Wilson which stops this side of adoration,' noted Callaghan. 'HW does show himself on these sort of occasions to be a spiteful and mean little man.'[11] However, on the *In Place of Strife* crisis, he also wrote, '[i]t shows the folly of publishing diaries written in the heat of battle. I had my faults too.'[12]

The wider significance of Wilson's commitment to trade union reform was obscured by the conflict with the TUC over the so-called penal clauses of the doomed draft Bill. But, in his speech to the 1969 TUC Congress, the Prime Minister reminded delegates what his government had achieved for trade unions, workers and their families. Wilson emphasised the 1965 Redundancy Payments Act that gave cash compensation to workers who lost their jobs as a result of industrial restructuring. He reminded the TUC of the substantial effort to improve industrial training, to better working conditions in merchant shipping and increase support for occupational health, as well as introduce earnings-related unemployment benefit. He pointed out the growth in social benefits to better the conditions of working families. Wilson also emphasised his government's commitment to the cause of equal pay by statute law for women workers. He was also keen to remind the TUC of the positive proposals for workers and trade unions contained in the industrial relations Bill planned for the forthcoming parliamentary session. The newly formed Commission on Industrial Relations was created as a voluntary body to spread good labour practices in industry, like the establishment of company-wide procedure agreements, and to help trade unions to modernise their obsolete structures with the assistance of a state-supported trade union development fund. It was agreed that workers should enjoy the statutory right to belong to a trade union and enjoy legal protection from unfair dismissal. There were even proposals to give trade union negotiators the right of access to company information and provide for the appointment of worker representatives to company boards.[13]

The high drama over *In Place of Strife* diverted attention from how far Wilson was willing to go in assisting the trade unions to modernise themselves. If Labour had won the 1970 general election, it is possible but not probable that industrial relations would have improved significantly. However, the growth of labour militancy in the low-paid public-service sector and resulting wage-push inflation meant that many of Wilson's positive plans for the trade unions were lost, at least for the time being.

THE SOCIAL CONTRACT

After the turmoil of the *In Place of Strife* crisis and its aftermath, Harold Wilson, as opposition leader following Labour's defeat in the June 1970 general election, was keen to re-establish close relations with the trade unions and repair the damage. He did so through the creation of a new joint body established between the Labour Party and the TUC known as the Liaison Committee. This turned out to be a key institution for the 1970s that formed a real partnership and gave genuine substance to a programme for government under the concept of the Social Contract. Wilson was not the initial driving force behind this; he often seemed like a back-seat driver. The crucial figure in its development was Jack Jones, the Transport and General Workers' leader. But it was Wilson who became the chief enabler of what was seen as the institutional means for restoring the historic, contentious alliance between the political and industrial wings of the labour movement, the first such committee since the National Council of Labour in the 1930s. Most importantly, the new committee included shadow Cabinet members, at the insistence of the TUC. It was not to be a talking shop but a practical body to assist future government action.

Wilson agreed to important changes to please the trade unions. He promised that a future Labour government would repeal the hated 1971 Industrial Relations Act that had enforced a new legal framework on their activities. He also accepted that he would not introduce any statutory or voluntary prices and incomes policy. Wilson agreed a TUC-driven set of proposals for government, including a boost for old-age pensions, an attack on low pay, the introduction of industrial democracy, food subsidies and a massive house-building programme. He came to see the advantage of the new committee as an alternative policy-making body to the party's National Executive, which was moving to the left under the messianic influence of Tony Benn. He envisaged the new committee would ensure a regular consultation between a future Labour government and the TUC. The so-called Social Contract was to take pride of place in the party's February 1974 general election manifesto. Wilson, upon his return to power, had to resolve the miners' strike and end the three-day working week. He wanted to demonstrate he could work in close partnership with the TUC. Proof of his benign intentions towards the trade unions was his decision to make the veteran left-winger Michael Foot Employment Secretary, to the delight of the trade union leaders, who met Wilson at No. 10 within twenty-four hours of the government's formation.

During his seven months as Prime Minister between the two 1974 general elections, Wilson more or less implemented the TUC-inspired programme in its entirety. Food and housing subsidies were introduced. Short-term benefits for the unemployed and sick were raised. The Trade Union and Labour Relations Bill swept away the Conservative measure to deal with organised labour. For its part, the TUC endorsed a voluntary pay policy, which called for restraint as part of the wider social agreement.

Speaking to the 1974 TUC Congress, Wilson told delegates that the Social Contract was being honoured. He spoke of his government being based on 'voluntary cooperation in a responsible democracy'.[14] 'We have learned as never before how totally dependent we are each upon the other,' he argued. 'Every one of us now knows we can inflict serious and often terrible damage upon one other section of the community. There is no need to go on flexing muscles to prove it.'[15] He emphasised the key role he believed that trade unions should play in the social-democratic state he hoped to create, and did so by drawing on the rich story of Labour's past:

This is the time to recall Britain to the ideals that inspired the labour movement in harder times, when the going for Britain had never been so good and the going for so many of our people had never been worse. Those were the days when the textile workers of Lancashire were prepared to starve rather than support slavery in America; the miners in South Wales or Durham or in other coalfields, themselves living on or below the poverty line, were never so poor that they could not provide help for the family of a comrade who had been killed in the pit or whose life had been destroyed by black lung.[16]

But it soon became clear that the trade unions would find it difficult to meet their obligations to the government. Many Cabinet ministers believed that, while they were keeping their promises to the trade unions, they were getting little from them in return. Wage increases continued to roar ahead of price rises in a self-destructive frenzy that threatened to push the country into hyper-inflation through the winter of 1974–75. The situation was becoming unsustainable, as Wilson himself recognised sporadically, although he was reluctant for understandable reasons after his 1964–70 experiences to intervene with any compulsory wage restraint, despite mounting pressure for executive action from his hard-pressed Chancellor Denis Healey. But, by June 1975, the government could not stand back any longer.

The mounting crisis was resolved by a last, skilful round of negotiations headed by Wilson himself that brought the country back from the brink of economic catastrophe. He was helped enormously by Jack Jones, who at last accepted that the trade unions would have to take direct responsibility for wage restraint if only as a temporary respite. Wilson warned Jones that the TUC would need to rein in the pay demands of trade union members or face the prospect of the government's collapse as more right-wing Cabinet ministers broke away in a replay of the creation of the National Government in the 1931 crisis. In the event, the TUC General Council voted narrowly to support a £6-a-week pay-increase limit for all and the government agreed to establish back-up statutory powers if the voluntary position failed to hold. The outcome was a strategic triumph for Wilson and his style of government. As he later wrote, '[t]en years of history under successive governments have proved that in our democracy any formula for the statutory imposition of pay limits would prove to be the *ignis fatuus* of policy. A British government in peacetime must proceed by leadership, agreement and consensus.'[17] In his final dealings with the trade unions, Wilson achieved a settlement on pay that kept all sides together. In doing so, he vindicated yet again his determination to ensure Labour Party unity:

> To bridge a deep political chasm without splitting a party or provoking dramatic ministerial resignations is sometimes regarded as something approaching political chicanery. This is to subordinate the realities of 200 years of democratic politics to the demands of sensationalism. The highest aim of leadership is to secure policies adequate to deal with any situation, including the production of acceptable new solutions and policies without major confrontations, splits and resignations.[18]

THE LOST OPPORTUNITY

In a dedication to both of his two rather dull narrative histories of his governments, Wilson used the same quotation from Aneurin Bevan's last speech in the House of Commons on 3 November 1959:

> I would describe the central problem falling upon representative government in the Western world as how to persuade the people to forego

> immediate satisfactions in order to build up the economic resources of the
> country ... How can we persuade the ordinary man and woman that it is
> worthwhile making sacrifices in their immediate standards or foregoing
> substantial rising standards to extend fixed capital equipment through-
> out the country?[19]

Bevan's wise words were very much part of Wilson's philosophy of government. He wanted to harness the goodwill and participation of the trade unions
in what he saw as his social-democratic project. He sought to convince them
to shoulder responsibilities in restraining the material appetites of their own
members for their own long-term good. Wilson believed other democratic
countries, especially in northern Europe, had showed what was possible.
But he also came to recognise reluctantly that the British trade unions could
not achieve a similar success without constant external pressure from the state.
TUC General Secretaries George Woodcock and, later, Len Murray accepted
that the trade unions could not become social partners in a corporate state.
They believed they could reach deals involving compulsory wage restraint
with governments for only short periods of time in national economic emer-
gencies. The TUC did not regard itself as an Estate of the Realm. Both men in
their different ways believed Wilson was always asking too much of the TUC,
despite his honourable motives. While Woodcock thought that democratic
governments should respond to the trade unions by creating the conditions
for cooperation through social-democratic measures, he did not accept they
should be asked to rein in the wage demands of their members. For his part,
Murray liked to quote the words of the nineteenth-century Bookbinders'
Union General Secretary Frederick Rogers, that there must be an independent life within the state to prevent government becoming tyranny, and the
trade unions would be chief among those who should call that independent
life into being. While they welcomed the role of the state in assisting trade

unions by the establishment of minimum standards in the workplace and creating the wider framework to ensure responsible wage-bargaining, they did not
accept that the state should interfere on a permanent basis in pay determination in the so-called national interest. Trade unions were above all collective
bargainers and not instruments of government. In their basic functions, they
were economic liberals that sought to advance and protect their democratic
freedoms. Wilson believed this limited view of trade union purpose was no
longer good enough in the modern world. With power must come responsibility. But, contrary to conventional wisdom on the right and the left, most
of the trade unions were too weak organisationally to shoulder what Wilson
wanted and not too strong. They represented sectional interests in the work-
places and their members saw them as guardians for what they regarded as
limited, piecemeal objectives in a competitive labour market.

Wilson tried to change the culture of workplace trade unionism by argument and persuasion, except during the *In Place of Strife* crisis. He was keen
to modernise the trade unions so they could join with employers and government in helping to resolve the country's deep-rooted economic and industrial
problems. Bodies like the tripartite Advisory Conciliation and Arbitration
Service, Health and Safety Commission and Equal Opportunities Commission provided hope of a more responsible trade union movement involved
in public policy-making and administration. Industrial democracy proved a
step too far but, again, Wilson was keen at least for the issue to be discussed.

The trade unions, however, failed to respond in what were only modest
steps forward in social partnership. In the turbulent years of Wilson's governments, worker individualism and workplace power grew more formidable
as older notions of solidarity became weaker. Customs and practices at work
remained indomitable. But, without a national consensus, there could only
be internecine strife, disintegration and sectionalism. Under Wilson, the so-
called social wage meant higher taxes on working people and alienated many

voters. The upsurge in wage demands was not a sign of rising contentment among workers but stemmed from a sense of fear and insecurity. Moreover, it reflected the realities of the free-market economy. Workers and the trade unions that sought to represent their disparate demands did not really share the benign vision of Wilson's industrial-relations model.

Wilson had offered what turned out to be the last real attempt at establishing a northern European system of industrial relations in Britain. Under his successor, James Callaghan, the Social Contract fell apart in the Winter of Discontent. But the trade unions were always prisoners of their own past and it would be wrong to criticise them. In later years, some of their leaders, notably Jones and Scanlon, looked back with nostalgia to Harold Wilson and his industrial-relations strategy. They had spurned the Social Contract as a permanent way to run the political economy and yet at the time they could not have done otherwise. Their own members rebelled against it if it meant wage restraint. Britain was not to become a social-democratic state; the long, sad decline of British trade unionism had begun. Wilson had sought a better way but he could not achieve what he wanted. It was a national tragedy and a lost opportunity. His failure cleared the way for Margaret Thatcher, the return to the delusion of free collective bargaining and, above all, the abandonment of full employment that was at the core of the Wilson approach.

NOTES AND REFERENCES

1.   TUC Annual Report, 1964
2.   Ibid.
3.   Ibid.
4.   Ibid.
5.   B. Castle, *Fighting All the Way*, p. 418
6.   D. Healey, *The Time of My Life*, p. 341
7.   B. Castle, *Fighting All the Way*, p. 434
8.   J. Callaghan, *Aide Mémoire*, June 1969, Callaghan Papers
9.   J. Jones, *Union Man: An Autobiography* (London: HarperCollins, 1986), p. 204

10.   H. Wilson, *The Labour Government, 1964–70*, p. 654
11.   J. Callaghan, *Aide Mémoire*
12.   Ibid.
13.   TUC Annual Report, 1974
14.   Ibid.
15.   Ibid.
16.   Ibid.
17.   H. Wilson, *The Labour Government, 1964–70*, p. 675
18.   Ibid.
19.   Ibid., dedication in both his histories of his governments

8

EDUCATION POLICY

Jane Martin

'*Labour wants to mobilise the entire nation in the nation's business.*
It wants to create government of the whole people by the whole people.
Labour will replace the closed, exclusive society by an open society
in which all have an opportunity to work and serve, in which brains
will take precedence over blue blood, and craftsmanship will be
more important than caste.'[1]

HAROLD WILSON'S VISION of a New Britain captured the mood of the time. Education was at the centre of the distinctive claims made by the Labour Party regarding its belief in social justice to bring about a fairer and better society. Amid assertions that British society was still too class-ridden, led by an outdated Edwardian establishment mentality, Wilson denounced the power elite for having failed the country and demeaned Britain's influence in a world of superpowers and new economic groupings. The comprehensive school, presented as an efficient way of equalising opportunities, was an integral part of Wilson's plans to deliver a new, swinging, meritocratic generation.

This chapter has used political interviews and speeches, private political papers, published political diaries, biographies and autobiographies to offer a revaluation of education policy during Wilson's leadership. It is structured as a narrative, describing the level of political debate, the context and particularities of educational developments of the period, interleaved with some selected voices of the powerful as well as the many whose webs of influence provoke and guide the exercise of power. I am not presenting these voices as somehow representative of the period; they are here to bring to life the experience of policy and practice that is the focus of this chapter. I go on to explore the legacy and impact of Wilson, his ideas and ambitions for education. Many of the themes that he addressed remain relevant today: how to create a more equal society, debates about the principles and purposes of education, questions of radical, cultural transformation and the operation of knowledge and power.

The narrative is organised in four sections. It starts by demonstrating the continuing power of the past as a backdrop to the Wilson government's education programme. Section two focuses on the long fight over comprehensive secondary education. The third section centres on the question of numerical expansion in higher education, including the creation of the Open University. Finally, the chapter considers the advocacy of compensatory education, before concluding with an assessment of social paralysis and social change on the issue of education during Wilson's premiership.

BACKGROUND TO THE WILSON GOVERNMENTS' EDUCATION PLANNING

The ideal of common or community schools has behind it a long history within the British labour movement, but it has struggled against a vicious circle of class-conditioned assumptions institutionalised in the education system. Universal, basic elementary education was introduced in the period from 1870 to the first decade of the twentieth century. Grant-aided, academic secondary education was established after 1902, though it was confined to a fraction of the nation's youngsters, accessible through the payment of fees or through competitive scholarships from the elementary schools. In 1922, the infant Labour Party advocated secondary education for all, but this formal commitment concealed disagreements of aim. For example, many in the Fabian Society supported the development of specialised and differentiated schooling as the means by which the 'clever' working-class child would rise. Conversely, opponents hotly criticised the notion of a ladder of opportunity for the few. Both the London Labour Party and the National Association of Labour Teachers championed the comprehensive (originally multilateral) school. The only way of achieving educational equality and ensuring that social inequality did not reproduce itself in the schools, they said, was to establish a system whereby all kinds and curricula of adolescent education were under one roof. When Labour won control of the London County Council in 1934, it made history as the first local authority to endorse comprehensive schools.

The 1944 Education Act made secondary education universal and free. But this did not mean that all children then received what before this date had been described as secondary education. The same post-war Labour administrations that created the modern welfare state enshrined selection on the basis of academic attainment or aptitude at age eleven and 80 per cent of the nation's children were placed in Britain's non-selective secondary modern schools, many of which were, in fact, the old elementary schools renamed. Predictably, parents favoured the higher-status grammar schools. 'With all places free, and maintenance grants available, the simple right of class and purse was abruptly replaced by an annual pitched battle of childish wits and nerves,' wrote journalist Harry Hopkins. As 'the anguished protests of "scorned" middle-class parents filled the suburban air and the newspapers

... it now began to appear that "ruin" came ... from having had the misfortune to have conceived a child who "failed" the eleven plus'.[2]

Despite the express intention of those who designed the new system of secondary education that all school types should be accorded 'parity of esteem', it was hard for secondary modern schools to live down the tradition of the elementary school. Under-funded and under-staffed, these schools would always bear the mark of failure, while some pupils were being creamed off by the grammar schools and could draw little prestige from the manual occupations that most of their pupils entered at fifteen. Post-war research confirmed beyond a shadow of doubt that selection advantaged the children of middle-class parents and that social class was a major influence on educational achievement. The few working-class children who made it to grammar school would find that they had to accommodate to the prevailing middle-class values, or rub up against them. Consequently, they would either leave at the earliest opportunity or they would survive within the grammar school but become alienated from their family and neighbourhood.[3] Government reports drew attention to 'wastage of talent' among working-class leavers and opposition to the educational apartheid came from the experience of teachers, children and parents aware that selection rested on spurious educational thinking (to do with IQ testing) that made it acceptable for many, if not most, children to fail.[4]

Anthony Crosland's *The Future of Socialism*, published in 1956, claimed that modern socialism was concerned to improve welfare and secure justice between individuals. For Crosland, education remained 'the most divisive, unjust, and wasteful of all the aspects of social inequality'.[5] While he wanted a new system built around the comprehensive school, the new emphasis on human capital theory made education an issue around which the party could coalesce. In the 'white heat of technology' speech at the Labour Party conference in Scarborough in 1963, Wilson put it like this:

We simply cannot as a nation afford to neglect the educational development of a single boy or girl. We cannot afford to cut off three-quarters or
more of our children from virtually any chance of higher education. The
Russians do not, the Germans do not, the Americans do not, and the Japanese do not, and we cannot afford to either.[6]

In 1964 and 1966, Labour was pledged to the abolition of selection, comprehensives, the raising of the school-leaving age to sixteen and the continued
growth of higher education. What happened can be seen as a continuation of
divided aims and the 'access' agenda dating back to the 1920s.

EQUALISING OPPORTUNITIES I:
THE COMPREHENSIVE MOMENT

In public life, Tony Benn became Postmaster-General. In private, he and his
wife Caroline had made their home in Holland Park Avenue, ten minutes'
walk from Holland Park, the new state comprehensive secondary school that
opened in west London in September 1958 and which they chose for their
children's education. In his diary, Benn recorded his pleasure at Wilson's
decision to appoint Michael Stewart, an ex-teacher and National Union of
Teachers-sponsored MP, as his Education Secretary. Benn described Stewart
as 'a passionate believer in comprehensive education'.[7]

In mid-January 1965, Stewart put a major policy paper to the Cabinet setting out his approach to comprehensive reorganisation strategy. He sought
first approval for a circular that requested local authorities to submit plans
for reorganisation and, second, agreement that this would be backed up by
legislation to deal with any recalcitrant local authorities. Stewart 'presented
reorganisation as likely to extend grammar-school education to a wider section

of the population' and 'rebutted charges that sound grammar schooling was about to be destroyed'.[8] The Cabinet, led by Wilson, refused to agree to legislation. Only Fred Peart and William Ross, both ex-teachers, supported Stewart. Edward Short, Wilson's Chief Whip and former head of a secondary modern school, voiced the most extreme disillusionment in his autobiography: 'In spite of a lucid explanation by Michael, the Cabinet rejected his plea and decided that the case for comprehensive schools should be put to the local authorities in a carefully drafted circular which asked for their co-operation.'[9]

Accordingly, Stewart's successor as Education Minister, Anthony Crosland, asked authorities to submit plans for the reorganisation of education along comprehensive lines. This came in Circular 10/65 of July 1965. The junior Education Minister, Reg Prentice, wanted the circular to 'require' local authorities to become comprehensive, but Crosland favoured change through agreement, on a voluntary basis rather than through compulsion, as he noted in conversation with Maurice Kogan.[10] Senior civil servant Toby Weaver went so far as to express his admiration for Crosland as 'the first person to stop talking about comprehensive reorganisation and to take a decisive step towards it'.[11] That he did not always find this easy is evident from Susan Crosland's biography, where she claimed her husband was

> driven mad by the obtuseness of those who claimed grammar schools
> did not affect comprehensives despite the undeniable fact that the for-
> mer creamed off the more gifted children ... 'If it's the last thing I do, I'm
> going to destroy every fucking grammar school in England,' he said. 'And
> Wales. And Northern Ireland.'[12]

Outside Whitehall, those wanting to accelerate change set up the Comprehensive Schools Committee (CSC). Active campaigner Brian Simon recorded that the 'dynamic energy' was initiated by Information Officer Caroline Benn.[13]

The committee headquarters were the Benn family home. 'They used to meet there in the daytime when I was at the ministerial office,' Tony recalled. 'My house really became a centre of campaigning on comprehensive education.'[14] In his diary, he noted 'an amusing confrontation' between Caroline and Crosland at the 1965 Labour Party conference. Crosland was unhappy at reading press reports about the new committee 'but obviously knew nothing about it. His inclination was to be scornful but when Peter Shore showed him the list of sponsors, he was somewhat taken aback.'[15] In the 1960s and '70s, Caroline conducted an annual survey of reorganisation plans, edited *Comprehensive Education*, the CSC journal, co-authored the major report on the comprehensive reform, *Half Way There*, was chair of governors of Holland Park School, a co-opted member of the Inner London Education Authority and an official on a Labour Party education committee.[16]

Ann Glennerster heard Caroline speaking on the radio about her decision to send her elder sons to Holland Park. Ann herself was a product of the elite St Paul's School for Girls in London, but retained strong memories of a childhood visit to a secondary modern school with a friend. She remembered being 'very conscious that they were thirteen years old, didn't know any more than me, I could only have been nine years old and they were going to leave school at fourteen'. Ann had joined the Young Fabians and met Shirley Williams, who persuaded her to write a Fabian Society pamphlet on social work, through which she met her future husband, a young Oxford graduate working for the Labour Research Department. Howard Glennerster got to Oxford despite failing his eleven plus and never wanted a child of his to experience this early rebuff. Later, at the London School of Economics, he became friends with David Donnison, who had been educated at a public school, a negative experience for him. Both men wanted something different for their children and the children of other people. In Howard's words: 'We were strong supporters of comprehensive schools, very conscious that the grammar-school lobby was good at getting their message out but we were not. We wanted to change this.'[17]

Weakness, vacillation and the splits within the Labour Party over tactics saw Edward Short produce his own abortive Bill and the Department of Education's Circular 10/70 withdrawing the comprehensive circular, issued with admirable speed a mere twelve days after the Conservative election in June 1970. When Labour returned to power in 1974, it took over a year before Fred Mulley introduced legislation empowering the Secretary of State 'to call for proposals to complete reorganisation'. In Short's own words: 'In spite of all the efforts of Tony [Anthony] Crosland and his successors, of whom I was one, the government's refusal to legislate and the Chancellor's refusal to make funds available meant that comprehensive reorganisation was often a botched-up job from the start.'[18] Caroline Benn agreed: 'The weak nature of the 1976 Education Act was the last chapter in a history of failure to legislate effectively on comprehensive reform, beginning in 1965 with the crucial decision not to legislate at all.'[19]

Alongside the stopping of free school milk in secondary schools, the postponement of the raising of the school-leaving age created the greatest anger. A stronger Education Secretary than Patrick Gordon-Walker, who had no conception of pupils leaving school at fifteen, would have been loath to abandon a long-held pledge of the labour movement affecting the majority of the nation's children. But Gordon-Walker insisted he would rather spend the money on universities. Wilson described the postponement as 'difficult, not to say repugnant', but agreed it was necessary given the need to cut public spending.[20] Benn was adamant against. When Richard Crossman asked Crosland just who would be affected by the decision, Crosland was stung to reply: 'Only 400,000 children. But they're not our children. It's always other people's children. None of us in this room would dream of letting our own children leave school at fifteen.'[21] Lord Longford resigned, saying: 'I felt if I swallowed this, there was nothing I wouldn't swallow.'[22] George Brown 'thought it was one of the greatest betrayals a Labour government, so overwhelmingly composed of university graduates, could make of the less privileged people who, after all, had elected it'.[23]

Meanwhile, there was still the unsolved problem of the private sector. Crosland set up a Public Schools Commission (overriding his expert adviser, A. H. Halsey), which produced two reports. This was not a clear clarion call for the abolition of private education. CSC advocated absorbing the private schools into the state system but only one member, John Vaizey, rejected the recommendation to offer more assisted places.[24] Caroline Benn produced evidence to show how public money bolstered the private sector considerably despite its undermining of comprehensive schools.[25] She briefed her husband well, but Wilson didn't want to discuss it. Tony Benn described the report as 'ghastly'.[26] When Labour abolished direct grant status (in 1975), the unintended consequence was to grow the private sector, as most of the schools chose to become fully independent.

EQUALISING OPPORTUNITIES II:
HIGHER EDUCATION EXPANSION

By the 1950s, just 4 per cent of eighteen- and nineteen-year-olds attended university. More children were staying on voluntarily than had been expected and in 1955 there simply weren't enough university places available for a quarter of the candidates who achieved the entry requirements by acquisition of two A-Levels. Upon taking office, Labour adopted the recommendations of the 1963 Robbins Report for higher education expansion but soon ran into difficulties of cost. In part, at least, this explains why Crosland adopted 'the binary principle', challenging the view that higher education was synonymous with university education. Instead of relying solely upon the creation of new universities to increase the numbers, there was the proposed creation of new institutions (a development specifically precluded by Robbins) called polytechnics.

Crosland first outlined the government's policy for a dual system of higher education in a speech at Woolwich Polytechnic in April 1965. Susan Crosland said the permanent politicians of the Department of Education and Science suggested the policy to her husband but he seized it, amended it and made it his own. 'Let us now move away from our snobbish, caste-ridden hierarchical obsession with university status,'[27] he said. Crosland recognised, as Robbins had not, that there was a public sector of higher education, with distinctive principles and purposes, alongside the universities:

> On the one hand we have what had come to be called the autonomous sector, represented by the universities, in whose ranks, of course, I now include the colleges of advanced technology. On the other hand, we have the public sector, represented by the leading technical colleges and the colleges of education.[28]

If the universities could be said to be in an 'autonomous' tradition established by Royal Charter, the public-sector colleges were in a 'service' tradition, which was valuable in itself and should not be subsumed by the other.

The outcome was the 1966 White Paper, *A Plan for Polytechnics and Other Colleges*, which made clear the government's intention to designate a limited number of polytechnics based upon institutions already carrying on higher degree work and these would become points of development for higher education in the public sector. Eventually, thirty new polytechnics were designated. The polytechnic concept was local, vocational and relevant to the needs of industry and technology. Pluralist in their qualifications, important innovations during this period included the development of sandwich courses, involving alternation between periods of formal instruction and practical experience.

Perhaps the most important innovation was the Open University (OU), which had its roots in Labour's passion for adult education and Wilson's enthusiasm for meeting the demands of the new scientific and technological revolution. His visits to the USSR in the early 1960s taught him that 60 per cent of Soviet engineers acquired their degrees by correspondence courses, backed by radio tuition, followed by a year at university. The idea matured while Wilson was lecturing at Chicago University as the guest of Senator Benton, proprietor of the *Encyclopaedia Britannica.* There he saw Chicago's scheme of extra-mural teaching (based in part on television) and the work done by *Encyclopaedia Britannica* in producing educational films.[29] Wilson, as Prime Minister, offered the Scottish socialist politician Jennie Lee, with wide experience in the Workers' Educational Association and the labour movement, a job. She was to be the first Minister for the Arts and she was to define his institution-building.[30]

The academic establishment opposed the project; it would devalue the university degree and not give students a first-rate version of higher education. Lee and Wilson ploughed ahead and Labour's 1966 manifesto included a promise to establish a 'University of the Air' using the latest broadcasting technology: 'This open university will obviously extend the best teaching facilities and give everyone the opportunity to study for a full degree. It will mean genuine equality of opportunity for millions of people for the first time.'[31] Three years later, the Open University got its Royal Charter. Although a limited number of working-class people enrolled, it had the widest class reach of all British universities, the largest student body and the highest proportion of female students. Open-access and flexible distance teaching allowed women previously denied higher education to combine study with domestic and/or work roles. For the many women teachers who wished to upgrade their qualifications from a teaching diploma to a degree, the Open University provided an opportunity to do this.

Individually and collectively, these initiatives, including the restructuring of the colleges of education to address the question of teacher supply,
changed the shape of higher education in Britain, although the biggest share
of the expansion took place in the universities and unequal funding patterns continued. Spending per student at universities in 1971 was £1,284 per
head, against £920 in colleges of education and £720 in advanced courses
in further education.[32] Within the universities, male students continued to
outnumber female, although the gap narrowed slightly. Female students
were more likely to be found in the polytechnics and colleges of education.
In part-time further education, the steady increase in the numbers of students on part-time, day release courses was achieved through the greater
participation of females. Males attending evening classes were more likely
to be found in the colleges of technology and colleges of advanced technology, whereas female students were more likely to be found in evening
institutes, which generally taught to a lower level and offered more directly
vocational qualifications.

EQUALISING OPPORTUNITIES III:
PLOWDEN'S EDUCATIONAL PRIORITY AREAS

Educational Priority Areas (EPAs) were a recommendation of the 1967
Plowden Report on primary education. Plowden's focus on the under-achieve-
ment of 'deprived' children was foreshadowed by the Newsom Report's
concern for 'Education in the Slums', four years earlier, with its call for social
policy to alleviate the influence of poor home background. Arguably, Newsom
and Plowden rediscovered poverty for the 1960s administrators of British
education. Essentially EPAs were an attempt to direct attention and resources
to children whose education was affected by the co-existence of deprivation,

slum housing, widespread poverty, unskilled employment or actual unemployment. Initiatives included an expansion of nursery schooling in EPAs and financial inducements to teachers working in EPA primary schools.

Plowden's emphasis on the *cultural* barriers to a child's capacity to make full use of educational opportunities contrasted with the predominant approach of government reports in the immediate post-war period where the barriers were assumed mainly to be material and financial. Getting the EPA principle accepted and securing an extra £16 million to be spent exclusively on buildings was one of the things that gave Crosland 'most satisfaction'.[33] The approach owed something to the Kennedy/Johnson 'War on Poverty' in the USA, plus the British tradition of community studies and small-scale innovation that Michael Young had promoted around the Institute of Community Studies in east London. Secondary schools did not get EPA treatment but the government set up a national EPA action-research programme under the leadership of A. H. Halsey, who directed the compensatory education programme from Oxford. Five areas were designated to test out innovative ideas that could be extended if proven successful, in what Halsey called 'experimental social administration'.[34]

George Smith, member of the West Riding EPA, said later the idea of an 'EPA area' began to unravel under a series of challenges linking area-based policies with individual pathology, and as research studies showed it to be a rather blunt instrument. In Halsey's words, '[w]e learnt painfully that educational reform had not in the past and was unlikely in the future ever to bring an egalitarian society unaided'.[35] Ben Pimlott considers Wilson 'an egalitarian by instinct and conviction, as well as by birthright. His was a Lib–Lab, Nonconformist, free-thinking egalitarianism, fertilised by the hardships suffered by his family in the 1930s, by irritation at the social snobberies of Oxford and Whitehall.'[36] Pimlott, therefore, calls his attempt to increase social equality in education unsurprising.

CONCLUSION

To return to the quotation with which we started, Wilson's aim was to spell out what life under a Labour government would be like. Paul Foot commented in 1968 that Wilson's targeting of the old-boy network, his frustration with the distinction between amateurs/gentlemen and players/professionals, 'was no more than a meritocrat's irritation with an incompetent and amateur aristocracy: the cry of the scholarship boy angrily knocking at the bolted door of the bourgeoisie'.[37] That Wilson aspired to meritocracy is surely beyond dispute. He repeated *ad nauseam* his vision of a society 'in which brains will take precedence over blue blood'.[38] A distinct echo of Michael Young's famous equation, writing in 1958, I+E=M – intelligence plus effort equals merit.[39] Brian Simon argued Labour in power displayed a lack of political will on the question of comprehensive reorganisation.[40] My argument is not that Wilson lacked political will, but that his slogan 'grammar schools for all' was very different from what campaigners like Simon and Caroline Benn meant by comprehensive schools.

Half Way There contains the important statement: 'A comprehensive school is *not* a *social* experiment; it is an *educational* reform.'[41] Caroline Benn believed in the concept of human genius but she did not think it could be defined by, and limited to, the world of IQ testing, and opposed all attempts to commandeer it for the purpose of preserving a secondary-school system designed for the production of a meritocracy. 'Giftedness is what education itself helps to create and release and the purpose of the education system is to help foster as many gifts as possible in as many children as possible. Selection for giftedness … stunts our chances of helping the gifted,' she said. High-quality education in free-standing, community comprehensive schools 'is the only way we can openly ensure attention to all equally and, at the same time, protect and reveal the full range of human gifts'.[42] By 1977, the proportion of pupils educated in comprehensive schools was 78.6 per cent.[43] Unlike the divided education system of the post-war period, comprehensives emphasised by their very existence the notion that extending one's education was a normal thing for ordinary children to do.

Yet a profound ambiguity lay at the heart of Wilson's education policy – at least as it applied to schools. Tony Benn was a devoted ally of the comprehensive concept, disappointed by the slow progress of reform. He recalled a meeting of the inner Cabinet in December 1969, when Fred Peart questioned why Short's Education Bill had not come forward. Wilson, it seems, disliked the wording. '"It says we shouldn't select people by aptitude or ability and surely that is not what it is about," he said. "It is about getting comprehensive schools, not an attack on the grammar schools." Thus he revealed with staggering simplicity that he doesn't understand the party's education policy at all.'[44] Anxious to repudiate the idea that comprehensive reorganisation entailed one type of secondary school being abolished in favour of another, there was a degree of confusion in Wilson's approach. A policy of absorbing the grammar schools and making them available to all without any discussion of whether that was what was needed (or the limitations of an outdated grammar-school model) suffered from an incoherence that left the door open for educational and political conservatives, like the Black Paper writers, to suggest that only by a system of elitist education can high standards be maintained.

There remains a strong political prejudice against comprehensive schools. In their main purpose they challenge the idea of keeping all 'clever' children socially separate. Michael Stewart thought it 'nonsense' to try to keep politics out of it. He did not see comprehensive schools as a more efficient meritocratic engine of inequality; he wanted to use them as an instrument in pursuit of an egalitarian society:

> A system of education is bound to have some effect on the character,
> as well as the intellectual development, of pupils; and society has some

right to decide, and in fact always does decide what that influence shall
be. For many years the public schools had been praised for inculcating the
quality of leadership; this assumes a society in which leaders and followers
are distinguished at birth and trained for their respective duties. We who
believe in comprehensive schools have in mind a society in which people
of different attainments and occupying very different positions will have
learnt to respect each other.[45]

Education changed in the 1960s and '70s, but neither comprehensives nor
polytechnics disturbed the hegemony of the traditional institutions. This is
what critics meant by paralysis. Alan Dawe, *Tribune*'s education correspon-
dent, announced his resignation from the Labour Party on 24 September 1965,
the same day CSC was launched: 'We are not right to view the Labour Party
and its latter-day works as having had anything to do with socialism. They
don't, they won't, and it is time we faced up to it.' While some rejected the
idea of the brain-race, there was no complete re-examination of the content
of secondary education and most newly established comprehensive schools
had to assimilate the two existing trends handed down from the grammar
and secondary modern schools. Few arguments were made in favour of radical cultural transformation of the kind Tony Benn envisaged when he wrote,
'[t]he public ownership of knowledge is also one way of describing comprehensive life-long education to allow us all to have access to it'.[46]

There was no ambiguity surrounding Wilson's proposals for a University
of the Air. 'Cabinet colleagues claimed that they were never in doubt that the
OU would happen, because Wilson wanted it to: "What the Prime Minister
wants, he gets," said Ted Short. All they could do, say Jim Callaghan and Roy
Jenkins, was to argue about the price. As Tony Benn said: "Wilson was the
real political drive behind it" – he willed it; it was therefore "unstoppable".'[47]
Joe Haines, Wilson's press secretary, noted, '[i]t will always remain to Wilson's

credit that despite the economic and political difficulties, some of them Oxbridgean elitists, who surrounded the project, he forced it into existence. It is a better and more enduring monument to his life than any other achievement.'[48] Tony Benn also believed, as Wilson himself came to believe, that it was one of the finest achievements of his premiership, 'the one for which – above almost anything else in his career – he most wished to be remembered'.[49]

NOTES AND REFERENCES

1. H. Wilson, *The New Britain: Labour's Plan Outlined by Harold Wilson*, p. 9
2. H. Hopkins, *The New Look: A Social History of the Forties and Fifties* (London: Readers Union, Secker & Warburg, 1964), p. 150
3. B. Jackson and D. Marsden, *Education and the Working Class* (Harmondsworth: Penguin, 1962)
4. See C. Chitty, *Eugenics, Race and Intelligence in Education* (London: Continuum, 2009)
5. C. A. R. Crosland, *The Future of Socialism* (London: Constable & Robinson, 2006), p. 216
6. H. Wilson, *Purpose in Politics*, p. 19
7. T. Benn, *Out of the Wilderness: Diaries, 1963–67* (London: Hutchinson, 1998), p. 208
8. E. Short, *Whip to Wilson* (London: Macdonald, 1989), p. 105; see D. Dean, 'Circular 10/65 Revisited: The Labour Government and the "Comprehensive Revolution" in 1964–65', *Paedagogica Historica*, 34/1, (1998), pp 63–91 for a full account
9. D. Dean, 'Circular 10/65 Revisited', pp 73–4; E. Short, *Whip to Wilson*, p. 104
10. M. Kogan, *The Politics of Education* (Harmondsworth: Penguin, 1976), p. 191
11. S. Crosland, *Tony Crosland* (London: Coronet, 1983), p. 144
12. Ibid., p. 148
13. B. Simon, *A Life in Education* (London: Lawrence & Wishart, 1998), p. 103. The committee was launched at a press conference on 24 September 1965: see T. Benn, *Out of the Wilderness*, p. 324
14. Tony Benn to Jane Martin, 20 December 2013
15. T. Benn, *Out of the Wilderness*, pp 325–6
16. See J. Martin, 'Building Comprehensive Education: Caroline Benn and Holland Park School', *Forum*, 57:3, (2015), pp 363–85
17. Ann Glennerster to Jane Martin, 30 September 2013; Howard Glennerster to Jane Martin, 30 September 2013
18. E. Short, *Whip to Wilson*, p. 108
19. C. Benn, 'A New 11-Plus for the Old Divided System', *Forum*, 22:2, (1980), p. 36
20. H. Wilson, *The Labour Government, 1964–70*, p. 484; see also C. Ponting, *Breach of Promise*, p. 132; B. Castle, *The Castle Diaries, 1964–76* (London: Weidenfeld & Nicolson, 1984), p. 348
21. Quoted in C. Griggs, *The TUC and Education Reform 1926–70* (London: Woburn Press, 2002), p. 262
22. H. Wilson, *Labour Government 1964–70*, p. 482; M. Craig, *Longford: A Biographical Portrait* (London: Hodder & Stoughton, 1978), p. 149

23. G. Brown, *In My Way*, p. 175

24. J. Vaizey, 'Boarding Schools and Social Divisiveness', *The Public Schools Commission*, First Report (London: HMSO, 1968), p. 213

25. The Comprehensive Schools Committee Evidence to the Public Schools Commission, *Public and Comprehensive Schools*. Caroline Benn papers, DC/CB 26 Comprehensive Schools Committee, Comprehensive Education 1967–71; Caroline Benn, Labour Party Education Sub-Committee 1975. Also listed as NEC Education Sub-Committee 1969–84, boxes 1–5

26. Tony Benn, *Office Without Power: Diaries, 1968–72* (London: Arrow, 1989)

27. S. Crosland, *Tony Crosland*, p. 159

28. Quoted in R. Lowe, Schooling and Social Change 1964–1990 (London: Routledge, 1997), p. 39

29. H. Wilson, *Memoirs: The Making of a Prime Minister*, p. 194

30. P. Hollis, *Jennie Lee A Life* (Oxford: Oxford University Press, 1997), p. 302

31. W. Perry, *Open University: A Personal Account by the First Vice-Chancellor* (Milton Keynes: The Open University Press, 1976), p. 16

32. D. Rubinstein and C. Stoneman (eds), *Education for Democracy* (Harmondsworth: Penguin, 1972), p. 9

33. M. Kogan, *The Politics of Education*, p. 197

34. A. H. Halsey, 'Plowden: History and Prospect', *Oxford Review of Education*, 13:1, (1987), p. 5

35. G. Smith, T. Smith and T. Smith, 'Whatever Happened to EPAs? Part 2: Educational Priority Areas – 40 Years On', *Forum*, 49:1, 49:2, (2007), pp 141–56; A. Halsey, 'Plowden: History and Prospect', p. 7

36. B. Pimlott, *Wilson*, p. 510

37. P. Foot, *The Politics of Harold Wilson*, p. 327

38. H. Wilson, *The New Britain*, pp 9–10

39. M. Young, *The Rise of the Meritocracy* (London: Thames and Hudson, 1958)

40. B. Simon, 'The Politics of Comprehensive Reorganisation: A Retrospective Analysis', *History of Education*, 21/4, (1992), pp 355–62

41. C. Benn and B. Simon, *Half Way There: Report on the British Comprehensive School Reform* (Harmondsworth: Penguin, 1972), p. 64

42. C. Benn, 'The Myth of Giftedness (Part II)', *Forum*, 24/3, (1982), pp 83–4

43. C. Benn and C. Chitty, *Thirty Years On* (Harmondsworth: Penguin, 1997), p. 88

44. P. Foot, *The Politics of Harold Wilson*, p. 308

45. M. Stewart, *Life and Labour: An Autobiography* (London: Sidgwick & Jackson, 1980), p. 103

46. T. Benn, *Arguments for Socialism* (Harmondsworth: Penguin, 1980), p. 172

47. P. Hollis, *Jennie Lee*, p. 304

48. J. Haines, *Glimmers of Twilight: Harold Wilson in Decline* (London: Politico's, 2003), p. 18

49. B. Pimlott, *Harold Wilson*, pp 513–14

9

SOCIAL POLICY

Robert M. Page

I N A CAMPAIGN speech at Southampton shortly before the 1964 general
election, Harold Wilson described Alec Douglas-Home as a 'nineteenth-
century patrician' for referring, during an appearance on the BBC's TV
Election Time programme, to a prospective social security benefit for those
aged over eighty as a 'donation'. Wilson's mocking response to the then Prime
Minister captured his tribal antipathy to privileged, 'reactionary' Tories as well
as his own deep-rooted commitment to the welfare state, which he believed
had done much to improve the lives of ordinary citizens in post-war Britain.
He was particularly scathing of the thirteen wasted years of Conservative rule,
which had failed to address the 'indefensible pockets of shameful poverty and
injustice' in British society.[1]

After defeating George Brown for the party leadership in 1963,
Wilson identified the modernisation of both the economy and the welfare
state as the central task for the next Labour government in order to redress the
wilful neglect of previous Conservative administrations (1951–64). Wilson
was opposed to parts of his predecessor Hugh Gaitskell's political agenda,

particularly the proposed abandonment of the party's commitment to public ownership, believing that this would only serve to perpetuate the damaging war between the fundamental and revisionist wings of the party. Nevertheless, he was in agreement with much of the party's existing economic and social agenda that had been set out in the policy document to which he had made a substantive contribution – *Signposts for the '60s*.[2]

Wilson's ambitious proposals for the improvement of the welfare state reflected many of the 'revisionist' social-democratic ideas that Crosland had developed in his influential book *The Future of Socialism*. The 'fundamentalist' notion that increased public ownership and industrial democracy were essential features of a socialist economic strategy had given way to the idea that it was now possible to achieve egalitarian ends by effective forms of state intervention and direction and by the active encouragement of improved co-operation between both sides of industry. Significantly, social policy was now seen as the key arena for promoting greater equality within society.

The main challenge facing Wilson and his prospective Labour government was to decide on an effective set of egalitarian social policies. This was no easy task given the complexity of policy formation in areas such as social security. During the party's lengthy period in opposition, painstaking plans were, for example, drawn up for both a National Superannuation scheme and an Income Guarantee for pensioners. Under the former, the flat-rate contributory and benefit arrangements designed by Beveridge were to be replaced by a new earnings-related scheme, which would limit the growth of private provision by tying most citizens into a more generous state system. In the case of the Income Guarantee, poorer pensioners were to be provided with a supplementary benefit to lift them out of poverty. The novel aspect of this scheme was that Inland Revenue data would be used to calculate these payments, thereby eradicating, it was hoped, the problem of take-up associated with the stigmatising means tests operated by the National Assistance Board.[3]

Labour's egalitarian social strategy also needed to be sensitive to demographic changes. The party was faced with a significant increase in the
proportion of citizens that the former Conservative leader Harold Macmillan had described as either 'resting' (those over retirement age) or 'learning'
(infants and those below the school-leaving age). The growth in the proportion of this so-called 'dependent' population, from just under 50 per cent in
the early 1940s to some 60 per cent by the mid-1960s, necessitated an increase
in social expenditure in order to maintain existing service levels, let alone to
meet the manifesto commitment of ensuring that they would be 'fit for the
1960s and '70s'.[4] Moreover, acceptance of the idea that enhanced levels of
social expenditure would depend on a growth dividend gave rise to the possibility that the party's social agenda would be blown off course in the event
of the economy misfiring.

Wilson and his colleagues also had to contend with emerging social-
scientific evidence that cast doubt on the supposedly egalitarian impact
of existing welfare benefits and services. Ground-breaking work by Brian
Abel-Smith and Peter Townsend at the London School of Economics (LSE),
for example, indicated that poverty was still a major and growing problem despite the creation of the post-war welfare state. These academics
drew attention to the fact that poverty could be experienced by a significant
number of citizens engaged in paid work as well as by those outside the
labour market.[5]

Finally, Wilson and his colleagues were faced with the challenge of devis-
ing an optimal mix of universal and targeted provision that would help them
realise their egalitarian ambitions. Over-reliance on the former might prove
costly unless steps were taken to recoup some of the expenditure through
complementary, progressive tax measures, while provision geared towards
those in the most acute need, particularly in the area of social security, might,
as was noted previously, have an adverse impact on take-up.

THE LABOUR PARTY
MANIFESTO 1964

Labour's plans for social reform were clearly set out in their 1964 general election manifesto. In an effort to counter the Conservatives' 'austere' approach to social security, which had 'imposed poverty standards on the retired, the sick and the unemployed', Labour promised to raise National Insurance benefits and link them to increases in earnings. Retirement pensioners would receive a non-means-tested Income Guarantee and a new 'wage-related scheme' would be 'grafted onto the existing flat-rate National Insurance scheme'. The position of widows was to be improved by higher-rate benefits and the abolition of the earnings rule. A new socially just redundancy payments scheme was also scheduled to be introduced.

Various remedies were also proposed for the NHS, which had been 'starved of resources' and had failed to 'adapt sufficiently to modern needs'. Prescription charges were to be abolished and plans put in place 'as rapidly as possible' to recreate a 'completely free health service'. There was to be increased hospital capacity to meet growing demand for treatment and an expansion in the number of qualified medical staff. Community care services – 'the most neglected of all health services in recent years' – were to be improved by means of expanded home help and other domiciliary services.

In the area of housing, the Conservatives were castigated for their desire to decontrol rents, which had created the conditions for so-called 'Rachmanism',[6] and for allowing interest rates and land prices to spiral out of control, with the consequence that another generation of ordinary families were condemned to live in 'squalid and overcrowded' conditions. To rectify these shortcomings, Labour proposed to set up a Land Commission to buy land for building and rebuilding at fair, rather than 'exorbitant' prices.

Labour also promised to underwrite cheap loans for prospective owner-occupiers and for local authority building programmes. The 1957 Rent Act would be abolished and security of tenure was to be restored for tenants. Older homes were to be modernised and slum clearances accelerated. While Labour did not want to be drawn into an 'election auction' on the number of new homes that they would build, not least because of uncertainties about the capacity of the construction industry, they believed that a target in the region of 400,000 new homes per annum was deliverable.

After securing a narrow victory in the October 1964 general election, the external economic pressures, which were to prove a constant irritant for successive Wilson administrations, soon cast a shadow over Labour's social agenda. The adverse reaction of the foreign exchange markets to Labour's announcement in the November Budget that they would tackle the problem of pensioner poverty by means of an 18.5 per cent increase in the basic state pension led to a sharp rise in the UK bank rate. A subsequent Cabinet decision to backdate this pension increase was rescinded in the face of continued market volatility. Many Labour supporters quickly became disillusioned by Labour's continued willingness to cut social expenditure if economic circumstances so 'dictated'. Nevertheless, the lingering possibility that large parts of Labour's social programme would not be implemented because of the party's slender parliamentary majority dissipated following Wilson's decision to call a general election in March 1966, which saw Labour increase its overall majority to ninety-seven seats. The party's 1966 general election manifesto – *Time for Decision* – reaffirmed that there would be no change in the party's approach to economic and social policy.

Most commentators have opted to review the Wilson governments from 1964 to 1970 as if they were a single government rather than 'separate' administrations. This convention will be adopted in the assessment of the welfare record of the Wilson 'government' that follows.

THE WILSON GOVERNMENT AND
THE WELFARE STATE, 1964-70

Social Security

By the time Labour left office in 1970 after six years in government, its two flagship social security policies, the Income Guarantee and National Super-annuation, had fallen by the wayside. The Income Guarantee for pensioners had been strongly promoted by Douglas Houghton, who, as Chancellor of the Duchy of Lancaster from 1964 to 1967, was given Cabinet responsibility for both social security and health. The technical difficulties involved in developing a scheme of this kind, coupled with the costly decision to prioritise improvements in the living standards of existing pensioners and other claimants by an across-the-board rise in benefit rates, effectively scuppered this proposal.

Wilson's appointment of one of his closest Cabinet allies, Richard Cross-man, as the new Cabinet overlord for social security and health in April following the brief tenures of Houghton's successors, Patrick Gordon Walker and Michael Stewart, led to plans being formulated for the introduction of a modified National Superannuation scheme.[7] Relying heavily on the expertise of LSE academics such as Richard Titmuss and Brian Abel-Smith, a White Paper, *National Superannuation and Social Insurance*, was eventually published in January 1969. The subsequent Bill failed, however, to reach the statute book owing to Wilson's decision to call a general election in 1970.

Despite the failure to introduce the Income Guarantee or National Superan-nuation, Wilson's supporters could point to a number of positive developments within the field of social security from 1964 to 1970. These included benefit increases, the introduction of earnings-related unemployment and sickness benefits, and the abolition of the restrictive-earnings rule for widows. The replacement of the National Assistance Board by a new, semi-autonomous body – the Supplementary Benefits Commission – under the 1966 Social Security Act was also intended to enhance the position of claimants. In an effort to resolve the problem of the low take-up of benefits caused by stigma and bureaucratic complexities, the new body emphasised the welfare rights of claimants and reduced the discretionary powers of officials. Other progressive developments included the introduction of rate and rent rebates and a redundancy payments scheme.

Housing

Wilson's recognition that Labour would need to deliver an effective housing policy if it was to retain electoral support led him to persuade Richard Crossman to become his first Minister of Housing in 1964. The two pressing issues facing Crossman were the need to tackle the negative effects of the Conservatives' 'pro-landlord' Rent Act of 1957, which had given rise to Rachmanism, and the need to press ahead with an ambitious housing drive. In an attempt to resolve the first of these issues, Crossman extended the remit of rent tribunals to those in furnished as well as unfurnished properties, granted tenants security of tenure and introduced 'fair rents'. In terms of house-building, a White Paper was published in 1965 that committed the government to an annual target of 500,000 new homes by 1970. Although some 400,000 homes were built in both 1967 and 1968, Crossman's 'drive' faltered in 1969 as the adverse fall-out from the currency devaluation of 1967 began to feed through. Although the number of completions was impressive by contemporary standards, the decision to rely in part on experimental, prefabricated, 'system-build' techniques rather than traditional construction methods proved problematic over time as concerns started to be raised about the quality and durability of these new homes. In addition, the new high-rise estates that had been commissioned by a number of local authorities, with the aid of generous central government subsidies, proved far from popular with many council tenants, who criticised the lack of local amenities and the absence of balconies and gardens. The publication of the White Paper *Old Houses into New Homes* in 1968 was one of the first signs that Labour had begun to recognise that, with housing supply now exceeding demand (except in London and the south-east), it now needed to shift its focus from the construction of new homes to the renovation of the existing housing stock.

Wilson and his ministers also recognised that they needed to demonstrate to their 'aspirational' supporters that they were as supportive of homeowners as of council tenants. To this end, a number of measures were introduced to support prospective homeowners, including exemption from capital gains tax, low-interest loans for those on modest incomes and the provision of 100 per cent mortgages. By the time Labour had left office in 1970, there had been a steady increase in owner-occupation, which now made up around 50 per cent of all tenures.

Health and Personal Social Services

Shortly after returning to power in 1964, Labour moved quickly to honour their manifesto pledge of abolishing prescription charges. This commitment proved relatively short-lived, however, as Kenneth Robinson, the Minister of Health from 1964–68, 'opted' to reintroduce these charges, albeit with exemptions for children, older people and those with chronic forms of ill-health as part of the Treasury's expenditure squeeze in 1968, rather than cut the hospital-building programme. This pressure to control spending also meant that Labour failed to meet its ambitious, real-terms, annual NHS spending target of 4.8 per cent of GDP during the Wilson era. It did manage, though, to achieve a rate of growth significantly in excess of the level achieved by the previous Conservative administrations.

Robinson also moved decisively to deal with the growing crisis in General Practice, where threats of mass resignations posed a major challenge to the delivery of effective health services. A generous pay award and the introduction of a new GP charter, which boosted practice allowances and provided low-cost loans for the creation of group practices, proved effective in placating this section of health professionals.

While Wilson and influential ministers such as Crossman recognised the need to modernise and improve existing health and social services, the abject quality of some post-1945 provisions was brought into sharp relief with the publication of the Report of the Committee of Inquiry into allegations of ill-treatment of patients at the Ely Hospital, Cardiff, in 1969. The report revealed harrowing evidence of the inhumane treatment meted out by nursing and other staff to vulnerable patients suffering various forms of mental illness and disability within a closed institution. The report highlighted the major overhaul of service quality that would be needed if Labour was to move beyond the austere range of welfare services introduced by the post-war Attlee governments.

One of the final acts of the Wilson government was to establish a more unified system of local authority-run personal social services, following the publication of the Seebohm Report in 1968. It was hoped that the new social services departments would provide a more streamlined service to both children and adults. Although there were turf wars over which particular services the new departments would exercise control over, this development was widely regarded as a positive step forward in terms of improving the resourcing and status of what came to be known as the 'fifth' social service.[8]

The failure of Wilson and his fellow 'socialist' ministers to deliver the improvements to welfare services that many of their supporters had been anticipating led to increasing levels of 'friendly fire' being directed at the government, not least from the plethora of newly established campaigning

groups. The Wilson government's unwillingness to increase family allowances after returning to office in 1964 was the catalyst for the formation of
the Child Poverty Action Group in 1965. Unable to persuade ministers
of the urgent need to pursue a more vigorous anti-poverty strategy, the group
sent a critical memorandum to Wilson shortly before Christmas of that year.
Timed to coincide with the publication of Abel-Smith and Townsend's work
The Poor and the Poorest, the memorandum generated significant media
interest in Labour's continuing difficulties in resolving the problem of poverty. A number of other campaigning groups soon emerged, championing
groups such as the homeless (Shelter, Campaign for Homeless and Roof-
less), lone-parent families (Gingerbread), the low-paid (the Low Pay Unit)
and disabled people (the Disablement Income Group). By the time of the
1970 general election, the Child Poverty Action Group was once again in
the media spotlight after their controversial and damaging claim that the
poor had got poorer during the Wilson era. Although this charge was refuted
by government ministers and by some of their remaining academic sympa-
thisers, such as Richard Titmuss and Brian Abel-Smith, the claim reflected
the profound sense of disillusionment among many Labour supporters and
activists with regard to the achievements of the Wilson governments in the
area of social policy.

Subsequent reviews of the Wilson government's record on welfare expenditure during the period 1964–70 suggests that Labour did indeed keep its
promise to outspend the Conservatives. They also managed to enhance the
overall living standards of the poorest groups in society and secure a modest
reduction in the level of inequality in society.[9] Despite these achievements,
though, there was a sense that Labour lacked a clear 'socialist' vision and
that they were all too willing to abandon policy commitments in the face of
adverse economic pressures. While the limited improvements they were able
to make might have been a cause for celebration in other eras, they failed to

resonate with either their core supporters or the wider electorate, who opted for Edward Heath and the Conservatives in the 1970 general election.

WILSON AND THE WELFARE STATE, 1974–76

Following the turbulent years of the Heath government, Wilson confounded the experts by leading Labour to a wafer-thin victory in the February 1974 general election. A bold, avowedly left-wing manifesto, *Let Us Work Together – Labour's Way out of the Crisis*, was prepared for the election to tackle the prevailing crises in British society. The manifesto promised to eliminate poverty and, in that most memorable of post-1945 election statements, pledged to 'bring about a fundamental and irreversible shift in the balance of power and wealth in favour of working people and their families'.[10] Greater equality was to be achieved through full employment, improved housing and increased benefits for pensioners, the unemployed and the sick, which would be uprated in line with earnings. Disabled people were to be given additional support, new children's allowances were to be introduced and the Conservatives' 1972 Housing Finance Act repealed. Compulsory purchase would be used to ensure that development land would be freed up for the construction of new homes, hospitals and schools. NHS prescription charges were once again to be abolished, private health care phased out and a wealth tax introduced. The manifesto also promised to improve women's rights in areas such as employment, education, training and social security.

In an effort to break free from the shackles of governing without an overall majority, Wilson called and won another general election in October 1974 (though he only secured an overall majority of four seats). In his introduction to this manifesto – *Britain Will Win With Labour* – he reiterated his determination to bring about a more just society, underpinned by a Social

Contract between the government and the trade unions, which was designed
to enhance the overall living standards of more disadvantaged citizens. The
social policy commitments contained in the October 1974 manifesto were very
much in line with those contained in the February 1974 version, though there
were some additional commitments. These included a promise to extend
eligibility for the £10 Christmas bonus to a wider group of claimants and
increased family allowance payments. New benefits for disabled citizens and
their carers were also to be introduced. In housing, the government promised
that there would be a major effort to tackle homelessness, overcrowding and
squalor. Council tenants were to be provided with greater security of tenure
and rent levels were to be set at affordable levels.

By the time Wilson announced his unexpected resignation to the Cabinet
on 16 March 1976, just five days after his sixtieth birthday, significant progress
had been made in meeting a number of these manifesto pledges, despite the
economic difficulties that continued to beset his government. Wilson's decision
to appoint Barbara Castle as Minister of State for Health and Social Security
(March 1974–April 1976) provided a major impetus in this regard. Following
repeated attempts by previous Labour and Conservative governments to institute new pension proposals, Castle and her junior minister Brian O'Malley
managed to secure cross-party agreement to pave the way for the introduction of a new State Earnings Related Pension Scheme in 1975. Although the
new arrangements were less ambitious than Labour's initial plans for National
Superannuation, involving as they now did a significant role for non-state
providers, the new scheme, which was to be phased in over two decades, met
some of Labour's egalitarian aims. Those with interrupted working careers or
significant variations in pay, most notably women, were to be provided with
enhanced benefits based on their best twenty years of paid work.

Castle also prepared the ground for the introduction of Child Benefit,
which would be payable for first as well as subsequent children. This new

weekly benefit, which replaced both child tax allowances and family allowances, was underpinned by a deliberate decision to transfer resources from
the father's 'wallet' to the mother's 'purse'. There were protracted internal
discussions about the possibility of an electoral backlash from male voters,
who also faced the prospect of lower take-home pay as a result of changing
tax thresholds. Fears were also expressed that the new rate proposed for
Child Benefit might be inadequate. Following Wilson's departure in 1976 and
Callaghan's subsequent decision to sack Castle, it seemed that the introduction
of Child Benefit might be delayed, but following staunch rear-guard action
by supporters, involving the publicising of confidential government papers
that had been 'leaked' to the Child Poverty Action Group, Callaghan and his
ministerial sceptics agreed to phase in the new benefit in 1977.

During her time in office, Castle had to resolve long-standing disputes
with both consultants and hospital doctors, who were now willing to engage
in more traditional forms of trade union activity such as working to rule
and taking strike action. Given that Castle was also charged with honour-
ing the manifesto commitment to phase out pay beds in NHS hospitals, this
proved to be no easy task. Following lengthy and fraught discussions and
intermittent strikes, both these issues were only resolved after Wilson agreed
to enter the fray, promising a Royal Commission on the NHS and agreeing
to a modified plan relating to the phasing out of pay beds. One of Castle's
other egalitarian achievements was the introduction of a new NHS funding
mechanism, devised by the Resource Allocation Working Party. The new funding formula attempted to redirect health resources to geographical areas and
specialisms in greatest need.[11]

During Wilson's final two years in office, Labour also secured a freeze in
council rents and published a housing Bill that, following the subsequent
passage of the Housing (Homeless Persons) Act of 1977, provided greater
protection to those at greatest risk of homelessness, such as lone parents.

ASSESSING WILSON AND THE WELFARE STATE

Evaluations of Wilson's attempts to enhance welfare provision from 1964 to
1970 and subsequently from 1974 to 1976 need to be undertaken with a recognition of the many other issues that demanded governmental attention during
this era. These included long-standing economic and industrial problems as
well as the Rhodesian crisis, the Vietnam War, the retention or otherwise of
an independent nuclear defence capability, trade union reform and membership of the Common Market.

Left-wing critics have taken Wilson to task for his failure to implement
the bold socialist strategy that Labour supporters had eagerly anticipated.
The second-stage socialist advance, which would build on Attlee's earlier
achievements, simply failed to materialise. Wilson's willingness to confront
the trade unions, bear down on wages, impose welfare cuts and persist with
'Cold War' politics were seen as conclusive evidence of a non-radical mindset.
This left critique was set out in a number of publications, such as the *May Day
Manifesto 1968*, which signalled the emergence of new-left thinking that sought
to break free from the confines of the 'orthodox' Marxism of the Communist
Party as well as the revisionist Labour doctrines developed by Crosland and
implemented by Wilson.[12] Rejecting the idea that a modern, egalitarian, socialist
society could be created within the confines of a more socially responsive form
of capitalism, the new left were seeking a much more fundamental reformula-
tion of economic and social policy. In particular, they were highly sceptical
of the Fabian notion that the state could be a vehicle of substantive change
within a capitalist society. Even if Wilson had been willing to pursue a more
radical welfare agenda, this was never likely to have truly satisfied his most
fervent left-wing critics. In addition, those such as Townsend, who believed
it *was* possible to achieve socialist outcomes through concerted forms of state
action, also expressed frustration at the limited degree of egalitarian progress

that had been made during the Wilson era. A particular source of concern was Wilson's reluctance to press ahead with more radical initiatives unless the economic outlook was adjudged sufficiently favourable.

Wilson's willingness to water down or abandon more radical policy proposals reflected his pragmatic instincts and his desire to maintain party unity at all costs. For Wilson, it was better to pursue a modest set of policy objectives that would ensure party unity and retain popular support than opt for a set of politically contentious egalitarian measures that might pave the way for the return to power of a reactionary Conservative administration.

Although Wilson's pragmatism led many commentators and associates to regard him as unprincipled, cynical and even untrustworthy, this was not the impression that held sway among ordinary Labour voters. For them, Wilson was seen as someone who was amusing, down to earth, with hobbies and interests similar to their own and who really did have their best interests at heart. When Paul McCartney, along with his fellow Beatles received a Variety Club of Great Britain personality of the year award from the then opposition leader in 1963, he declared that 'good old Mr Wilson' deserved a medal too. While many seasoned commentators might have been willing to award Harold Wilson a gold medal in respect of his sparkling performance as opposition Labour leader, few were likely to have been so inclined on the basis of his overall welfare record during 1964–70 and 1974–76. With the benefit of hindsight, though, might there be a case for the award of at least a silver medal? Despite all the tribulations he faced, Wilson did succeed in making improvements to the welfare state and reducing income and wealth inequalities. While his cumulative endeavours did not amount to a welfare 'revolution', they were a step forward. While many might have been disappointed by the slow pace of democratic-socialist advance during the Wilson era, it is by no means certain that a more radical leader could have achieved more egalitarian outcomes given entrenched, class-based opposition to progressive social reform of any kind.

NOTES AND REFERENCES

1.   H. Wilson, Speech at Birmingham Town Hall, 19 January 1964, in H. Wilson, *The New Britain*, p. 11

2.   Labour Party, *Signposts for the '60s* (London: Labour Party, 1961)

3.   See S. Thornton, *Richard Crossman and the Welfare State* (London: I. B. Tauris, 2009)

4.   *The New Britain*, Labour Party general election manifesto, 1964

5.   See B. Abel-Smith and P. Townsend, *The Poor and the Poorest* (London: Bell & Sons, 1965)

6.   The term Rachmanism derives from the intimidatory methods used by Perec Rachman, the landlord of a large number of rental properties in the Notting Hill area of London, to 'persuade' sitting tenants paying low controlled rents to vacate their homes so that higher-paying tenants could be moved in

7.   Crossman eventually became Secretary of State in a newly created combined Ministry of Health and Social Security

8.   See P. Townsend (ed.), *The Fifth Social Service* (London: Fabian Society, 1970)

9.   See, for example, W. Beckerman (ed.), *The Labour Government's Economic Record 1964–70* (London: Duckworth, 1972); P. Townsend and N. Bosanquet (eds), *Labour and Inequality* (London: Fabian Society, 1972); and R. Whiting, *The Labour Party and Taxation: Party Identity and Political Purpose in Twentieth-Century Britain* (Cambridge: Cambridge University Press, 2006)

10.   *Let Us Work Together*, Labour Party general election manifesto, 1974

11.   See N. Timmins, The Five Giants (London: HarperCollins, 2001), pp 339–40

12.   See R. Williams, *The May Day Manifesto 1968* (London: Penguin, 1968)

10

SOCIAL AND SEXUAL LIBERALISATION

Peter Dorey

'There is mounting evidence of depravity in the Labour Party ... Labour Members of Parliament back loosening of homosexual laws. Labour Members of Parliament peddle abortion. We urgently need a government of moralists ... The long hair of Mr Wilson's intellectuals on the back benches will strangle him.'[1]

INTRODUCTION

THE 1964–70 LABOUR governments led by Harold Wilson have become synonymous with a series of social reforms that, to their supporters, liberated millions of people from repressive prejudice and puritanical intolerance but, according their critics, unleashed an era of licentious behaviour and moral depravity, the deleterious consequences of which still affect Britain today. These reforms entailed the liberalisation of Britain's abortion and divorce laws and the legalisation of homosexuality (the terms 'gay' or 'same-sex relationships' were not generally used in the 1960s; rather more derogatory or offensive terms prevailed). Other civilising or liberalising measures were also enacted during the 1960s, such as the abolition both of the death penalty and of theatre censorship, as well as the provision of contraceptive advice to unmarried women, but space will preclude consideration of these three reforms.

On most of these issues, Harold Wilson's own views were ambivalent or agnostic, and he personally played little active part in the relevant legislation. However, his ambiguous stance was not solely attributable to his personal views (or lack of) on these issues, but also owed to his political position as Labour Party leader from 1963–76, Prime Minister from 1964 until 1970, and again from 1974 to 1976, with much of his time and energy expended on struggling to maintain party unity.[2] As such, Wilson tended to place himself above the political fray on many of these issues, either because some of the reforms were considered to be controversial in the PLP itself or because some Labour voters were certainly not socially liberal on penal policies or sexual issues. Indeed, several Labour MPs appeared similarly lukewarm about many of these reforms, precisely because they feared a hostile reaction from some of their more socially conservative (or authoritarian) working-class constituents. As we will see, this was to prove a particular concern with regard to the legalisation of homosexuality.

Perhaps more importantly, though, was the fact that much of Wilson's 1964–70 premiership was concerned with a plethora of serious economic and industrial problems (including the ill-fated attempt at trade union reform via *In Place of Strife*), pursuing British membership of the European Economic Community (EEC) and military intervention in Northern Ireland. It is perhaps not surprising, therefore, that the liberalisation of the laws pertaining to abortion and divorce, and the legalisation of homosexuality, are conspicuous by their absence in many essays on, and biographies of, Harold Wilson, these focusing almost entirely on economic, industrial and foreign affairs,[3] while Pimlott's 800-page biography alludes to Wilson's (cautious) views on such issues merely in a cursory sentence or two, and then only *en passant*.[4]

CONTEXT

When Labour's Anthony Crosland published, in 1956, the 'bible' of social-democratic revisionism, *The Future of Socialism*, he urged the party to pay more attention to social or lifestyle issues, rather than constantly highlighting economic objectives, such as more public ownership (nationalisation), higher taxation of the rich and further wealth redistribution. In one particularly noteworthy passage, Crosland urged the Labour Party to address:

> the more serious question of socially imposed restrictions on the individual's life and liberty … the divorce laws, licensing laws, prehistoric (and flagrantly unfair) abortion laws, obsolete penalties for sexual abnormality [*sic*], the illiterate censorship of books and plays, and remaining restrictions on the equal rights of women. Most of these are intolerable, and should be highly offensive to socialists, in whose blood there should always run a trace of the anarchist and libertarian, and not too much of the prig and the prude.[5]

Three years later, in the run-up to the 1959 general election, Roy Jenkins similarly recommended that the Labour Party should place a much stronger emphasis on liberating individuals from repressive restrictions on their lifestyles, so that people would be free to live how they wanted to, provided they were conducting what John Stuart Mill termed 'self-regarding actions', which therefore did not impact negatively on other individuals or society.

In this context, Jenkins claimed that hanging (often known as capital punishment, or simply the death penalty) was 'barbaric ... the ghastly apparatus of the gallows', described the law against homosexuality as 'brutal and unfair', condemned the restrictions on abortion as 'harsh and archaic', and argued that the divorce laws 'caused a great deal of unnecessary suffering'.[6]

These, along with other repressive and out-dated restrictions on individual liberty, such as theatre censorship, gambling laws and licensing laws – what Jenkins terms 'social archaisms' – were in urgent need of reform or repeal, Jenkins insisted: 'We gain nothing, and lose a great deal, by keeping subject to the penalties of criminal law, personal actions and conduct which should be matters of personal choice and do no harm to society.'[7]

LEGALISATION OF HOMOSEXUALITY

In Britain today, where same-sex couples can get married and adopt children, it should not be forgotten just how much hostility homosexual men faced until relatively recently, this not uncommonly manifesting itself in physical assaults (commonly known as 'queer-bashing'). This stark attitude towards sexuality was reflected and reinforced by the fact that, since 1885, sexual activity and relationships between men had been illegal,[8] hence Oscar Wilde's allusion to 'the love that dare not speak its name'.

Although Winston Churchill's 1951–55 government had established a committee, chaired by Sir John Wolfenden, to examine the manner in which the law treated homosexuality (and prostitution), Conservative ministers declined to act when the committee's report claimed that '[w]e do not think it is proper for the law to concern itself with what a man does in private, unless it can be shown to be so contrary to the public good that the law ought to intervene in its function as the guardian of the public good'.[9]

Homosexual activity thus remained illegal for another decade, until Harold Wilson's second (1966–70) government presided over the introduction of the Sexual Offences (No. 2) Bill.[10]

This legislation emanated as a Private Member's Bill, introduced by Leo Abse in December 1966, although as with many such Bills, its success in reaching the statute book was heavily dependent on tacit governmental support. In this instance, Abse's Bill benefited from support from key Cabinet ministers, not least from Roy Jenkins, whose reputation as a social liberal was considerably enhanced by his role, as Home Secretary, in providing practical support for the Sexual Offences (No. 2) Bill, even though he informed the Cabinet's home affairs committee that the government's official stance towards such Bills was one of 'benevolent neutrality'.[11]

However, what was most notable about the enactment of the Sexual Offences (No. 2) Bill was the rather ambiguous stance of many Labour MPs and ministers, whose attitude was often that of 'hate the sin, love the sinner'. Many Labour parliamentarians who supported Abse's Bill nonetheless strongly disapproved of, or were even disgusted by, the idea of two men engaging in sexual activity together, to the extent that even Abse felt obliged to describe homosexuality as an 'ailment' and 'terrible fate', but one that was compounded by the law effectively compelling homosexuals to choose 'between celibacy or criminality'. Moreover, reflecting his penchant for Freudian psychoanalysis, Abse suggested that homosexuality was often a consequence of domestic circumstances and family upbringing, whereby an absent or ineffective father sometimes resulted in young boys developing an unhealthily close emotional attachment to their mothers. In such cases, boys sometimes 'grow up to have men's bodies but feminine souls', and as such, warranted compassion, not condemnation; to be pitied, rather than punished.[12] In effect, the 'enlightened' approach to homosexuality advanced by Abse still depicted it as a consequence of a defective family upbringing, rather than an innate or inherent individual characteristic; nurture, not nature.

Many other Labour proponents of legalising homosexuality similarly couched their arguments in terms of compassion or pity for homosexuals, because to have actually expressed approval of homosexuality, or directly acknowledged such relationships as a legitimate source of sexual pleasure for some men, risked 'stirring up … violent opposition'.[13]

Even Roy Jenkins was at pains to emphasise that:

> [i]t would be a mistake to think that … we are giving a vote of confidence
> or congratulation to homosexuality. Those who suffer from this disability
> carry a great weight of loneliness, guilt and shame. The crucial question,
> which we are nearly at the end of answering, is, should we add to those
> disadvantages the full rigour of the criminal law?[14]

Jenkins and Abse evidently believed that the answer was a resounding 'no'.

Harold Wilson did not publicly make his own views known, but some of his closest colleagues sensed that he found the issue somewhat distasteful, and that his willingness to let Crossman and Jenkins assist Abse, by enabling his Bill to reach the statute book, owed more to a desire to get the matter resolved swiftly, lest it cause Labour problems near the next general election. Ever the supreme political pragmatist, therefore, Wilson permitted the legislation more for tactical reasons than because of any personal approval. Indeed, Crossman claimed that, as 'a perfectly sincere Sunday Methodist' who held 'a number of moral convictions', Wilson was 'against the legal reforms to deal with homosexuality or abortion'.[15] Another commentator suggests that part of Wilson's apparent social and moral conservatism on such issues derived from concerns about the potential for public disapproval, and thus 'the electoral harvest that might be reaped, particularly in areas like his own constituency of Huyton [Liverpool] with a large Catholic vote',[16] a suggestion echoed by Hindell and Simms with particular regard to the liberalisation of abortion in the latter half of the 1960s.[17]

LIBERALISATION OF ABORTION LAW

Between the general elections of 1964 and 1966, no less than three Private Members' Bills were introduced concerning abortion, two in the House of Commons (one by a Labour MP, and one by a Conservative) and one in the Lords (tabled by a Labour peer). None of these Bills were successful, owing in large part to insufficient parliamentary time – a perennial problem for most Private Members' Bills. As such, abortion was only legally permitted if and when a doctor judged that continuation of a pregnancy would make the woman a physical or mental wreck.

A fourth Private Member's Bill to reform the law pertaining to abortion was introduced by the Liberal MP David Steel shortly after the 1966 general election. Initially titled the Medical Termination of Pregnancy Bill, but later changed simply to the Abortion Bill/Act, the legislation decreed that a pregnancy could be terminated if certain conditions were met, namely:

- The continuation of a pregnancy would pose a serious risk to the life, or physical or mental well-being, of the woman.
- There was a substantial risk that the unborn child would suffer such mental or physical impairment as to be seriously handicapped.
- Either of these two conditions were confirmed by two registered doctors, their judgement being formed in good faith.
- Any such abortions had to be conducted in a National Health Service hospital or other medical institution approved by the Secretary/Minister of State for Health.

This Bill was given its Second Reading by 223 votes to twenty-nine, with the government's stance again being that of neutrality (whereupon Labour MPs were granted a free vote), albeit with all but one of its ministers voting in support. However, lengthy debates and numerous amendments tabled during Committee Stage[18] – reflecting the medical complexities involved, ethical issues raised and considerable Conservative hostility – meant that the Bill did not return to the floor of the House until June 1967, by which time it was in danger of running out of time in that parliamentary session. This would mean that a fourth abortion law reform Bill introduced by a back-bench MP or peer within the previous two years would fail to reach the statute book, not because of lack of political support *per se*, but because of the House of Commons' legislative timetable and procedural rules (namely no 'carry-over' of Bills to the next session).

Once again, the sympathy of the government, and particularly of the Home Secretary Roy Jenkins, led to parliamentary time being made available to enable the Bill to pass through Report Stage and onto its Third Reading prior to a relatively smooth passage through the House of Lords. As Richards remarked:

> There can be no doubt that the success of the Abortion Bill was due in great measure to the benevolence of ministers. Their assistance was especially valuable in preserving the measure from shipwreck in the dangerous seas of the parliamentary timetable.[19]

However, a few ministers found abortion law reform deeply unpalatable, most notably Shirley Williams (a staunch Roman Catholic), who was the only Labour minister to vote against the Bill at Second Reading, although she was subsequently joined by six other Labour ministers in the vote on the Third Reading, including the Cabinet minister Anthony Greenwood.

DIVORCE LAW REFORM

The 1969 Divorce Reform Act was another landmark measure of social liberalism, passed during Wilson's 1966–70 premiership. It too emanated from a Private Member's Bill introduced initially by the Labour MP William Wilson in early 1968, but, when this ran out of time, an almost identical (Private Member's) Bill was introduced in the following parliamentary session (1968–69) by another Labour backbencher, Alec Jones, but with extensive and energetic support from Leo Abse. Moreover, as with Abse's recent promotion of homosexual law reform, Jones and his supporters could cite the recommendations of a major inquiry, this time under the auspices of the Archbishop of Canterbury, whose report, *Putting Asunder – A Divorce Law for a Contemporary Society*, was published in 1966. Indeed, another report into Britain's divorce law was published in the same year, by the Law Commission (which had conducted a parallel inquiry), entitled *Reform of the Grounds for Divorce: The Field of Choice*.

Both reports argued that the status quo was unfair and untenable, primarily because the main criterion for divorce was adultery. However, even in the absence of such infidelity, instead of guaranteeing the holy sanctity of marriage and ensuring that couples remained happily married 'until death us do part', the erstwhile divorce law ensured that some couples endured long lives of private misery and sullen resentment. Moreover, some women found themselves trapped in a marriage with a husband who was (or subsequently became) emotionally and sexually abusive and/or physically violent; these women were often compelled to suffer in silence, while publicly presenting an image of domestic bliss and marital harmony.

It was in this context that Jones – himself formerly a solicitor who had dealt with many divorce cases – introduced his Divorce Reform Bill, which received its Second Reading (the debate on a Bill's principles) in December 1968.

The Bill provided a new statutory basis for dissolving a marriage, namely, 'irretrievable breakdown', this to be defined by one (or more) of five criteria: adultery; unreasonable behaviour; desertion for two years; separation for two years with mutual consent; separation for five years regardless of consent. The last two criteria also meant that it was no longer necessary for the partner seeking a divorce to prove that their spouse was directly and demonstrably 'at fault' (as had previously been the case, particularly in instances concerning adultery), hence the notion of 'no-fault divorce' became enshrined in law.

As William Wilson's Bill had suffered from a lack of parliamentary time, Jones's virtually identical legislation prompted the Cabinet to agree that, in this instance, sufficient parliamentary time would be made available by the government, even while again maintaining a stance of formal neutrality, and thus permitting a free vote.[20] Or, as the government's Solicitor-General, Arthur Irvine, explained: 'This is a matter of great importance in terms of social policy and social conduct in this country. It is a non-party matter and, in that context, the government [is] facilitating the opportunity which the House has to arrive at a conclusion.'[21]

Although a clear majority of Labour MPs did vote for the Divorce Reform Bill during the sundry Divisions as it wended its way through the House of Commons, there was some residual opposition, with nineteen Labour MPs voting against it at Second Reading stage in mid-December 1968,[22] while Harold Wilson either abstained or was not present in the House during the debate and Division. However, some of the opposition that emanated from the Labour back benches was not derived from antipathy to divorce law reform per se, but reflected concern about the potential financial destitution that some women (and their children) might suffer as a consequence of divorce, an issue that was subsequently addressed more directly by the 1970 Matrimonial Proceedings and Property Act. Indeed, although the Divorce Reform Bill entered the statute book in 1969, it did not come into effect until January 1971, precisely so that those affected would be covered financially in the 1970 Act.

EXPLAINING THE WILSON GOVERNMENTS' SUPPORT FOR SOCIAL REFORM

The obvious question following this brief overview is why Harold Wilson's 1964–70 premiership heralded such a strong tranche of social and sexual reform, especially as Wilson personally was not renowned as an enthusiast of these liberal measures, save, perhaps, the abolition of the death penalty, which he detested. One of his biographers noted that, although Harold Wilson was strongly egalitarian on social issues like racial and sexual equality, the issues we have discussed in this chapter 'did not interest him greatly'. For example, he was 'cautious about abortion, partly because of the Catholic vote' in some of Labour's urban heartlands in the north of England.[23]

The Importance of Key Individuals

Despite this apparent caution, Wilson subsequently appointed Roy Jenkins as Home Secretary in December 1965, presumably fully cognizant of his social liberalism and associated desire – previously signalled in *The Labour Case* – to transform the Home Office into a progressive and forward-thinking department, which would subsequently be at the forefront of progressive social reform, rather than a bastion of stuffy conservatism and reactionary traditionalism.[24] Wilson himself only devoted one sentence to this appointment in his 836-page memoir of the 1964–70 Labour governments, merely noting that appointing Jenkins as Home Secretary 'marked a revolutionary change in both the out-dated administration of the department and in Home Office attitudes'.[25] Beyond this, Wilson made absolutely no reference to reform of the laws on abortion, divorce or homosexuality, the memoir instead focusing strongly on the economic and industrial problems that dogged his premiership.

However, it has been suggested that even if Wilson made 'no direct reference to wider issues of morality', his appointment of Jenkins strongly implied 'willing acceptance of what was to come', considering that Jenkins had 'such an explicit and radical agenda' of social reform.[26] Or, as Pimlott observed, Wilson 'was happy to accept ... a liberal reform programme that had the backing of the Labour Party intelligentsia, as well as of his own, inspired choice of Home Secretary'.[27] In fact, Jenkins himself recalled that, having been appointed Home Secretary, he conveyed 'some of my ideas about letting fresh air into the Home Office', in response to which Wilson 'became enthusiastic'.[28]

Having thus been appointed as Home Secretary, Jenkins became the prime progenitor of the social reforms outlined above, along with a few others, most notably the abolition of theatre censorship, for, as the esteemed author of a recent biography notes, 'these reforms would not have happened when they did ... without Jenkins's drive and determination'.[29]

Jenkins's active role in facilitating the enactment of these reforms – for example, he actively cooperated and consulted with David Steel and other sponsors of the abortion law reform Bill during its passage through Parliament[30] – ensured his enduring reputation for social liberalism. Although whereas liberals and the left view this legacy as one worthy of congratulation for liberating millions of individuals from private misery and sexual repression, the stance of many Conservatives has been one of condemnation, blaming Jenkins for measures that unleashed forces of moral decay and social disintegration and crossed the line between liberty and licentiousness.

However, vital though his role clearly was, Jenkins also benefited from considerable support, either verbal or practical, from other individuals, to the extent that these landmark social reforms might otherwise have failed to reach the statute book. Certainly, Leo Abse was a key figure, having introduced the 1967 Sexual Offences Act as a Private Member's Bill, and then actively supporting Alec Jones's Private Member's Bill to reform the divorce law. With regard to the parliamentary proponents of divorce law reform, apart from William Wilson and then Alec Jones (the sponsors of the two Private Members' Bills), it has been argued that

> Leo Abse was the dominant figure ... His eagerness, experience boundless
> energy ... and his close personal relationship with several ministers and
> other key individuals who were holding key positions in various depart-
> ments of the governments and Parliament, were vital factors in the success.[31]

Meanwhile, Labour's Health Secretary, Kenneth Robinson, has been credited with playing a crucial role in supporting David Steel's Bill, having himself previously introduced a Private Member's Bill to reform the law on abortion.[32]

Also crucial to the enactment of these social reforms was the practical support provided by Richard Crossman as Leader of the House of Commons, primarily in arranging or adjusting the parliamentary timetable to ensure that the Bills received enough parliamentary time to complete their legislative stages. This was vitally important given that Private Members' Bills are usually allocated a few Fridays only, when attendance in the House is often sparse owing to most MPs travelling back to their constituencies and/or families for the weekend. On each occasion, when it became apparent that one of these Bills was likely to run out of parliamentary time, Crossman – often in tandem with Roy Jenkins[33] – persuaded the Cabinet to make time available in the government's own legislative timetable.

Crossman himself benefited from considerable assistance from Labour's Chief Whip, John Silkin, the latter playing a vital role – in tandem with Crossman – in organising the government's legislative timetable to create sufficient time for these Private Members' Bills (the formal neutrality of the government notwithstanding), and also ensuring that sufficient numbers of Labour MPs were always present during the relevant parliamentary debates and Divisions.[34] Certainly, Silkin's role was readily acknowledged by Jenkins himself.[35]

Changes in the Parliamentary Labour Party

A further explanation for the 1964–70 Wilson government's legalisation of homosexuality, and the liberalisation of the laws pertaining both to abortion and divorce, was the changing composition and demographics of the Parliamentary Labour Party, and resultant generational transformation, in terms of both membership and social attitudes. Those Labour MPs who were *least* enthusiastic about these social and sexual reforms, especially the legalisation of homosexuality, tended to be older and/or working class (at least in origin), or middle class themselves but representing working-class constituencies. For example, having once claimed to 'strongly favour the Bill' to legalise homosexuality, Richard Crossman, on another occasion, referred contemptuously to the 'Bugger's Bill' as 'an extremely unpleasant Bill', and claimed that:

> working-class people in the north jeer at their Members [of Parliament] at the weekend and [are] asking them why they're looking after the buggers at Westminster instead of looking after the unemployed at home. It has gone down very badly that the Labour Party should be associated with such a Bill.[36]

Several other Labour MPs, such as Dick Taverne[37] and Kevin McNamara,[38] expressed similar concerns about Labour's leadership seemingly prioritising homosexuality over unemployment and other economic issues, while a weekly meeting of Labour backbenchers heard the complaint that Labour risked being viewed as 'the party which cares more about the "odd people" in society, such as murderers and homosexuals and the like, rather than the ordinary hard-working members of the community'.[39]

One of Crossman's Cabinet colleagues, George Brown – 'who often liked to cast himself as a representative of working-class common sense'[40] – was particularly appalled, apoplectically warning that '[t]his is how Rome [the Roman Empire] came down', and that, as such, 'society ought to have higher standards ... must have rules. We've gone too damned far on sex already.'[41] Similar disdain emanated from the chair of the Parliamentary Labour Party, Emmanuel 'Manny' Shinwell, who harboured 'contempt for the intellectuals who would bring disastrous opprobrium upon the Labour government'.[42]

Such sentiments seemed to be shared by Jenkins's successor at the Home Office, James Callaghan, who 'viewed most of the mood of permissiveness with dismay', and although he agreed that homosexuals should not suffer criminal punishment or persecution, 'homosexuality in itself was something he disliked intensely'. His disdain for the 'permissive revolution' owed much to the fact that he 'embodied ... traditional working-class virtues', and, like Shinwell, harboured 'contempt ... of the unrepresentative and destructive view of the bourgeois chattering classes'.[43] This perhaps derived both from his upbringing in the naval town of Portsmouth, and his later being the MP for Cardiff South, a constituency that included Cardiff's docks.

Meanwhile, although David Owen, a GP, spoke in favour of the Sexual Offences (No. 2) Bill during its Second Reading – when he argued that those who suffered from the 'symptom of homosexuality' should not suffer further by being subject to the criminal law for what they did in private[44] – as an MP for the naval town of Plymouth, he was fully aware that 'homosexual behaviour ... was strongly disliked' by many local people, and that, as a consequence, 'my stance was bound to upset some of my constituents'. Thus did Owen recall an older train-driver and trade union stalwart telling him at a local Labour

Party meeting: 'David, I accept that you're all in favour of abortion ... and family allowances for unmarried mothers ... but I do draw the line at buggery.' The disjuncture between such sentiments, and the generally more liberal stance of many (more middle-class) local Labour Party members, meant that the latter occasionally 'felt the backlash in Plymouth pubs'.[45]

Meanwhile, some of the strongest intra-party opposition to abortion law reform emanated from Labour MPs, such as the brothers Peter and Simon Mahon, who represented seats in north-west England, particularly parts of Merseyside and various 'working-class Lancashire constituencies whose voters were the Roman Catholic descendants of Irish immigrants'.[46]

In contrast, much of the support for the Wilson governments' social and sexual reforms emanated from the PLP's increasing intake of younger, university-educated and middle-class MPs,[47] most of whom held rather more liberal or 'progressive' attitudes on such issues – a key factor emphasised by Marsh and Chambers,[48] and Richards.[49] Indeed, in the summer of 1967, Crossman claimed that:

> at the moment, many more of our backbenchers are enthusiastic for the
> social measures contained in the Private Member's Bill than they are for
> the government's own legislation like leasehold reform and steel nation-
> alisation. All that, they feel, belongs to the government up there, whereas
> homosexuality and abortion are issues on which backbenchers can
> enforce their own discipline, and where they are free to vote according
> to their own consciences.[50]

Or, as Hindell and Simms observed, these Private Members' Bills provided back-bench MPs 'with opportunities to make a reputation as legislators without the patronage of government or the backing of a civil service staff'. On such occasions, backbenchers 'were no longer lobby-fodder'.[51]

Although Harold Wilson's own stance on such reforms was, as we noted above, ambiguous and ambivalent, and his public pronouncements on such issues were conspicuous by their absence, he allowed such reforms to be enacted anyway, and, in so doing, helped to reinforce the modernising image with which he sought to burnish his 1964–70 government.

Furthermore, such measures also enshrined an egalitarian ethos, with homosexual law reform placing gay men on a more equal legal footing with their heterosexual counterparts (although changing the law did not in itself eradicate homophobic attitudes), while reform of Britain's divorce law made it easier (than hitherto) for women to divorce their husbands and, as such, served to promote greater sexual equality. Meanwhile, abortion law reform also, indirectly at least, facilitated greater social equality because it made it easier for poorer women to seek an abortion (provided that the relevant criteria were met). Previously, working-class women with unwanted pregnancies often had to rely upon dangerous back-street abortions, whereas middle- or upper-class women could usually afford a more discreet (and infinitely safer) Harley Street procedure.

CONCLUSION

Although the 1964–70 Labour governments are renowned for enacting several measures of social liberalism and sexual liberation, Harold Wilson himself remained above the political fray in these cases. He refrained from expressing his own views on such issues, either in public speeches or in Cabinet meetings, and there is scant reference to such reforms in the archives of Wilson's papers at the Bodleian Library, Oxford. However, the general consensus among his biographers and academic commentators, as well as some of his closest colleagues, is that Wilson was *not* enthusiastic about the legalisation of homosexuality or the liberalisation of Britain's abortion and divorce laws. However, it has always been unclear whether this stance reflected a personal disdain for such measures (as Crossman suggested), a simple lack of interest (due to his preoccupation with economic and industrial policies), or apprehension that such reforms might have damaging repercussions for the Labour Party electorally (particularly among some of its 'socially authoritarian' working-class or Catholic supporters).

Yet, regardless of his own enigmatic and equivocal stance on these issues, Wilson did appoint Roy Jenkins as Home Secretary in full knowledge of the latter's liberal views on social and sexual matters, and did not advise him to tone down his reforming zeal. Moreover, as Prime Minister, Wilson chaired the Cabinet meetings that agreed, in response to requests from Jenkins and Crossman, to make parliamentary time available (via the government's own legislative timetable) to ensure that the relevant Private Members' Bills successfully completed all of the necessary legislative stages to reach the statute book. There is no record, in the Cabinet minutes, of Wilson expressing any demurral on such occasions; he merely allowed his ministerial colleagues to air their views and then summarised – as most Prime Ministers do – the overall view (or balance of opinion) of the Cabinet as a whole, which was mostly supportive of these reforms.

Regardless of his own personal views on these social and sexual reforms, permitting his colleagues to pursue them nonetheless suited Wilson's more general desire to be seen to be the leader of a Labour government committed to a programme of modernisation, even if his own priorities were with modernising the economy, industry and political institutions. Wilson was probably not enthusiastic about these social and sexual reforms, but he was nonetheless strongly opposed to discrimination and the unjust treatment of disadvantaged sections of society, and this ensured that he certainly did not oppose or obstruct them. In this crucial respect, his social egalitarianism and political pragmatism combined to ensure that his 1964–70 governments enacted several landmark reforms and, in so doing, immeasurably increased individual liberty by legislating against erstwhile sources of private misery.

NOTES AND REFERENCES

1. G. Nabarro, Speech to the Society for the Protection of Unborn Children (SPUC), 2 July 1967, quoted in K. Hindell and M. Simms, *Abortion Law Reformed* (London: Peter Owen, 1971), p. 102

2. However, our focus is on the first of Wilson's premierships, because this was when these major social reforms were enacted. His 1974–76 term was dominated by other issues, namely the economy, the Social Contract (with the trade unions) and the referendum on Britain's membership of the (then) European Economic Community

3. See, for example: P. Foot, *The Politics of Harold Wilson*; T. Hennessey, 'Harold Wilson', in C. Clarke and T. S. James (eds), *British Labour Leaders* (London: Biteback Publishing, 2015); K. O. Morgan, *Labour People*; P. Shore, *Leading the Left* (London: Weidenfeld & Nicolson, 1993); P. Ziegler, *Wilson*

4. B. Pimlott, *Harold Wilson*

5. C. A. R. Crosland, *The Future of Socialism*, p. 355

6. R. Jenkins, *The Labour Case* (London: Penguin Books, 1959), pp 136–7

7. R. Jenkins, Speech to London Labour Conference, 13 May 1967, reproduced in R. Jenkins, *Essays and Speeches* (London: Collins, 1967), p. 286

8. Sexual relations between women had never been similarly outlawed, apparently because no one had the courage to explain to Queen Victoria how two women could possibly engage in such activity together!

9. Wolfenden Committee, Report of the Committee on Homosexual Offences and Prostitution (HMSO, Cmnd 247, 1957), para. 52

10. This reflected the fact that a separate Private Member's Bill on this issue had been introduced by a Conservative MP, Humphrey Berkeley, in early 1966, but its progress interrupted by the general election in March that year. In those days, Bills that had not completed their parliamentary stages were not 'carried over' to the next session

11. TNA CAB 134/2852, H (66) 6, Minutes of a meeting of the Cabinet's home affairs committee, 18 January 1966

12. Hansard, HC Debs, Vol. 738, col. 1078, 19 December 1966

13. C. Davies, *The Strange Death of Moral Britain* (New Jersey: Transaction, 2007), p. 95

14. Hansard, HC Debs, Vol. 749, col. 1511, 3 July 1967

15. R. H. S. Crossman, *The Crossman Diaries* (London: Mandarin, 1991), pp 159–60; diary entry for 11 December 1966

16. A. Holden, *Makers and Manners: Politics and Morality in Post-War Britain* (London: Politico's, 2004), p. 118

17. K. Hindell and M. Simms, *Abortion Law Reformed*, p. 195

18. Ibid., pp 180–87

19. P. G. Richards, *Parliament and Conscience* (London: Allen and Unwin, 1970), p. 111

20.   TNA CAB 128/43, CC (68) 46th Conclusions, 12 November 1968

21.   Hansard, HC Debs, Vol. 775, col. 1073, 17 December 1968

22.   B. H. Lee, *Divorce Law Reform in England* (London: Peter Owen, 1974), p. 168

23.   B. Pimlott, *Harold Wilson*, p. 487

24.   J. Campbell, *Roy Jenkins* (London: Vintage, 2014), p. 260

25.   H. Wilson, *The Labour Government, 1964–70*, p. 191

26.   A. Holden, *Makers and Manners*, p. 119

27.   B. Pimlott, *Harold Wilson*, p. 487

28.   R. Jenkins, *A Life at the Centre*, p. 177

29.   J. Campbell, *Roy Jenkins*, p. 298

30.   TNA CAB 129/130, C (67) 90, Memorandum by the Secretary of State for the Home Department [Office], 'Medical Termination of Pregnancy Bill', 31 May 1967

31.   B. H. Lee, *Divorce Law Reform in England*, pp 166–7; P. G. Richards, *Parliament and Conscience*, pp 149–50; J. Campbell, *Roy Jenkins*, p. 297

32.   D. Marsh and M. Read, *Private Members' Bills* (Cambridge: Cambridge University Press, 1988), p. 114; and P. G. Richards, *Parliament and Conscience*, p. 106

33.   TNA HO 291/198, Note of a Meeting between Jenkins and Crossman, 6 September 1966

34.   See, for example, TNA PREM/13/1563, Silkin to Wilson, 21 September 1966

35.   See, for example, TNA CAB 129/127, C (66) 144, Memorandum by the Secretary of State for the Home Department [Office], 'Homosexual Law Reform', 24 October 1966

36.   R. H. S. Crossman, *The Crossman Diaries*, pp 159–60; diary entry for 11 December 1966

37.   D. Taverne, *The Future of the Left: Lincoln and After* (London: Jonathan Cape: 1974), p. 38

38.   Labour Party Archives, Minutes of a meeting of the Parliamentary Labour Party, 29 June 1967

39.   Ibid., 12 May 1965

40.   D. Sandbrook, *White Heat: A History of Britain in the Swinging Sixties* (London: Little, Brown, 2006), p. 469

41.   B. Castle, *The Castle Diaries, 1964–76*, p. 54; diary entry for 11 February 1966

42.   L. Abse, *Private Member* (London: Macdonald, 1973), p. 149

43.   K. O. Morgan, *Callaghan*, pp 319, 321

44.   Hansard, HC Debs, Vol. 738, col. 1110, 19 December 1966

45.   D. Owen, *Time to Declare* (London: Penguin, 1992), p. 104

46.   C. Davies, *The Strange Death of Moral Britain*, p. 191

47.   See P. Dorey, 'The social background of Labour MPs elected in 1964 and 1966', in P. Dorey (ed.), *The Labour Governments, 1964–70* (London: Routledge, 2006), pp 24–33

48.   D. Marsh and J. Chambers, *Abortion Politics* (Toronto: Junction Books, 1981), p. 18

49.   P. G. Richards, *Parliament and Conscience*, pp 181–2

50.   R. H. S. Crossman, *The Crossman Diaries*, p. 409; diary entry for 4 July 1967

51.   K. Hindell and M. Simms, *Abortion Law Reformed*, p. 231

11

SPORT POLICY: AN UNHERALDED SUCCESS STORY

Kevin Jefferys

WHEN THE WORDS 'Harold Wilson' and 'sport' are used in conjunction, they are often associated with the feel-good effect England's famous victory in the 1966 football World Cup was supposed to have had on Labour's election victory of that year. This widespread perception is misleading on various grounds. In the first place, as public quiz aficionados well know, voters went to the polls months before a ball was kicked: the election was held in March 1966; the World Cup final did not take place until July. Secondly, sport nevertheless *did* have a place (albeit limited) in the electoral history of the Wilson era. This was mainly associated, however, not with 1966, but with the run-up to the 1970 contest; ironically, an election in which, far from being triumphant, Labour was soundly beaten. In addition, the enduring mythology about the 1966 World Cup implies that very little else of note occurred in the relationship between

sport and politics during Wilson's tenure as Prime Minister, which was far
from the case. None of the key biographers of Wilson give any attention to
sport.[1] Even those historians who conclude that, whatever his failings, Wilson
should be credited with significant achievements – for example, the creation
of the Open University and moves towards equal pay for women – make no
mention of sporting issues.[2] This chapter sets out to show that, fifty years
on from '1966 and all that', sport policy should be added to the list of credit-
able advances presided over by Wilson; until now, it has remained one of the
unheralded success stories of his premiership.

It will be argued here that Labour's approach to sport after 1964 was characterised by considerably greater urgency than anything that came before. State
intervention of a sort alien to pre-1964 administrations of all political colours
became the order of the day. A Sports Council, resolutely opposed by the
Macmillan and Douglas-Home Conservative regimes of the late 1950s and early
1960s, was rapidly introduced by Wilson in 1965; not with the intention of
securing state control but aimed at creating a viable partnership between statutory authorities and voluntary sports organisations. There were even signs that
Labour regarded sport as a potential electoral asset: a far cry from the prevailing
orthodoxy in the 1950s. Sport, of course, remained, in the eyes of politicians
and voters alike, a long way from being a front-line issue. But Wilson was the
first incumbent of 10 Downing Street to sense that it might prove beneficial for
his party to associate itself more closely in the public mind with one of Britain's
national obsessions. Within six months of Labour coming to power in 1964, an
internal Treasury memo noted (disapprovingly, in view of the financial implications) that within the corridors of power 'there has been a marked increase of
interest in sport'. And, later in the decade, a private report by a Conservative
study group, recognising the need to make up lost ground, noted that whatever
its perceived failings on core economic issues, 'sport is one sphere in which the
Government is thought by the public to have been successful'.[3]

THE INTRODUCTION AND EARLY HISTORY
OF THE SPORTS COUNCIL, 1964–66

Sport in Britain was traditionally a voluntary activity, overseen mainly by individual national governing bodies responsible for administering and fund-raising on behalf of hundreds of separate sports. It was widely assumed that sport and politics did not 'mix'. By the 1950s, a small number of MPs were complaining that Britain's infrastructure of sporting facilities was deeply inadequate compared with other advanced industrialised nations. Sport, reformers argued, was a valuable means of countering problems such as youth alienation at a time of rising affluence, and required investment at all levels: from the casual participant to elite performers. Britain's unpaid amateur athletes, in particular, were struggling to compete on the international stage against the likes of their state-sponsored Soviet counterparts at events such as the Olympics. But Tory administrations after 1951 continued to maintain that sport should be left to run its own affairs. This stance prevailed, despite the publication of the influential Wolfenden Report on Sport in 1960. Although small changes followed, when the Conservatives lost office nothing had been done to implement Wolfenden's central recommendation – that of introducing a 'Sports Development Council' to act as a focal point for the building of a new generation of athletic tracks and facilities, such as multi-purpose leisure centres.

As part of the 'New Britain' campaign that brought Wilson to power in October 1964, Labour promised a more progressive, interventionist approach to sport. Although not known as a sportsman in his youth, Wilson was a keen follower of football, capable of reciting all the names of Huddersfield Town's 1938 FA Cup final team. Ahead of the election, there was talk in Labour circles of appointing a senior Cabinet figure to oversee both sport and the arts, working through the Arts Council (first established in the Attlee years) and a newly introduced Sports Development Council. On further reflection, Wilson decided it would be a simpler and more effective way forward to appoint – as he wrote in his later account of the 1964 administration – a number of junior ministers 'with special responsibilities for subjects essential to Britain's economic and social development which had not been given an adequate priority in the past'.[4] With this in mind, he offered to Birmingham MP Denis Howell the position of Under-Secretary of State with special responsibility for sport at the Department of Education and Science (DES). Howell, prominent among the parliamentary advocates of reform in sport and an experienced football referee in his spare time, was the crucial figure in all that followed. While Wilson acted as facilitator, Howell was the man who really ensured that the term 'sport policy' for the first time became meaningful.

Wilson's interview with Howell a few days after the election victory illustrated the extent – and limits – of the Prime Minister's involvement in this fledging sphere of government activity. Wilson told Howell he had the exciting opportunity of becoming Britain's first-ever Minister for Sport. After accepting the offer, Howell asked what approach the Prime Minister wished to see pursued. On this, Wilson said (probably covering for a lack of detailed knowledge) that policy was in the minister's hands: 'I think you know what needs to be done, otherwise I would not be appointing you.' Feeling emboldened, Howell enquired if there was money to spend, only to be told not: 'The country's broke.' But Wilson was more receptive to the idea of including sports figures in future Honours Lists, thereby initiating a trend whereby modern politicians sought to gain reflected glory from the triumphs of leading sports personalities. To his surprise, Howell also received a positive response when, thinking out loud, the difficulties of England hosting football's World Cup in 1966 came to mind. He understood the previous administration had promised little more than police escorts for teams during the tournament, whereas Howell knew from conversations with football friends that there was much to be done by way of preparation. 'How much do you want?'

Wilson asked. Howell recollected that at the time he had not the 'faintest idea' but, reluctant to lose his opening, suggested half a million pounds, to which Wilson agreed. 'I thanked him again and ... left No. 10, astonished at my good fortune and overwhelmed by my interview with the Prime Minister.'

Although the role of Sports Minister was thus created without any carefully defined sense of the scope of the post, Howell pushed ahead with an energy that was to be widely lauded. His initial priority was to overcome residual opposition in Whitehall circles to the fulfilment of Labour's manifesto pledge to introduce a Sports Council. Within weeks, Howell had sketched out plans for an advisory body, which he would chair, and secured approval from a Cabinet committee to go ahead. There was grumbling from the Ministry of Housing and Local Government, which had long-established oversight of local authority recreational provision, that it was being treated in a 'high-handed fashion', but any objections were rapidly swatted aside. Howell encountered stiffer opposition when he requested Cabinet committee backing for plans such as improvements to football stadiums ahead of the World Cup. Unlike the creation of the Sports Council, this required approval for the early injection of extra sums of money, and the Treasury spokesmen present pointed to the extremely unhelpful economic backcloth. Howell was getting concerned about the outcome when the chairman of the committee suddenly curtailed discussion and nodded the proposals through. 'Clearly, he had been well-briefed beforehand,' Howell reflected. 'Harold Wilson had kept his part of the bargain.'[5]

On 3 February 1965, Howell told the House of Commons that the government was establishing a Sports Council 'to advise them on matters relating to the development of amateur sport and physical recreation and to foster cooperation among the statutory and voluntary organisations concerned'. In a brief statement, the Sports Minister outlined the membership of the council, which included prominent sports figures of the day, and indicated the key areas in which it would advise the government. These included the future provision of facilities and likely capital expenditure, regional planning, the development of coaching schemes and participation by amateur British teams in overseas events, including the Olympics. The announcement was well received in the press, and, in the months that followed, Howell looked to build upon his early success. By April 1965, the Sports Council was up and running via four main sub-committees, and the minister presented figures to the Commons underlining the seriousness of the government's intent. The level of direct Exchequer assistance to sport and physical recreation in England, Wales and Scotland, he reported, would rise from £915,000 in 1964–65 to £1,571,000 in 1965–66, an increase of 70 per cent. 'Not enough,' he believed, 'but a good start.'[6]

Another of Howell's preoccupations in 1965 was working on preparations for the World Cup. He quickly realised that big improvements – such as more and better seating – were required at several antiquated stadiums earmarked for fixtures. Treasury civil servants (and a few vociferous Tory spokesmen) were alarmed at the prospect of direct funding to professional sport, which was traditionally expected to pay its own way without recourse to state aid. Treasury officials at first appeared unaware of the deal struck between Wilson and the Sports Minister, and one complained: 'Mr Howell regards himself as having a roving commission with responsibilities to no one except the Prime Minister.'[7] In due course, however, an agreement was brokered under which the government would cover 50 per cent of the cost of stadium improvements of a permanent nature and 90 per cent for temporary installations. Howell reported the details to the House, confident that the World Cup had received a major promotional boost and that everything would be ready in time.

By the summer of 1965, the Sports Minister had developed a considerable public profile, junior though he was in the government hierarchy. His outgoing personality made him a favourite with many journalists, happy to report on his World Cup plans and on advances proclaimed by the Sports Council. Announcements about financial support for governing bodies, extra funding for national teams competing overseas, and the imminent creation of regional sports councils were greeted by the *Daily Telegraph* as among the 'most significant and exciting ever uttered about British sport'.[8] But Howell's assertiveness was not universally acclaimed. One civil servant complained that the impression was being given that the 'Sports Council *itself* was making grants', when in reality its role was advisory. Within Whitehall, more active means were soon being sought to rein in the Sports Minister. In September 1965, Treasury pressure forced the DES into issuing a letter stating that in the wake of Chancellor Jim Callaghan's pronouncements about holding down public spending, projects in the pipeline for new sports facilities financed by local authorities (many pump-primed by the Sports Council) would have to be postponed for the time being.

Although the new restrictions marked a step back, Howell still had reason to be satisfied with his record thus far. So, too, did the Prime Minister. Seeking to escape the constraints of a small parliamentary majority, Wilson called an election in the spring of 1966, claiming that great progress had been achieved in spite of financial constraints. Among the achievements he listed at the election was the creation of a Sports Council. Wilson's optimism proved justified and, following Labour's comfortable victory at the polls, Howell returned to his post at the DES secure in the knowledge that sport policy could be developed over the lifetime of a full parliament ahead. As the World Cup finally got under way in the summer, Howell's careful planning paid dividends. The success of the tournament, culminating in England's dramatic 4–2 win over West Germany on 30 July, captured the imagination of the nation, much of which watched the final on television. The Sports Minister reported to the Commons that over £400,000 had been given in grants and interest-free loans to help clubs improve their facilities. In view of the outcome, even those who felt professional sport should fend for itself were silenced. There was, Howell recollected, not 'a word of criticism inside or outside the House – no one dared!'[9]

The period between 1964 and 1966, therefore, witnessed radical changes in the relationship between sport and politics. By appointing a Sports Minister, Wilson provided a means of coordinating government policy and raising funding levels more systematically than ever before. But, at the same time, it would be wrong to suggest that Labour inaugurated what Wolfenden termed a 'new deal', emulating the game-changing investment levels found in some European nations such as West Germany. After a heady honeymoon period, Howell found himself increasingly frustrated by the Treasury's drive for cutbacks. At a private meeting with Treasury Chief Secretary Jack Diamond, Howell complained about the strongly held feeling of the Sports Council that 'sport was getting less than a fair deal, especially compared with the arts, in the allocation of public funds'. He noted that Labour was committed at the 1964 election to a direct expenditure on sport of £5 million per year; yet DES estimates for 1966–67 amounted to only £1.6 million. Howell said he realised sport had progressed, but he was 'particularly embarrassed' by big rises pencilled in for the Arts Council, which was also administered via the DES. Jack Diamond reminded Howell that it had never had been the case that expenditure in one sphere should be levelled up or down to be in line with another area. Nor should it be forgotten, Diamond added, that 'the present Government had done more in one and a half years than its predecessors did in four'.[10]

SPORT AND POLITICS, 1966-70

Howell's reputation as Minister for Sport continued to rise after 1966. Under his chairmanship, the advisory Sports Council worked assiduously, for example offering unprecedented levels of travel and subsistence expenses to Britain's unpaid Olympic athletes at the 1968 Mexico Games. However, the second half of the 1960s brought fresh challenges and difficulties. Pressure grew for a streamlining of Whitehall machinery for dealing with sport, and financial constraints continued to thwart Howell's wish to see more rapid progress in the building of new facilities. One colleague wrote in a 1967 letter that Howell felt 'he could use a lot more money and thinks he has been unfairly treated compared with Jenny [*sic*] Lee'.[11] This reference to Arts Minister Jennie Lee, Nye Bevan's widow, showed that sport's treatment *vis-à-vis* the arts was a running sore for Howell. Not long afterwards, the government suffered the humiliation of devaluation: an event followed by a sharp slump in Labour's popularity and by renewed restrictions on public spending. When the Sports Council published a major review of its work in 1969, commentators were struck by its sober tone; although Howell spoke of progress, it was clear fresh advances were dependent on the return to a more favourable economic climate.

Despite ongoing frustrations, Howell earned recognition for his endeavours in the autumn of 1969 when he was moved and raised in status from Under Secretary to Minister of State level, one rank below that of Cabinet minister. As part of a general restructuring of Whitehall departments, Howell was transferred from the DES to the Ministry of Housing and Local Government (MHLG), which became the lead department for sport. From the vantage point of the sporting world, Howell's retention of his earlier brief was a welcome sign of continuity, though by the time he moved to the MHLG he was embroiled in a protracted and messy controversy over sporting links with South Africa. Aided by the growth of mass audiences on television, major events such as the Olympics and the football World Cup had raised the profile of international sport considerably in public consciousness by the mid-1960s. Cricket, too, for long England's premier summer sport, also attracted considerable media scrutiny, and erupted into wider public debate initially as a result of the so-called D'Oliveira affair. Howell confided to Wilson that the powers-that-be at the Marylebone Cricket Club (MCC) seemed to be 'very naive about the potential political repercussions' in the controversy over whether Basil D'Oliveira should be part of an English team to tour South Africa, though fortunately firm on the point that the trip should be cancelled – as it was – following pressure by the apartheid regime to influence England's team selection.[12]

The D'Oliveira affair was only the prelude to apartheid-related agitation that continued until the eve of the 1970 election. In early 1969, the MCC, looking to mend some fences, invited the South Africans (arguably the strongest team in the world at the time) to take part in a tour of England in mid-1970. This decision galvanised the growing anti-apartheid movement in Britain, notably a 'Stop the Seventy Tour' (STST) group led by the Liberal student activist Peter Hain, a native of South Africa. STST came to national attention when it spearheaded protests against a rugby tour over the winter of 1969/70 by an all-white South African team. The Springboks were hounded by protestors, who variously blockaded the team bus or pelted it with eggs, attempted pitch invasions and released smoke bombs to disrupt play. Although several newspapers attacked the protestors for infringing freedom of movement (*The Times* lambasted them as 'thugs and hooligans'), by the time the Springboks returned home, STST felt vindicated and ready to do all it could to jeopardise the proposed cricket tour. With the MCC refusing to call it off, the government inevitably became drawn into a growing shouting match. In March 1970, a meeting of senior Cabinet ministers gathered at Chequers. According to Tony Benn's diary, Wilson was giving serious consideration to a June general election, but feared the prospect of polling taking place at the same time as noisy agitation at barbed-wire-protected cricket grounds.[13]

During April, the Sports Minister was asked by Wilson to chair a small committee to keep him abreast of the developing situation. Howell confirmed

that there were no legal grounds for denying the South African team entry
to Britain. As a result, the best course was for the government to refrain from
direct intervention but to give 'tacit support' to any moves that 'might achieve
a useful result'.[14] Peter Hain believed STST was instrumental in making the
issue such a hot potato, though party rivalry in the run-up to the election was
arguably more important. Although the Prime Minister stated publicly that he
did not support 'violent methods', such as digging up pitches, his assertion
that protestors had the right to demonstrate against apartheid was interpreted
by the Conservatives (and several newspaper editors) as an incitement to law-
breaking. When Wilson appeared on television on 30 April, urging the Cricket
Council to reconsider its stance, Tory leader Ted Heath quickly countered
by backing the tour. The deadlock was only broken in mid-May when an
election date was announced. With the cricket authorities prevaricating, Jim
Callaghan as Home Secretary decided the time had come to act; he met with
MCC officials to argue that, on the grounds of 'broad public policy', cancellation was desirable. The following day, the Cricket Council announced that,
with 'deep regret', it was calling off the tour.

Reaction to the news of the abandonment of the tour was mixed. Anti-
apartheid campaigners claimed a great victory, one that left South Africa
increasingly isolated in the sporting world. Some cricket enthusiasts (and
many Conservatives) were aghast that sport and politics were becoming so
intertwined, and Howell was left uneasy at this first major intervention by
post-war politicians in the decision-making processes of sporting authorities. He was nevertheless relieved, like his colleagues, that the issue would no
longer overshadow the election. Public opinion polls indicated that a majority
of voters were opposed to the cancellation of the tour, though once the decision was made the issue was soon forgotten. Some MCC insiders believed
the government's position could cost Labour half a million votes. This might
have had some credence if the tour had gone ahead, resulting in endless media

stories about disruption and law-breaking but, in the event, agents for all parties were able to report that the subject of the cricket tour was not raised on the doorstep; a survey immediately after the election found that less than 1 per cent of voters mentioned it.

The settling of the dispute paved the way, it seemed, for more prosaic internal sporting matters to return to the fore in the run-up to the 1970 election. Unwilling to adopt a strategy that promised higher public expenditure, the Conservatives – concerned that Howell controlled sport policy too closely via the advisory Sports Council – focused on the need for a more independent, executive body. This left Wilson, as in 1966, believing he held the upper hand on sport. Labour's manifesto claimed the government's support for leisure over recent years had been 'immense' and that such support would continue into the 1970s. But, unlike in 1966, a generally serene campaign for Labour was not to be followed by re-election. The prospect of prolonged anti-apartheid protests may have gone away, but in the run-up to polling day ministers were confronted with another unwelcome development on the international sporting front: England's exit from the Mexico World Cup. Confidence was high as the defending champions progressed through the group stages, each England match attracting huge audiences on television. But, on Sunday 14 June, just four days before voting took place, England squandered a two-goal lead and lost 3–2 to West Germany in the quarter-finals. The blame was put on a mixture of goalkeeping errors in the absence of the bug-stricken Gordon Banks and the decision to withdraw key players to preserve their energies for an anticipated semi-final.

After recovering from a steep dip in 1968–69, Labour had retained a small but steady lead in opinion polls for several months ahead of the election. In the Nuffield study of the 1970 campaign, David Butler and Michael Pinto-Duschinsky wrote that on 15 June there was a short break in the glorious summer weather: 'The change, like the World Cup defeat, may have contributed to a switch in mood.'[15] There was to be much talk in due course of a late swing to the Conservatives, sufficient to give Heath a comfortable forty-seat majority. Howell was among those who believed the defeat in Mexico was a contributory factor. He wrote in his memoirs of a definite mood-shift in the final days, with England's abrupt defeat the talk of the factories as he toured his constituency. Butler and Pinto-Duschinsky argue, however, that if there was a late swing of public opinion, it was more likely to have resulted from the announcement, the day after the World Cup exit, of adverse trade figures. After nine months of good returns, a large deficit for May was immediately seized upon by Heath. With the benefit of hindsight, about half of all Tory and Labour candidates at the election agreed with the notion of a late move-ment of opinion. Of those among this group who reflected on the causes, most put it down to the trade figures; only a handful agreed with the Labour MP who bemoaned 'the damned germ in Gordon Banks's tummy that punctured the mood of euphoria'.[16]

LABOUR POLICY AFTER 1974:
THE WHITE PAPER ON SPORT AND RECREATION

As a result of Wilson's two narrow election victories in 1974, the framework for government oversight of sport underwent further change. The introduc-tion by Heath of an executive Sports Council in 1972 – secured by Royal Charter – was designed to free it from political interference. Independent members of the new body, such as the eminent athlete Sir Roger Bannister, the first chairman of the chartered council, would, it was hoped, determine strategy, while politicians were confined to agreeing the appropriate level of funding in an annual vote. But Denis Howell's acceptance in 1974 of Wilson's invitation to resume his duties as Sports Minister – this time based at the Department of the Environment (DOE) – produced a fresh twist. Howell set out to tilt the balance in the sport–state partnership further back towards ministerial influence, even if this meant accepting he could not return to the level of authority he had exercised as chairman of the advisory council.

In July 1974, Wilson informed Parliament that Howell would henceforth be called the 'Minister for Sport and Recreation': a conscious broadening of remit aimed at facilitating high-level coordination of the state's approach to leisure provision as well as sport. Anxious to impose himself on policy to a greater extent than favoured by Bannister, Howell also sought a figure-head with whom he might 'do business' when Sir Roger resigned in the autumn of 1974. The incoming chairman of the executive council, Sir Robin Brook, a former Olympic fencer, fitted the bill; and, according to senior Sports Council official John Coghlan, Howell and Brook's effective working relationship brought the council in the mid-1970s 'to a pinnacle of prestige and effectiveness in the field'.[17]

The high reputation of the council was not based on any increased funding. In a period of alarmingly high inflation, sparked by the global hike in oil prices, public spending was again under intense scrutiny, and Howell faced an even greater task than he had in the 1960s in persuading the Treasury to loosen the purse strings. Chancellor Denis Healey was a sufficiently tough customer that he even faced down pressure from the Prime Minister to direct more funds towards sport. In February 1975, anxious about press criticism, Wilson wrote to Healey about the 'genuine concerns' of those in sporting circles that progress was being stymied. In preparing a response, one of the Chancellor's aides hinted privately that Wilson seemed susceptible to the wily ways of the Sports Minister. With Howell's blessing, Robin Brook complained that the Sports Council budget for 1975-76, £7.85 million, barely kept pace with inflation, compared with a substantial real-terms increase for the Arts Council, set to receive £26.15 million. Shortly afterwards, Healey formally wrote to the Prime Minister. 'I should of course like to have been able to help,' he wrote, but it was too often overlooked that local authority financing of the arts was 'very small compared with support for sport'. In the light of sport already having a greater share of public expenditure in totality – more than four times the level for the arts – there was little scope for more assistance.[18]

Unable to secure much extra funding, Howell nevertheless proclaimed a landmark moment when, in August 1975, the government published a White Paper entitled *Sport and Recreation*. Although he knew a broad statement was likely to be a slow burner, rather than having an immediate impact, Howell saw the merits of Labour setting out its stall. Whereas state involvement prior to 1974 centred primarily on organised sporting activity, both for elite performers and club-level enthusiasts, interest was gradually turning towards the importance of 'sport for all', leisure provision for the masses. A top priority in the White Paper was urging the Sports Council and local authorities to give greater attention to developing facilities in deprived urban areas. More broadly, Howell was keen to include a statement of first principles as a means of underlining Labour's commitment to the cause even in hard times. He personally penned the conclusion to the White Paper and, in a unique departure, he outlined what he called a 'Government philosophy for sport and recreation – a leisure service', in which sport and recreation contributed to the well-being of individuals and communities.[19]

The fact that Howell was able to proceed with a comprehensive overview of policy was an achievement in itself. Ahead of publication, the Treasury again sought to intervene, asking Wilson not to go ahead on the grounds that – though the document was carefully worded – the government should not risk giving any impression 'which inevitably implies the desirability of extra expenditure on Sport and Recreation'. The Prime Minister was briefed that the argument for publishing was finely balanced. The severity of the economic situation meant extra spending was entirely out of the question; on the other hand, the White Paper would be a timely morale booster for interested parties in the sporting world. Yet again (and for the last time, as it turned out, prior to his resignation), Wilson proved himself a loyal friend to sport. He scribbled his view on the briefing paper, saying further amendments had been made to the text to meet the concerns of the Treasury and, as a result, publication should go ahead. Although Howell's persistence won the day, he was prevailed upon to begin the press launch by emphasising that no new spending was in the offing; only then could he talk about 'sport for all'. Howell's subdued tone inevitably coloured reactions to the White Paper. Robin Brook welcomed the document on behalf of the Sports Council but added: 'Policy alone is not enough. There must be adequate resources.'[20]

CONCLUSION

Despite concerns that the White Paper contained more rhetoric than substance, by the time Harold Wilson shocked the political world with his sudden departure in March 1976 there was much of which he could be proud in terms of sport policy. Before his arrival in Downing Street in 1964, the approach of both Labour and Conservative administrations had been largely uncoordinated, ambiguous and low key. But, in the years that followed, sport established itself as a legitimate area of government concern and, at times, claimed a political profile unimaginable in the 1950s. In part, this occurred because growing media and commercial interest in international sport drew politicians into uncharted waters. The ministerial interventions that followed sometimes reflected well on the government (as in the hosting of the 1966 World Cup), though at other times resulted in protracted anxiety, notably over the anti-apartheid protests associated with rugby and cricket during 1969–70.

It was in the more domestic context, however, that Wilson made a planned and conscious choice to prioritise sport in an unprecedented way. Although created in hasty fashion in 1964, the advisory Sports Council pushed forward on various fronts, including giving support to national coaching schemes and assisting local clubs in updating their facilities. Sports Council pump-priming for local authority capital costs towards new facilities helped to underpin a huge increase over time in the construction of multi-purpose leisure centres, up from a handful in the early 1960s to nearly 450 by the end of the 1970s. One of its members, Bernard Donoughue, later reflected that serving on the Sports Council was rewarding and satisfying: 'Strong leadership and high profile by Howell, plus [a] clear sense he was supported by Prime Minister Wilson' meant it was able to 'make a difference'.[21]

Yet, in spite of significant progress, Wilson's later reflection that sporting facilities in Britain had been 'revolutionised' under his watch was difficult to square with the scale of investment, especially when compared with that taking place in some other European nations during the same period. Direct Exchequer spending on sport had still not reached the levels proposed by the 1960 Wolfenden Report when Wilson departed from Downing Street, and local authority funds had been continually squeezed. In its various guises, state investment in sport remained only a tiny fraction, less than 1 per cent, of total public expenditure. Nor had Labour devoted much attention to resolving, as it pledged in 1964, where sport fitted precisely into a 'basic philosophy of the fullness of life'; whether 'sport for all' was a genuine ambition and right, or whether – as seemed increasingly the case in the troubled 1970s – sport policy should primarily serve other social purposes, such as tackling youth crime or improving public health.

Whatever the shortcomings, in the final reckoning, Wilson deserves credit for creating a benevolent political environment in which sport could be taken seriously. The same could not be said of all his successors in Downing Street

(John Major and Tony Blair being prominent exceptions). The lion's share of responsibility for the higher profile secured by sport in the corridors of power during the 1960s and 1970s ultimately rested with Wilson's trusty lieutenant, Denis Howell. His championing of sport, at a time when it formed only one element of his portfolio of ministerial duties, was the product of both ideological conviction – the belief that the state needed to actively assist sport without directly controlling it – and a pragmatic sense that Labour's image would be enhanced through a progressive approach. It was a testimony to his success that the Conservatives under Heath recognised it was no longer possible to simply sideline sport, or to retreat to a stance of non-intervention (although Margaret Thatcher later attempted to do so in the 1980s). At the victory banquet in London on the evening of England's 1966 World Cup triumph, Harold Wilson took hold of the Jules Rimet trophy and went with the players to wave it aloft in front of jubilant fans outside. According to Stanley Rous of the Football Association, it was Denis Howell who really should have been taking the plaudits. It was he, Rous said – in words that apply to sport policy more broadly during the Wilson years – 'who worked hard to ensure all went off smoothly', taking 'a minute interest in every detail'.[22]

NOTES AND REFERENCES

1.   See, for example, B. Pimlott, *Harold Wilson* and P. Ziegler, *Wilson*
2.   For example, D. Walker, 'The First Wilson Governments, 1964–70', in P. Hennessy and A. Seldon (eds), *Ruling Performance* (Oxford: Basil Blackwell, 1987), pp 186–209
3.   Cited in K. Jefferys, *Sport and Politics in Modern Britain: The Road to 2012* (Basingstoke: Palgrave Macmillan, 2012), p. 78
4.   H. Wilson, *The Labour Government, 1964–70*, p. 10
5.   D. Howell, *Made in Birmingham* (London: Queen Anne Press, 1990), pp 140–43
6.   Ibid., pp 149–51
7.   Ibid., pp 164–6; Hansard, HC Debs, Vol. 705, cols 1081–863, February 1965
8.   TNA, Treasury papers, cited in K. Jefferys, *Sport and Politics*, p. 90
9.   *Daily Telegraph*, 15 July 1965
10.   D. Howell, *Made in Birmingham*, p. 175

11. TNA, Treasury papers, cited in K. Jefferys, *Sport and Politics*, pp 99–100
12. P. Noel-Baker papers, Churchill College Cambridge, cited in K. Jefferys, *Sport and Politics*, p. 103
13. D. Howell, *Made in Birmingham*, p. 204; see also P. Oborne, *Cricket and Controversy* (London: Sphere, 2004)
14. T. Benn, *Office without Power, Diaries 1968–72* (London: Arrow, 1989); entry for 8 March 1970, p. 247
15. TNA, Prime Minister's papers, cited in Jefferys, *Sport and Politics*, p. 113
16. D. Butler and M. Pinto-Duschinsky, *The British General Election of 1970*, p. 166
17. Ibid., pp 166, 334, 335
18. J. Coghlan, *Sport and British Politics Since 1960* (Brighton: Routledge, 1990), pp 128–9
19. TNA, Treasury papers, cited in K. Jefferys, *Sport and Politics*, pp 139–40
20. Department of the Environment, *Sport and Recreation*, Cmnd 6200 (London: Cabinet Office, 1975)
21. *The Times*, 8 August 1975
22. Lord Donoughue, email to author, 11 February 2014

12

HAROLD WILSON AND THE BRITISH CONSTITUTION

Jasper Miles

P RIOR TO THE 1964 general election, Harold Wilson employed a motoring analogy when describing the British state, arguing that: 'What matters is the driver. If the man behind the machine is a Labour man, the machine will move towards Labour. Not only Parliament, but the vast machinery of the State which it controls … are politically neutral, loyal to their political masters.'[1]

INTRODUCTION

The workings of the British constitution, with its traditional practices, was by the 1960s thought to be acting as a drag on the British economy, preventing the United Kingdom from keeping pace with European counterparts who were experiencing faster rates of growth. Elected in 1964 with a slim majority on a platform of 'efficiency' and 'modernisation', the Labour governments of 1964–70, especially when empowered with a large parliamentary majority after 1966, sought to address a number of concerns that had arisen during the thirteen years spent in opposition. Critics of the workings of Parliament, from both within and outside the Labour Party, tended to focus on the balance between the legislature and the executive. They considered that the executive had become too dominant and the wider British constitution was deemed to be unconducive to good governance for the last third of the twentieth century.

This chapter will outline the interest shown and reforms made by the Wilson governments towards different parts of the constitution, including the House of Lords, the House of Commons, electoral reform, the Civil Service and local government, specifically in England. Devolution to the constituent parts of the United Kingdom is explored elsewhere in the book. The arguments put for and against reform will be addressed in the main body of the text and the conclusion will set out the wider ideological and theoretical reasoning behind the different positions adopted in the Labour Party. Additionally, the role of Harold Wilson will be reviewed to examine whether he was the leading advocate or whether he followed the views of colleagues.

HOUSE OF LORDS REFORM

The Attlee government of 1945–51 had reduced the delaying powers of the House of Lords from two years to one, motivated by practical factors to ensure the government's nationalisation programme was enacted. However, generally, the Attlee government had displayed little interest in major parliamentary reforms, instead focusing on social and economic issues. Labour's 1964 manifesto stated: 'We shall not permit effective action to be frustrated by the hereditary and non-elective Conservative majority in the House of Lords', suggesting that, by the 1960s, reform in some capacity was desired. The slim majority won in 1964, however, prevented this being put to the test, resulting in the more controversial issues, such as House of Lords reform, being sidelined, not wishing to antagonise the peers without a strong mandate from the electorate.

Labour's 1966 manifesto revisited reform of the second chamber, stating legislation would be introduced 'to safeguard measures approved by the House of Commons from frustration by delay or defeat in the House of Lords'. The initial policy adopted by the Cabinet was to reduce the delaying powers of the House of Lords from one year to six months. Richard Crossman, the leading advocate of reform within government, was, in August 1966, appointed Lord President of the council and Leader of the House; therefore, responsible for constitutional reform. Crossman's preference was to tackle not just delaying powers but also composition, for reducing delaying powers alone could encourage peers to use their right to delay more regularly, especially against a Labour government. Abolition, leading to a unicameral system (the preferred position of the Labour left), was not on Crossman's agenda; he wrote in his diary, '[i]t's jolly useful to have a second chamber' and '[i]n reducing its powers, we mustn't reduce its utility'.[2] It was hoped a reformed chamber could be of greater assistance to the House of Commons in helping to deal with the business of legislation.

John Silkin, Labour's Chief Whip, devised the idea of a 'two-tier' system of peers, with 'Voting Peers' and 'Speaking Peers', the latter unable to vote in Divisions. At a two-day meeting of Cabinet in September 1967 at Chequers, the 'two-tier' policy was endorsed, along with the abolition of the hereditary principle. Labour backbenchers and Cabinet ministers evidently did not share Crossman's enthusiasm. In Cabinet, George Brown considered House of Lords reform a distraction 'from the real issues of unemployment', exposing Labour to criticism from its own supporters and rejecting the view that there was demand for reform. James Callaghan was also concerned that '[t]his was a kind of bread-and-circuses stunt – or at least would be regarded as such', although 'he would go along with it' if senior ministers were willing to endorse it.[3] The 'two-tier' policy drew criticism as it would have increased the Prime Minister's powers of patronage, strengthening the hand of the executive.

Crossman's proposal for all-party talks was approved in October 1967, a device that marginalised Cabinet opposition. A cross-party agreement was reached on the 'two-tier' system, although talks were terminated in June 1968, with the House of Lords voting against sanctions over Southern Rhodesia. Wilson sought to introduce a short, sharp Bill that would reduce the delaying powers of the Lords from twelve to six months.[4] Crossman, however, convinced the Prime Minister of the need to continue with the solution accepted by the all-party talks and to alter composition, in part fearing that new and more radical legislation would offer the Conservatives the opportunity to say the Labour government had reneged on the previous arrangement. Wilson backed Crossman's approach, resulting in the power of delay and composition being tackled in the same White Paper in November 1968.

James Callaghan, the then Home Secretary, introduced the Parliament (No. 2) Bill in the Commons, although he lacked any enthusiasm for reform and had been a voice in Cabinet arguing for the Bill to be abandoned. The Bill in the Commons was met by an 'unholy alliance' of the abolitionist left, led by Michael Foot, and the anti-reform right, led by Enoch Powell, filibustering the Bill, accordingly taking up significant parliamentary time and endangering Labour's legislative programme. In April 1969, Wilson abandoned the Bill, allowing time for the government to make progress with *In Place of Strife*. Wilson did emphasise that House of Lords reform would be resumed at a later date, a commitment that appeared in Labour's 1970 manifesto, although, given the opposition, divisions and weight of feeling in the party, such a commitment appeared dubious.

The 'two-tier' reform of the House of Lords failed to come to fruition for a number of factors. A lack of commitment in the Cabinet, in spite of Wilson's support for Crossman, resulted in a lack of unity and enthusiasm for the proposals, thought of as a distraction from the social and economic difficulties facing Britain. Moreover, while change was considered desirable, a difference of opinion existed on the best course of reform, with a significant section of the Parliamentary Labour Party demanding abolition. Furthermore, House of Lords reform was deemed not to be a salient electoral issue and, as with all other constitutional reforms, considered to have minimal traction with the working class.

HOUSE OF COMMONS REFORM

Shell writes that, in 1964, interest in the workings of the House of Commons was uppermost in Labour's mind, rather than reform of the House of Lords. Four reasons are put forward by Dorey and Honeyman: firstly, inferior economic growth in Britain was tied to the mechanisms of political institutions; second, the belief that decision-making had become remote from ordinary people; third, a new intake of university-educated Labour MPs who desired a participatory role in decision-making; and fourth, pressure from other sources, particularly academics.[5] Crossman's role included the remit to modernise the day-to-day operation and procedures of the House of Commons, providing impetus with the objective of increasing scrutiny of legislation and improving policy. Crossman wrote in 1966 that 'the modern House ... had lost its main function of controlling the executive' and therefore needed to 'reshape itself and redefine its functions if it ever wanted to be anything again'.[6]

On the topic of select committees, Wilson's preference was for a small number of specialist committees, simultaneously improving relations between the government and the Commons. Labour backbenchers would be occupied, making them less troublesome for the government. Crossman persevered with his predecessor Bert Bowden's notion that these committees should be investigatory rather than engaged in pre-legislative work. However, Cabinet ministers were critical; Michael Stewart deemed Labour backbenchers 'should be thankful that as a socialist government we want to keep the executive strong, not to strengthen parliamentary control', for which he was 'applauded by many around the [Cabinet] table'. Stewart 'could not understand how any socialist could propose to limit the powers of the Government by creating specialist committees to poach on their preserves' and Callaghan considered the proposal 'an outrage'.[7] Cabinet ministers were reluctant to accept any change that encroached on their authority or autonomy, accepting ministerial responsibility as a central tenet of the Westminster model.

Indeed, Crossman considered that Wilson's attitude towards select committees changed depending on his company: 'When he's alone with me he's always in favour of specialist committees but in Cabinet he's always accepting ministerial objections.'[8] Thus, it brings into question Wilson's personal view, and the sincerity with which he supported select committees. Regardless, from 1966–69, a number of mainly 'specialist' select committees were established, including those that had as their focus the subjects of agriculture, science and technology. Ministers were unhappy when, through the support of Wilson, they were informed that they had to appear in front of these committees. When Wilson conducted a reshuffle in 1968, moving Crossman to become Secretary of State for Health and Social Security, the government lost a key advocate for reform. Fred Peart, who replaced Crossman, lacked enthusiasm for select committees, resulting in interest waning over the remainder of the parliament.

The establishment of the Parliamentary Commissioner for Administration (PCA), more commonly known as the 'Ombudsman', offered the Labour Party the opportunity to alleviate concerns about the individual's relationship with the state. The Labour Party could also position themselves as 'reformers', as a Parliamentary Commissioner tied in with an 'open' and 'accountable' government, thus improving the relationship between the Commons, back-bench MPs and citizens, and the accountability of the executive to Parliament. Some Labour MPs were concerned about how the Ombudsman would impact on their representative role. The White Paper *The Parliamentary Commissioner for Administration* recognised the concern, stressing Parliament remain the arena in which redress of grievance is sought, and no intention to 'erode the functions of Members of Parliament in this respect'.[9] The Ombudsman was to investigate allegations of maladministration, a definition that remained purposely opaque. In practice, the Ombudsman was to be approachable only through MPs, thereby preserving their role as intermediary with the administration. Decisions were to be advisory, leaving untouched the principle of ministerial responsibility, and he could only examine matters for which ministers had direct responsibility to Parliament. This ruled out local government, the nationalised industries and the National Health Service. Notwithstanding, it would prove to be the most successful Commons reform introduced by the Wilson government.

Crossman had inherited from Bowden a commitment to trial morning sittings in the Commons and a trial scheme televising proceedings in the Lords and, while committed to neither, pursued both. Morning sittings were an attempt to end late nights, allowing MPs to finish earlier and return home at a more reasonable hour. While a noble intention, in practice it faced a number of difficulties and opposition from all sides of the House. Labour MPs came up against the logistical problem of travelling to and from northern constituencies, whereas Conservative MPs and middle-class Labour MPs, whose second jobs tended to be legal or financial, had morning meetings and therefore scheduling complications. In turn, the type of legislation brought forward for morning sittings was problematic. Non-controversial legislation did little to attract MPs to attend, whereas important government legislation placed strain on the commitments of ministers, who had other morning meetings, including Cabinet. Consequently, morning sittings were dropped in November 1967.

Crossman's programme of reforms for the House of Commons met opposition from both Labour ministers and back-bench MPs. Morning sittings proved unworkable in practice and, although select committees are now accepted, there was a distinct lack of keenness shown for the concept, impacting on the traditional role of the Commons and ministers. Subsequent governments would extend the role of the Ombudsman throughout society, emphasising the success of the policy introduced by the Wilson government.

ELECTORAL REFORM

The Labour Party, having replaced the Liberal Party as the main opposition to the Conservatives in the 1920s, experienced minority government in 1924 and 1929–31. Interest in proportional representation at Westminster duly faded as parliamentary representation increased. Winning a parliamentary majority in 1945 emphasised that a single-party government was capable of delivering social and economic reform to the benefit of the working class. Three successive general election defeats in 1951, 1955 and 1959 did not dampen Labour's enthusiasm for 'first past the post' (FPTP). Proportional representation was a minority pursuit both within Parliament and outside during the 1964–70 government. However, Wilson set up a Speaker's Conference on electoral law in 1965 with the then Speaker Harry Hylton-Foster presiding over the conference, later replaced by Horace King.

Proportional representation, in the form of the Single Transferable Vote (STV), was included in the terms of reference for the Speaker's Conference.

Yet this was just one of many electoral practices considered by the conference: reform of the franchise, with particular reference to the minimum age for voting and registration procedure generally; methods of election; conduct of elections, with particular reference to absent voting, the official mark on ballot papers and of electoral numbers on counterfoils; polling hours; polling day as a public holiday; provisions relating to undue influence, returning officers, use of broadcasting and cost of election petitions; and applications for relief were all up for discussion.[10] Wilson was concerned about the frequency of publishing the electoral register. After deliberation, the option of a twice-yearly publication was rejected, and publication was maintained at once a year.[11]

The Speaker's Conference produced three interim reports before a Final Report in February 1968, recommending a voting age of twenty, overwhelmingly rejecting a reduction to eighteen years of age by twenty-two votes to three. Indeed, it was deemed that reform of the franchise by reducing the voting age was 'constitutionally the most important issue arising out of the Speaker's Report'.[12] The Wilson government would go further than the recommendations of the Speaker's Conference, reducing the voting age to eighteen in 1969, thought to be advantageous to Labour, as young people were assumed to be more inclined towards voting for the party. On the motion of STV, the conference voted nineteen to one against; nineteen to one voted in favour of FPTP. Four meetings were spent discussing the Westminster electoral system and all Labour members of the conference made the case for FPTP, arguing that the purpose of a general election was the election of a government.[13]

The Wilson government of 1974–76 governed Great Britain in a different political climate; two elections in 1974 had given the Labour Party a slim majority and representation of the Liberal Party and the Nationalists had increased, with a decline in the vote share for the two main parties. As such, proportional representation returned to the political agenda and David Steel, the Liberal Chief Whip, asked Wilson a question on electoral reform.

In response, Wilson stated he had asked Lord Crowther-Hunt to conduct research into the matter, 'considering how it might best be tackled'. Crowther-Hunt the following year affirmed that he had made little progress and, importantly, the Prime Minister had asked him to 'play it long',[14] suggesting Wilson had no desire to give credence and fuel demands for proportional representation.

The Castle Diaries records that discussions on reconvening Ted Heath's Speaker's Conference that had ended owing to the Dissolution of Parliament in February 1974. Home Secretary Roy Jenkins claimed the conference had 'unfinished business left' and 'he was thinking of reconstituting it'. However, Jenkins wished to discuss STV, surmising that if the government did not include the matter it would appear only that Labour was not interested in reform. Consequently, Jenkins suggested the Speaker's Conference to examine it in a 'low-pressure way'. Foot came in emphatically: 'Once we get into this it will grow and grow,' he protested. 'Why hasten the conference at all?' Castle continues: 'If we were not careful we could see the end of any possibility of a Labour government.' It was 'obviously best ... to let this sleeping dog lie as long as possible. So we sent Roy away with a flea in his coalition ear.' In November 1975, Jenkins revisited the issue. Castle writes it was 'pleasant to have Roy Jenkins slapped down'. Ted Short sided with Jenkins, arguing there was 'great pressure for it' although 'we must watch it very carefully'. However, Castle declared that, 'the rest of us turned on them'. Denis Healey, '"with good pragmatic vigour", denounced the idea as "absolute madness"'. For Castle, only the hard core of Jenkinite coalitionists (Harold Lever, Shirley Williams and Reg Prentice) were in agreement, so Harold had to sum up that the idea was turned down, although 'those rightists will go on beavering away, with Harold and Jim as their instruments, until they have finally destroyed the Labour Party's independence and power to govern single-handedly'.[15]

From 1964–70, electoral practices, rather than proportional representation, were the focus, notably the extension of the franchise by reducing the voting age to eighteen. Demand for proportional representation increased in Wilson's second spell as Prime Minister, including from within the Labour Party, although the majority opinion remained solidly wedded to FPTP, believing that the system would revert back to stable, single-party, majority government in the future.

CIVIL SERVICE

The suitability of the civil service for an advanced industrial society like Britain became a key matter in the 1960s, given Labour's emphasis on 'modernisation' and the increasing importance of science and technology. The publication of the Fabian group report *The Administrators* in 1964 had called for a more professional, specialised and expert civil service. Wilson held the civil service in high regard, influenced by his role as a 'temporary' in World War Two, and subscribed to the view that it was the responsibility of ministers to get things done. Wilson rejected left-wing allegations of political bias and bureaucratic sabotage, deeming it 'nonsense' that a 'change of government means sabotage from the civil service'.[16] Still, Wilson did consider the civil service to lack drive, believing it to be dominated by an elite administrative class. In addition, a more dynamic and efficient civil service could assist Labour's plans for growth and scientific advance, allowing for expert planning to professionalise what was seen as the 'amateurism' of the civil service.

Wilson set up the Fulton Committee – chaired by Lord Fulton, who had worked alongside Wilson during World War Two – with a brief to 'examine the structure, recruitment and management, including training, of the Home Civil Service and to make recommendations'. However, impetus for reform stemmed from Thomas Balogh, economic adviser to the Cabinet in 1964–67 and then consultant to the Prime Minister in 1968. Balogh was supported by Crossman, who, in his evidence to the Fulton Committee, argued that reform was crucial, as the civil service simply took advantage of the existing departmental arrangements. Furthermore, Parliament needed to be strengthened by the introduction of specialist committees and outside advice. Indeed, a diary entry by Crossman pinned responsibility for the 'decline in the power of the politicians over the civil service machine' on Wilson, who, by enacting ministerial reshuffles, encouraged the civil service to take the upper hand.[17]

Published in 1968, the report identified a number of defects, comprising the view that the 'generalist' administrator was obsolete, the system of classes and grades was inefficient, there were too few opportunities for specialists to rise to top administrative posts, too few skilled managers, a lack of contact with the 'community' and a lack of personal management and planning. The core recommendations concerned recruitment procedure and training, a unified grading structure, the abolition of classes, securing greater mobility in and out of the civil service, and recasting its central management. Wilson immediately accepted the creation of a Civil Service Department (CSD), along with the establishment of a Civil Service College to 'provide major training courses in administration and management and a wide range of shorter courses' and the replacement of classes by a unified grading structure.

Fry writes that Wilson placed more emphasis on reshaping the machinery of central government and on creating new government departments than on the reform of the civil service. However, experience as much as advocacy, according to Fry, may have persuaded Wilson to make civil service reform a higher priority. Marcia Williams, Wilson's personal and political secretary, in an interview stated:

> There seemed to us to be a need to open up the civil service to promote a
> different attitude. This did not mean that we wanted the wholesale slaugh-
> ter of the civil service. Harold Wilson was an admirer of the civil service

but he thought that, like many other institutions by that time, it need[ed]
to change and he set up the Fulton Committee to bring this about.

Indeed, Wilson sought to maintain the constitutional arrangement whereby
civil servants were advisers and ministers were responsible to Parliament
for government policy.[18]

Fulton tied in with Wilson's 'technological revolution' and desire to update
the workings of the British state. Never one to miss an opportunity to appear
as a moderniser, Wilson embraced civil service reform, proving to be valuable
in the face of opposition from within Cabinet, emanating from Roy Jenkins
and Denis Healey. Jenkins, without consultation, was angered over the removal
of the management of the service from the Treasury. Healey later wrote that,
as 'Defence Secretary I had more urgent problems at the time', a view shared
by other ministers, according to Fry, who were weighed down with departmental duties. The matter, therefore, lacked importance. Additionally, two
Cabinet meetings were required before Fulton was accepted as, initially, only
Peter Shore and Tony Benn – who wrote a critical account of the civil service
in his diary – supported Wilson. Theakston affirms that the Fulton Report
was largely based on collectivist assumptions about 'big government' and a
belief in a large civil service. In terms of implementation, it was a process of
piecemeal adaptation, in part a result of the impact of other pressing events
occupying the government. Wilson, in the changed political climate on his
return to government in 1974, no longer had the eagerness to modernise.[19]

LOCAL GOVERNMENT

As with other reforms in this period, it had become intellectually and politically fashionable to pursue reorganisation of local government, with economies

of scale the motivation, considering bigger authorities to be more effective and
efficient. Indeed, J. L. Sharpe had published a Fabian pamphlet critical of the
small units that made up the present system and suggested that plans should
be made to bring everything up to a bigger scale, along with the end of the
two-country division.[20] Richard Crossman, in his ministerial role of Housing
and Local Government, was determined to accomplish reform. In an address to
the 1965 Conference of the Association of Municipal Corporations, he argued:

> The whole structure of local government is out of date, our county bor-
> ough and county councils as at present organised are archaic institutions
> whose size and structure make them increasingly ill-adapted to fulfilling
> the immensely important functions with which they are charged. The
> greatest obstacle, in fact, which prevents efficient councils from retaining
> public confidence is the obsolete constitutional framework within which
> they have to operate.[21]

There had been a growing dissatisfaction with the old structure of local government, which had remained largely unaltered since the Local Governments
Acts of 1888 and 1894. Redcliffe-Maud and Wood, in *English Local Government Reformed*, reflect on five areas of 'general agreement' as to why local
government suffered weaknesses and rose to prominence in this period:
too many authorities lacked sufficient resources; geographical boundaries
were out of date; complexity of the system, including issues of responsibility in delivering services; voter apathy in terms of interest and turnout; and
the overdependence of local authorities on central government for funds.[22]
The Wilson government acted and the English Commission set up by the
Local Government Act 1958 was abandoned; in its place, a Royal Commission
on Local Government in England started afresh in February 1966. A separate commission with the same remit was set up simultaneously for Scotland,

the Wheatley Commission, which reported in 1970. The terms of reference for the Royal Commission in England, chaired by Lord Redcliffe-Maud, were broad, yet contained the tension between efficiency and democracy:

> To consider the structure of local government in England, outside Greater London, in relation to its existing functions; and to make recommendations for authorities and boundaries and for functions and their division, having regard to the size and character of areas in which they can be most effectively exercised and the need to sustain a viable system of local democracy.

Redcliffe-Maud recommended 'unitary' authorities, an all-purpose council covering both town and country, with a population range of between 250,000 and 1 million. It was argued that the new structure had more potential for efficiency as responsibility for resources would lie with a single council. Democracy would benefit as the public could identify with the new authority, which greater reflected the new geographical situation, further enabling public understanding of where responsibility lay. One member of the commission, Derek Senior, wrote a significant and lengthy Memorandum of Dissent, instead advocating a 'two-level' system, comprising directly elected regional authorities and district authorities, allegedly more responsive to patterns of settlement, activity and community structure.

Wilson, in his statement to the Commons on the publication of the Redcliffe-Maud Report, said the government intended to advance progress and bring forward a Bill as soon as possible. Peter Jenkins, in *The Guardian*, felt that it was Wilson, keen to maintain his image as a reformer, rather than Anthony Greenwood (Crossman's replacement as Minister for Housing and Local Government), who was making the running. However, according to Crossman, there was, in addition, a more instrumental reason for Wilson's acceptance. Wilson was aware of the impending changes in parliamentary boundaries and acceptance of Redcliffe-Maud's proposals would allow the proposed boundary changes, thought to be disadvantageous to Labour, to be shelved, a view shared in Cabinet by Callaghan and Castle. Wood writes that Wilson was also shrewd enough to realise that local government reform was no longer a vote-losing issue, with only scanty evidence to suggest Conservative candidates had lost support in the outer suburbs of London in 1964 because of local government reform in London.[23]

The proposals of the Royal Commission were endorsed by the government with only minor amendments in a White Paper (*Reform of Local Government in England*) published in February 1970. The fifty-eight unitary authorities, and three metropolitan areas around Birmingham, Manchester and Liverpool, put forward by Redcliffe-Maud were altered in the White Paper. The number of unitary authorities was reduced to fifty-one and two new metropolitan areas in west Yorkshire and south-west Hampshire were added. The White Paper stated: 'Adoption of the unitary system wherever it is practical will make local government more efficient and more comprehensible to the public,'[24] emphasising both democracy and efficiency.

Redcliffe-Maud desired to strengthen the structure of local government in order to make the system both functionally and democratically more viable. The government White Paper was not, however, supported by the Conservative opposition, who disliked the unitary authority policy, and when the Labour government was defeated in June 1970, their proposals based on the Redcliffe-Maud Report were abandoned.

CONCLUSION

The Labour Party is often accused of 'constitutional conservatism', yet a great deal of time and energy was exerted under Harold Wilson seeking to reform the practices of the constitution. While the different attempts at reform had varying degrees of success, Wilson's first spell as Prime Minister (1964-70) sought to tackle the in-built Conservative majority in the House of Lords, mechanisms in the House of Commons, the alleged amateurism of the civil service, the supposed inefficiency of local government and electoral laws and procedures. However, barring the White Paper on local government reform, in the last two years of the parliament impetus for constitutional reforms waned or reforms were abandoned. Instead, the Wilson government focused attention on more 'practical' issues, such as industrial relations. While the Wilson government of 1974-76 saw the creation of the No. 10 Policy Unit and the extension of special advisers, the reforming zeal for parliamentary reform witnessed in the 1960s had abated, in spite of increasing demands for proportional representation.

Constitutional reform allowed Wilson to be the 'reformer', tying in with the wider ideas of modernising the British state and its ability to deliver economic growth. Yet, there was no coherent strategy of constitutional reform, and the Westminster model – parliamentary sovereignty, ministerial accountability, single-party government delivered through FPTP, general elections usually once every four or five years, granting a mandate to an executive able to deliver its manifesto pledges and unitary state with sovereignty residing at Westminster – remained intact. Indeed, ministers were disapproving of ideas that impacted on traditional notions of ministerial responsibility. Instead, a piecemeal approach was adopted in an attempt to update the constitution, allowing for more effective governance, in line with the prominent ideas of planning and efficiency. In spite of the reforms outlined, the Wilson governments had a general approval of the British constitution, with an overriding acceptance that 'the government must be able to govern'.

Ideologically, the Marxist analysis that the state is an instrument of the ruling class has had little traction within the Labour Party, which adhered instead to the Fabian view of a benign state, neatly summarised by Wilson's motoring analogy quoted at the beginning of the chapter. The Fabian approach to the British state professes that when governed by the correct people – Labour people – the arrangements of the British state are such that a parliamentary majority can enact the necessary social and economic reform. This approach was widely shared by others in the Cabinet and Parliamentary Labour Party. Crossman, the leading advocate of parliamentary reform, faced considerable opposition from individuals within Cabinet, not sharing the same enthusiasm for reforms designed to increase scrutiny of ministers, therefore challenging a central plank of the Westminster model.

A number of political factors shaped the debates on the constitution during Wilson's premiership: practical politics and governance; differences over the type of reform; and the electoral saliency of constitutional reform compared to social and economic policies. Underlying these tensions within the party has been a split between the 'elitists' and the 'pluralists'. The former, accepting the Westminster model, epitomised by Stewart's statement questioning the reasoning behind limiting the power of the executive, desire to have power concentrated in the centre, allowing the government to enact the 'socialist' manifesto pledge made at a general election. The latter aspire for power to be dispersed more widely in an open political system, such as the parliamentary reforms proposed by Crossman, with the legislature empowered to hold the government to account, having greater ability to influence and scrutinise. Over the course of Wilson's time in office, the 'elitist' position remained the dominant view towards the British constitution.

NOTES AND REFERENCES

1.   Quoted in D. Coates, *The Labour Party and the Struggle for Socialism*, pp 142–3
2.   R. Crossman, *The Diaries of a Cabinet Minister: Vol. 2, Lord President of the Council and*

Leader of the House of Commons 1966–68 (London: Hamish Hamilton/Jonathan Cape, 1976), p. 94; diary entry for 26 October 1966

3. Quoted in P. Dorey and A. Kelso, *House of Lords Reform Since 1911* (Basingstoke: Palgrave MacMillan, 2011), p. 143

4. H. Wilson, *The Labour Government, 1964–70*, p. 608

5. D. Shell, 'Parliamentary Reform', in P. Dorey (ed.), *The Labour Government 1964–70* (Abingdon: Routledge, 2006), p. 168; P. Dorey and V. Honeyman, 'Ahead of his time: Richard Crossman and House of Commons reform in the 1960s', *British Politics*, 5/2, (2010), pp 156–7; and see also P. Dorey, *The Labour Party and Constitutional Reform: A History of Constitutional Conservatism* (Basingstoke: Palgrave Macmillan, 2008), pp 61–62

6. R. Crossman, *The Diaries of a Cabinet Minister, Vol. 2*, p. 165; diary entry for 14 December 1966

7. Ibid., p. 130; diary entry for 17 November 1966 and p. 308; diary entry for 11 April 1967

8. Ibid., p. 347; diary entry for 9 May 1967

9. *The Parliamentary Commissioner for Administration*, Cmnd 3, para 4

10. *Conference on Electoral Law*, Cmnd 2880. Letter dated 28 December 1965, from Mr Speaker to the Prime Minister

11. TNA HO 328/129, see letter from Frank Soskice to Lord President of the Council, 20 November 1964; and Prime Minister's personal minute to the Home Secretary, 30 October 1964

12. TNA PREM 13/2076, Electoral Reform (C68, 74, 76), 29 May 1968

13. *Conference on Electoral Law*, letter dated 28 December, 1965; letter dated 8 February, 1966; letter dated 7 March 1966; and letter dated 9 February 1968, from Mr Speaker to the Prime Minister. For the discussions on proportional representation, see LSE Archives PARKER 4/2 A, 2, 9, 16, 23 November 1966

14. TNA CAB 198/6, Question for Oral Answer, Thursday 25 July 1974; and CAB 198/6, letter from Crowther-Hunt to Lord Harris of Greenwich, dated 24 March 1975

15. B. Castle, *The Castle Diaries 1974–76* (London: Weidenfeld & Nicolson, 1980), pp 69–70; diary entry for Thursday 4 April 1974; and p. 554; diary entry for Tuesday 18 November 1975. The Speaker's Conference would not be reconvened until July 1977, when Callaghan needed to win the support of the Ulster Unionists by increasing the number of constituencies in Northern Ireland

16. P. Ziegler, *Wilson*, p. 38; and N. Hunt *et al.*, 'Whitehall and Beyond' (1964), quoted in K. Theakston, 'Whitehall Reform', in P. Dorey (ed.), *The Labour Government 1964–70*, p. 150

17. TNA BA 1/6, *Civil Service Department: Committee on the Civil Service (Fulton Committee). Minutes, Papers and Report 1966–69*, quoted in V. Honeyman, *Richard Crossman: A Reforming Radical of the Labour Party* (London: I. B. Tauris, 2007), p. 113 and R. Crossman, *The Diaries of a Cabinet Minister: Vol. 3, Secretary of State for the Social Services* (London, Hamilton and Cape, 1977), p. 78; diary entry for Sunday 26 May 1968

18. K. Fry, *Reforming the Civil Service: The Fulton Committee on the British Home Civil Service of 1966–68* (Edinburgh: Edinburgh University Press, 1993), pp 5, 7 and Hansard, HC Debs, Vol. 724, cols 209–10

19. D. Healey, *The Time of My Life*, p. 405; K. Fry, *Reforming the Civil Service*, p. 243; K. Theakston, *The Civil Service Since 1945* (Oxford: Blackwell, 1995), p. 90; and K. Theakston, *The Labour Party and Whitehall* (London: Routledge, 1992), pp 113–40

20. J. L. Sharpe, *Why Local Democracy?*, Fabian Tract 361 (London: Fabian Society, 1965)

21.   Quoted in P. Richards, *The Reformed Local Government System* (London: George Allen
       and Unwin, 1973), p. 43
22.   Lord Redcliffe-Maud and B. Wood, *English Local Government Reformed* (Oxford: Oxford
       University Press, 1974), pp 23–31
23.   R. Crossman, *The Diaries of a Cabinet Minister, Vol. 3*, pp 509, 516; *The Guardian*, 8 July
       1969, 'Enter Maud in Strange Haste', cited in K. O. Morgan, *Callaghan: A Life* (Oxford:
       Oxford University Press, 1997), pp 362–4; B. Wood, *The Process of Local Government
       Reform 1966–74* (London: George Allen & Unwin Ltd, 1976), pp 71–2
24.   *Reform of Local Government in England*, Cmnd 4276, para. 18

13

DEVOLUTION

David S. Moon

2016 MARKS THE forty-year anniversary of the introduction of the 1976 Scotland and Wales Bill, the first serious attempt by a British government to bring about devolution in the two nations; a proposal described at the time by Harold Wilson as 'the most fundamental constitutional development in this century'.[1] Largely developed as a response to nationalist gains in the so-called 'Celtic fringe', the policy bitterly divided the Cabinet and party, facing sustained opposition up until the referendum defeats in 1979 under Wilson's successor as Prime Minister, James Callaghan. The 'decisions of principle' that underpinned the 1976 Bill would live on, however, as, with the development of Labour's new devolution policies in the 1990s, policy-makers revived key elements of 'Wilsonian' devolution – much to the detriment of subsequent legislation.

This chapter illustrates the particular political problems that Wilson faced in Wales and Scotland and his attempts to develop an adequate policy response from 1964 to 1976. It first focuses on the rise of political nationalism in the two nations, charting nationalist electoral gains and discussing the factors driving them. Subsequently, it traces the changing face of Wilson's policy response, from national planning to the promise of devolution, chronicling the opposition that this policy agenda faced through its development. The chapter concludes in the present, asking, forty years on, what legacy Harold Wilson has left for our contemporary, post-devolution politics.

WALES AND SCOTLAND:
THE RISE OF POLITICAL NATIONALISM

Wales and Scotland's electoral importance for the Labour Party was clearly demonstrated in 1964 when, without either nation's votes, Wilson would have been unable to form his government. Any threat to Labour's Welsh and Scottish votes was thus a major concern, explaining why, once a threat was perceived to them, Wilson would go on to expend so much political capital on devolution – a policy he had previously shown little interest in. The specific threat was the development of Welsh and Scottish nationalism into electorally successful entities. This threat was not immediately apparent, however.

Founded in 1925, Plaid Cymru was seen as a nuisance by Labour well into the 1960s. The party's electoral record was up until this point far from impressive. As a percentage of the Welsh vote, Plaid Cymru achieved just 0.7 per cent in 1951, 3.1 per cent in 1955 and 5.2 per cent in 1959. At the 1964 general election that brought Wilson to power, Labour secured 60.8 per cent of the Welsh vote, its highest-ever figure; by contrast, Plaid Cymru's twenty-three candidates had secured just 4.8 per cent of the Welsh vote. Welsh nationalism was, thus, little initial concern for the new Prime Minister. Even the 1966 general election, where Plaid managed an average of 8.3 per cent in the twenty seats contested, did little to unnerve Labour. In just a few months, this situation would markedly change.

In July 1966, at the famous Carmarthen by-election, Plaid Cymru's candidate, party president Gwynfor Evans, leapt from the third-place position he had achieved at the general election four months previously to first place, securing the then-largest swing against a government in the post-war period. Further mid-term contests also saw increases in Plaid's vote at Labour's expense. In May 1967, Plaid cut Labour's majority of 68.98 per cent in Rhondda West to just 9.1 per cent. Just over a year later, a by-election in July 1968 saw Labour's majority in Caerphilly of 59.7 per cent cut to only 5.2 per cent. The 1970 general election, in which Labour unexpectedly lost power, was Plaid's most successful, securing 11.5 per cent of the Welsh vote, but losing Carmarthen back to Labour. The party achieved a significant breakthrough at the two 1974 general elections, however, winning Caernarfon and Merioneth in February and regaining Carmarthen in October. All three seats were taken from Labour, feeding fears of a rising nationalist threat, but the reality was less impressive. Plaid's three seats were situated in Welsh-speaking west Wales and, while the nationalist vote was increasing in these communities, it simultaneously decreased elsewhere. Even if inflated, these fears fed into a sense that a swelling Welsh national consciousness was benefiting Plaid Cymru at Labour's expense.

In Scotland, as in Wales, when Wilson entered Downing Street, the nationalists were not perceived as threatening to Labour. The Scottish National Party (SNP) had achieved parliamentary representation in 1945, but only for a few months when they broke the war-time electoral truce. In 1959, the SNP secured less than 1 per cent of the Scottish vote. In 1964, the figure was 2.4 per cent. This figure doubled to 5 per cent by 1966, but in each case the SNP managed a smaller percentage share of the Scottish vote than Plaid Cymru was achieving in Wales. However, at the March 1967 Pollock by-election, the SNP secured 28.2 per cent of the vote in a Labour marginal, helping the Conservatives take the seat. Then, in November of the same year, the SNP

joined Plaid Cymru at Westminster, when Winnie Ewing won the Hamilton by-election with 46 per cent of the vote in a previously safe Labour seat.
Hamilton was seismic; Wilson recounts the fears it raised within Labour,
writing of its 'ominous portents' and asking: 'Was it just a Poujadist protest,
a short-lived reaction, or would it persist, with disastrous results, in a general
election? This was what everyone was asking.'[2]

The pattern continued with the 1968 local government elections, where
the SNP won almost 100 seats and deprived Labour of an overall majority in Glasgow. Just as Plaid lost Carmarthen in 1970, so too the SNP lost
Hamilton; this loss was offset, however, by their gain of the Western Isles
seat and a doubling of their share of the Scottish vote to 11.4 per cent.
Come the 1974 elections, the SNP overtook the Conservatives in total vote
share, becoming the second-largest party in Scotland with 30.4 per cent
of the vote and in second place in thirty-five of Labour's forty-one Scottish seats. With evidence mounting, the question for Wilson was no longer
whether the nationalist growth would persist, but since it evidently had, what
was happening and why?

FACTORS FUELLING NATIONALISM

At first glance, the reasons for Plaid Cymru's successes are far from obvious.
In many ways Wales fared well under Wilson. There was a significant amount
of administrative devolution, conferring formal recognition of Wales's particular national context. In 1964, Wilson introduced the position of Secretary
of State for Wales and founded the Welsh Office. The 1967 Welsh Language
Act, though limited in scope, was the first since the 1540s to increase rights to
use *Cymraeg* in legal settings and specified that, finally, in all future legislation
Wales had to be distinguished from England. In these two elements –

recognition of the status of the Welsh language and Wales's distinction from England – the act was another step affording official recognition to Wales's national status. The fact that, at the time the act was passed, Wilson presided over a Cabinet of which a quarter were Welsh, and in which four ministers spoke *Cymraeg*,[3] further illustrates the centrality of Welsh interests at the heart of Westminster.

After 1974, a number of bodies were created with the express purpose of promoting economic development, including the Welsh Development Agency, the Development Board for Rural Wales and the Land Authority for Wales. Other organisations of the British state were relocated to Wales, including the Driver and Vehicle Licensing Centre in Swansea, the Royal Mint in Llantrisant and the Census Office in Newport. Even the Investiture of the Prince of Wales in 1969, though viewed as symbolic of Welsh subjugation by nationalists, was seen by many unionists as a further boost to Wales's status within the union that 'would advertise this new Wales to the world and promote tourism'.[4]

Why, then, was it during Wilson's period as Labour leader that modern Welsh nationalism came of age? Several factors account for this shift. First, there was disillusionment within Labour's core vote linked to the economic problems suffered in Wales's industrial heartlands. Alongside the sterling crisis and subsequent cuts in government expenditure, between 1958 and 1968 50,000 mining jobs were lost with pits closed as the coal industry in Wales slipped into terminal decline. Wilson himself appears to have viewed such economic factors as key, noting in his personal account of the Carmarthen by-election that it was the same day George Brown moved the Second Reading of the Prices and Incomes Bill: 'I doubt if recent electoral history could produce another example of a government increasing bank rate, and foreshadowing a grim statement on a wide range of economic issues, at the moment of maximum electoral impact. We lost the election to the Welsh Nationalists.'[5] Further factors included the government's slow and reluctant response to the 1966 Aberfan disaster that was widely viewed as the betrayal of a Labour-loyal community in mourning, and the highly public and bitter arguments over *In Place of Strife*, which, with the historical dominance of the National Union of Mineworkers, was bound to raise opposition in Wales.

In Scotland, too, nationalists tapped into working-class frustration about industrial and economic policy. The establishment of the Highlands and Islands Development Board, meant to tackle rural economic decline, and the rescue of the shipyards meant that, initially, Wilson's government benefited from 'an aura of good feelings'.[6] The promise of the 'white heat of technology' soon began to cool, however, providing grievances that nationalists could exploit. In both cases, the identification of such factors as the explanation for Labour's woes tapped into the dominant narrative within the party's political thought that saw the problems facing Wales and Scotland as primarily economic, with nationalist support the result of the party's failure to adequately address material issues.

Yet, in Wales, something greater than economics was clearly at play. Beyond Labour's valleys heartlands perceived threats to cultural, environmental and linguistic identity and interests in Welsh-speaking Wales fuelled political nationalism. The flooding of Cwm Tryweryn and the Welsh-speaking community of Capel Celyn to construct a reservoir supplying Liverpool with water was a key inciting event; announced in 1955 and carried to conclusion in 1965 under Wilson, in the words of Huw T. Edwards, the action led 'the cream of Welsh youth ... into the ranks of the Nationalist Party'.[7] Plans announced in 1966, again by Liverpool City Council, to transfer several businesses from Merseyside to north Wales as part of a programme of industrial expansion faced similar nationalist protests, being viewed as a threat to 'the area's solidly Welsh-speaking status' that would render it 'little more than an English-speaking Liverpool "over-spill"'.[8] Duncan Tanner posits related concerns as the reason for Gwynfor Evans's victory in Carmarthen, describing it as 'largely because Labour policies on agriculture, regional development and education were successfully represented as a threat to the continued viability of small Welsh communities'.[9]

The ballot box was not the only area where Wilson's government confronted problems from Welsh nationalism. In Wales, '60s radicalism found expression, among other ways, in direct action and protests by new Welsh nationalist organisations. These were both peaceful (like *Cymdeithas Yr Iaith Gymraeg*, the Welsh Language Society, founded in 1962) and violent (such as the sporadic but well-organised bombing campaign carried out by the militant group *Mudiad Amddiffyn Cymru*, the Movement for the Defence of Wales (MAC)).[10] Indeed, between 1963 and 1969, there were twenty explosions across Wales, with a further six bombs that failed to detonate, targeting power and transport infrastructure, government buildings and the Royal Investiture. Finding a means to address nationalist sentiment in Wales thus included questions of civil order.

Represented politically in the form of the SNP, Scottish nationalism was (and is) 'civic' in nature, rather than the cultural-linguistic 'ethnic' variety then growing in Wales. This meant that, for Labour, the threat posed was both simpler and electorally more urgent than in Wales. The divisive civil disobedience of *Cymdeithas* and the bombing campaigns of the MAC were not replicated in Scotland. Instead, the SNP's campaign attached itself to Scottish claims to North Sea oil with the slogan 'It's Scotland's Oil!', constructing an easily grasped populist campaign that lacked the cultural-linguistic barriers attached to Welsh nationalism. However, the SNP's presence was felt even before the start of oil production, again pointing to a growing attachment to a separate national identity that went beyond materialist concerns. As the influence of the nationalist parties grew, Wilson's governments became ever more engaged with the question of devolution, seeing it as a means of holding off nationalist advances.

WILSON'S NATIONAL PLAN, 1964–70

Engagement with devolution was not immediate. Wilson's 1964 programme embraced a centralised and interventionist approach to governance, the Department of Economic Affairs (DEA) that Wilson set up pursuing a form of 'national planning' that, while containing a strong regional dimension, worked against any devolutionary instincts.[11] This attitude was expressed in Labour's March 1966 manifesto where, addressing regional economic problems, it stated: 'Labour respects the differences of culture and tradition of Scotland and Wales; nevertheless, we see the economic well-being of Great Britain as indivisible. The government has therefore set out measures which help both Scotland and Wales, within the context of a true National Plan.'[12]

Despite such nods to different cultures and traditions, this economistic mindset overrode the borders of any 'imagined communities'. This was demonstrated in November 1966 when, just four months after Gwynfor Evans's by-election victory, the Home Policy Committee's regional planning conference proposed dividing Wales in two for economic purposes. Wales 'made no sense'[13] for the planners, who advocated linking north Wales with Merseyside and south Wales with Bristol and the south-west of England. When, in 1967, Welsh Liberal leader Emlyn Hooson MP sought to introduce a Private Member's Bill 'to provide a scheme for domestic self-government of Wales and for connected purposes',[14] the government killed it off at the Second Reading.

During this period, between 1966 and 1970, constitutional discussions within the Wilson government were driven by Richard Crossman, whose primary concern was not nationalism, but reform of the 'machinery of government' (see Chapter 12). Crossman was an advocate not of national devolution, but of regionalism-all-round. In November 1967, he suggested to the Prime Minister that 'current proposals for further devolution to Wales and Scotland ought to be considered in relation to our whole attitude to regionalism including the role of regional councils in England'.[15] Crossman's proposals were stymied by opposition from Welsh and Scottish politicians, and a committee of junior ministers set up in 1968 to consider devolution was unable to reach agreement, offering only a bland, non-committal statement. Believing that nationalist advances had by then rendered his plans inadequate anyway, a disappointed Crossman saw the situation as evidence of 'Harold doing nothing about it, Harold allowing an issue ... to slip through his fingers'.[16]

As economic difficulties mounted towards the end of the '60s, Welsh Secretary George Thomas and Scottish Secretary Willie Ross – both anti-nationalists and anti-devolution – placed their emphasis on calls for central-government intervention to create new jobs in their respective nations. Recognising the *impasse* reached within his government over the issue of devolution, in late 1968 Wilson appointed a Royal Commission on the constitution (later known as the Kilbrandon Commission) timed to report after the general election – thereby kicking the issue into the long grass. The manifesto Labour fought and lost the 1970 election on included 'plans for an elected Council for Wales with extended powers', but rejected 'separatism or separate Parliaments or legislative assemblies in Wales and Scotland'.[17] Wilson spent the 1960s delaying, delegating and ultimately dismissing devolution as party policy. When next he entered Downing Street, circumstances necessitated far greater engagement with the issue.

TAKING DEVOLUTION SERIOUSLY, 1973–75

Re-elected in February 1974, Wilson found himself back in power but without a working majority. Faced with seven SNP and two Plaid Cymru MPs, Wilson required a credible policy that could reverse nationalist advances. Labour's manifesto failed to promise devolution, but in the face of nationalist gains,

Wilson looked back to the Kilbrandon Commission that he had set up four years previously. The commission's report had been published in autumn 1973, while Ted Heath was Prime Minister. It was widely deemed 'turgid and inconclusive' and a 'kill-devolution report',[18] with the eleven commissioners who signed the majority report unable to settle on an agreed position: 'Eight recommended legislative devolution for Scotland and six for Wales; three favoured a directly elected Welsh advisory council and one favoured a similar scheme for Scotland; [and] two recommended executive devolution for Scotland and Wales.'[19] Confusion was useful, allowing a split party room for manoeuvre. Labour's plans ultimately settled somewhere in the middle of this muddle; having decided upon devolution as a policy, however, Wilson struggled to establish support for it within the party.

Initially, backing was more forthcoming from Wales than Scotland. The Welsh pro-devolution side had enjoyed significant representation in Wilson's government throughout the 1960s with Jim Griffiths and Cledwyn Hughes as Secretaries of State for Wales, and Goronwy Roberts and Elystan Morgan government ministers. Hughes's replacement as Welsh Secretary by George Thomas in 1974 was a blow to devolutionists, but the policy also enjoyed support beyond Cabinet. The party in Wales's 1966 conference passed a resolution calling for an elected body,[20] an enthusiasm demonstrated again when, in preparing its evidence for the Kilbrandon Commission, the Labour Party in Wales shocked Central Office in London by supporting a directly elected body with powers over legislation and taxation.[21] This led to a major dispute between the two, resulting in a compromise whereby Labour went into the 1974 elections supporting the introduction of a directly elected assembly, but with executive functions only.

The situation differed in Scotland where, in 1958, a Labour Special Conference in Glasgow had voted to oppose Home Rule, arguing that only 'socialist planning on a United Kingdom scale' could solve Scottish problems.[22]

Anti-devolutionists such as Arthur Woodburn and Willie Ross dominated the Scottish leadership and, following publication by Wilson's government of a hastily drafted consultative paper, *Devolution within the United Kingdom: Some Alternatives for Discussion*, Labour's Scottish council voted to reject the policy by six votes to five, labelling devolution 'irrelevant to the real needs of the people of Scotland'.[23]

It was not only the Scottish party who were concerned with Wilson's devolution plans; much of the Cabinet were also. In his diary entry for 30 July 1974, Bernard Donoughue, head of the No. 10 Policy Unit under Wilson and then Callaghan, described a 'very depressing' Cabinet committee held to discuss the Kilbrandon Report. 'Everyone now getting frightened at what we are doing,' he wrote; Denis Healey, Roy Jenkins and Anthony Crosland all argued that devolution should be slowed down,[24] accepting manifesto proposals for electoral purposes but asserting that all discussions should be postponed until after the vote.[25] Wilson was insistent, however, that devolution would be party policy and, in September 1974, the government issued a White Paper: *Democracy and Devolution: Proposals for Scotland and Wales*. Wilson's exhaustion and lack of confidence in the plans were summed up by the benediction he offered the paper following the Cabinet's agreement: 'And God help all who sail in her.'[26] But while the White Paper was vague in many respects, it nevertheless contained a number of important 'decisions of principle' that would have a lasting impact. Bogdanor lists these as follows:

- There would be directly elected assemblies in Scotland and Wales.
- The Scottish Assembly would have legislative powers, the Welsh Assembly only executive powers.
- The assemblies would be elected by the first-past-the-post system.
- The assemblies would be financed by a block grant allocated by Parliament. There would be no devolution of revenue-raising powers.

- There would be no reduction in the number of Scottish or Welsh MPs at Westminster.
- The offices of Secretary of State for Scotland and Wales would remain, and the office-holders would continue to sit in the Cabinet.
- Devolution in England would be postponed for further consideration.[27]

With the White Paper published, pressure was applied to the Scottish party by London so that, just two days before the October election, it could be announced that agreement had been reached for a manifesto commitment to 'create elected assemblies in Scotland and Wales', the Scottish assembly having 'substantial powers over the crucial areas of decision-making'.[28]

In that October's election, though Wilson secured his overall majority, he found himself faced with a combined nationalist group of fourteen MPs: the SNP's vote had risen from 22 per cent to 30 per cent, securing them a further four seats, while Plaid Cymru increased their number of seats to three. As Labour's majority slowly but inevitably declined and then disappeared, this nationalist bloc became increasingly important. No doubt in response to this, the Queen's Speech promised 'urgent' action to create the promised directly elected assemblies, with a revised White Paper, entitled *Our Changing Democracy: Devolution to Scotland and Wales*, issued that November.

Continued divisions within the Cabinet meant that real progress remained difficult. These divisions were clearly displayed in January 1975 at an all-day Chequers meeting held to discuss devolution. Ted Short, the minister in charge of the government's devolution policy, presented his plans, which found support from Barbara Castle, Gerry Fowler, Willie Ross and the new Welsh Secretary John Morris. The majority of those present resisted them, however, again arguing that devolution was being pursued too quickly and should be slowed down. Taking this line were Richard Crossman, Elwyn Jones, Roy Jenkins, Fred Peart, Reg Prentice, Eric Varley, Anthony Crosland,

Merlyn Rees and Tony Benn, the latter of whom described the drive for devolution as 'part of the collapse of confidence of the English establishment'.[29] Speaking in supporting Short's plans, Wilson warned that devolution was the only way to avoid separatism, arguing that, 'we must get devolution rolling forward'. But, in a blow to Wilson's leadership, when Short subsequently claimed that the Cabinet committee had approved his papers in principle, Jenkins, Crosland, Prentice and Benn opposed him, and Wilson, unable to push the decision through, was forced to agree to delay the decision pending further debate.[30] In Cabinet the following week, Callaghan and Healey joined the devo-sceptics.

These Cabinet divisions continued through to next September, when an all-day meeting on devolution deteriorated into 'dreadful squabbling', 'like a monkey's tea party'. Again, Benn, Healey, Jenkins, Crosland and Callaghan opposed moves towards devolution. Wilson attempted to restore order and assert his leadership over the matter but, by this point, Donoughue recalls, he had become 'totally bored with the whole question' and 'privately admitted he had not read all the papers'. The government thus found itself in the strange position wherein the government was pledging devolution despite a majority of Cabinet members opposing the policy. The Prime Minister himself, in Donoughue's words, did 'not support it either really... His position is that we are committed to it: we proposed it, we put it in our manifesto, and we produced a White Paper – therefore we cannot go back on it. But he does not believe in it.'[31] Ultimately, Wilson and his Cabinet colleagues remained strongly attached to Britain's executive-dominated, centralised, parliamentary system, with devolution proposals compromised to accommodate this.

Wilson's enthusiasm would rally, in part because he came to believe that a Scottish Assembly would destroy the SNP. Wilson based this judgement on John Mackintosh's argument that the SNP was a coalition that would break up under the pressures of the assembly and requirement to cooperate with other parties.[32] Relaying these thoughts to Donoughue, a chipper Wilson even professed that 'he would personally love to be a member of the Scottish Assembly'.[33] If the Prime Minister had discovered his enthusiasm, and the Cabinet had finally, albeit half-heartedly, agreed to the plans, a significant proportion of Labour's back benches remained antagonistic. Debates in the House of Commons chamber had already demonstrated dissension within Labour's ranks as anti-devolutionists, such as the Welsh MPs Neil Kinnock, Leo Abse, Alfred Evans and Ioan Evans, and Scottish MPs such as Robin Cook and Tam Dalyell, expressed their passionate opposition to the government's proposals. Devolution, they argued, would divide the working class and give succour to the nationalist agenda.

WILSON'S RESIGNATION AND
DEVOLUTION'S DEFEAT, 1976-79

In November 1975, a second White Paper was published, based upon the same 'decisions of principle' as the 1974 paper, promising 'the creation of elected as well as administrative institutions distinctive to Scotland and Wales'.[34] This paper was the subject of four days of debate between 13 and 19 January. Opening the debate, Wilson declared:

> We reject the separation into independent political units of the countries that make up the United Kingdom. We reject the rigid and legalistic approach which is the very essence of proposals based on federalism. We reject as unworthy and totally inadequate to meet the needs of the people of Scotland and Wales a shadow assembly which has no real substance, on the one hand, and mere tinkering with administrative machinery, on

the other. We also reject the idea – perhaps many of us agree on this; not all of us – that because of the difficulties, the safest thing would be to do nothing, that as things are, so they shall remain.

The government's proposals, he stated, were 'based on two objectives: a decentralisation of power to the people and the unity of the United Kingdom'.[35] Wilson's statement turned out to be his last major contribution to the devolution debate. Less than two months after, on 16 March, he announced his resignation. Callaghan, who replaced him as Prime Minister on 5 April, was left to carry Wilson's devolution plans forward.

These plans were consolidated in a single Bill covering both countries, the Scotland and Wales Bill 1976, but this would eventually be withdrawn, on 22 February 1977, when the government's defeat on a guillotine motion meant to smooth its passage left it 'effectively dead'.[36] The motion was defeated by a majority of twenty-nine (312 to 283); twenty-two Labour MPs voted against and another twenty-three abstained. Leading a minority government and needing support from Liberal and nationalist MPs, Callaghan subsequently split the Bill in two and tried again. However, while ultimately passed by Parliament, the separate Scotland and Wales Acts of 1978 would never be implemented. The policy's credibility was destroyed by the referendum defeats in 1979, and the election of Margaret Thatcher, an avowed opponent of devolution, saw the Scotland and Wales Acts repealed.

CONCLUSIONS: WILSON'S LEGACY

Twenty years after the original Scotland and Wales Bill was withdrawn, the development of Labour's new devolution policies under Tony Blair saw policy-makers return to key elements of 'Wilsonian' devolution, most notably the 'decisions of principle' set out in 1974. New Labour's departure from these principles were not major, abandoning the third principle (first past the post) in both Wales and Scotland, and making limited changes in the Scottish case only to the fourth (proposing minor tax-varying powers) and fifth (agreeing a reduction of Scottish MPs).

Membership of a cross-party Scottish Constitutional Convention through-out the 1980s helped Labour produce a devolution settlement for Scotland free from the compromises of the 1970s, introducing a Scottish Parliament with primary legislative and tax-raising powers. In Wales, however, the party was far more divided over devolution and playing catch-up with Scotland. Subsequently, a constitutional policy commission, established to re-examine Labour's plans for Welsh devolution, produced a report recommending the resurrection of the 1970s devolution settlement: executive devolution, albeit this time with an assembly elected under a proportional system.

This 'Wilson legacy' has been detrimental for Wales. The ensuing 1998 Government of Wales Act founded a National Assembly for Wales that thus resembled in many ways the institution proposed in the 1970s. Constructed for compromise rather than good governance, the Welsh devolution settlement was plagued with inefficiencies and incoherence, and the first eighteen years of post-devolution politics have been consumed with the question of how best to reform the system. Key to these problems is a direct remainder of the 1970s proposals: the adoption of a 'conferred powers' model of devolution. This refers to a model wherein the central, 'sovereign' Parliament *confers* powers to a devolved assembly, allowing it to legislate in specifically defined subject areas. This is in contrast to a 'reserved powers' model, wherein a devolved body is granted the freedom to legislate on *any* subject area, provided it is not one specifically 'reserved' to the central Parliament. In 1998, Scotland received a reserved powers model; Wales maintained the conferred powers approach. The problem with the latter model is clarity. Different governments and institutions can and have disagreed in their interpretations of what is and is not conferred on Wales, as the Welsh government has found laws it passed referred to the Supreme Court by Westminster on the basis that legislative competencies are not devolved. The draft Wales Bill, under debate in 2016, promises to shift Wales to a reserved powers model but, facing sustained criticism, seems predestined to disappoint.

However, Wilson's main objectives in promoting devolution had less to do with good governance than dealing with the growing nationalist threat to Labour's Scottish and Welsh seats. Today, entering into devolution's fifth election cycle, the policy has proved a failure. If anything, devolution has exacerbated Labour's problems. It is true that, in parliamentary terms, Plaid Cymru have failed to break out of their heartland in *Y Fro Gymraeg*; however, within the National Assembly, the nationalist vote has been significantly higher, even carrying the party into coalition government with Labour in 2007. But in Scotland the situation is much worse. Wilson's anticipation that devolution would destroy the SNP has proven incorrect. In 2007, the SNP formed a minority government in Holyrood; in 2011, it secured a majority. In 2014, it held and only narrowly lost a referendum on Scottish independence; in 2015, it achieved Wilson's nightmare – decimating the Labour Party and winning all but three of Scotland's Westminster seats. Directly and indirectly, devolution has created an increasingly disunited Kingdom. If Harold Wilson was wrong, then, about the *effect* devolution would have, his description of devolution as 'the most fundamental constitutional development in this century' was certainly correct.

NOTES AND REFERENCES

1.   Quoted in L. Gunn, 'Devolution: A Scottish View', *The Political Quarterly*, 48/2, (1977), pp 129–39

2.   H. Wilson, *The Labour Government, 1964-70*, p. 447

3.   N. Johnes, *Wales Since 1939* (Manchester: Manchester University Press, 2012), p. 227

4.   N. Evans, 'The Investiture of the Prince of Wales', BBC Wales History, 25 June 2009, http://www.bbc.co.uk/wales/history/sites/investiture/pages/investiture-background.shtml

5.   H. Wilson, *The Labour Government, 1964-70*, p. 253

6.   B. McLean, 'Labour in Scotland since 1945: Myth and Reality', in G. Hassan (ed.), *The Scottish Labour Party: History, Institutions and Ideas* (Edinburgh: Edinburgh University Press, 2004), pp 34-50; p. 39

7.   P. Ward, *Huw T. Edwards: British Labour and Welsh Socialism* (Cardiff: University of Wales Press, 2011), p. 114

8.   W. Thomas, *Hands of Wales: Nationhood and Militancy* (Llandysul: Gomer, 2013), p. 105

9.   D. Tanner, 'Facing the New Challenge: Labour and Politics, 1970-2000', in D. Tanner, *et al.* (eds), *The Labour Party in Wales: 1900-2000* (Cardiff: Cardiff University Press, 2000), pp 264-93; p. 267

10.   W. Thomas, *Hands of Wales*

11.   Regional Planning Boards were introduced in 1965, but granted limited responsibilities

12.   D. Tanner, 'Richard Crossman, Harold Wilson and Devolution, 1966-70: The Making of Government History', *Twentieth Century British History*, 17/4, (2006), pp 474-578, http://tcbh.oxfordjournals.org/content/17/4/545.short

13.   Ibid., pp 558-9

14.   R. Deacon, *Devolution in Britain Today* (Manchester: Manchester University Press, 2006, 2nd edn), p. 76

15.   Quoted in D. Tanner, 'Richard Crossman, Harold Wilson and Devolution, 1966-70: The Making of Government History', p. 560

16.   Ibid., p. 567

17.   In 'General Election Manifesto 1970', in I. Dale (ed.), *Labour Party General Election Manifestos: 1900-1997* (London and New York: Routledge, 2000), pp 153-80

18.   L. Gunn, 'Devolution: A Scottish View', p. 131

19.   R. Deacon, *Devolution in Britain Today*, p. 78

20.   R. Merfyn and I. R. Jones, 'Labour and the Nation', in D. Tanner *et al.* (eds), *The Labour Party in Wales: 1900-2000*, pp 241-64; p. 256

21.   K. Morgan and G. Mungham, *Redesigning Democracy: The Making of the Welsh Assembly* (Bridgend: Seren, 2000), p. 133

22.   Quoted in F. Wood, 'Scottish Labour in Government and Opposition: 1964-79', in I. Donnachie *et al.* (eds), *Forward! Labour Politics in Scotland 1888-1988* (Edinburgh: Polygon, 1989), p. 101

23.   V. Bogdanor, *Devolution in the United Kingdom* (Oxford: Oxford University Press, 1999), p. 141

24.   Crosland was unimpressed with the issue generally. When told he had to attend Cabinet discussions he replied: 'Not interested in Devolution. Have no intention of wrecking my August holiday simply to hold a fatuous discussion about another White Paper.' Quoted in S. Crosland, *Tony Crosland*, p. 277

25.   B. Donoughue, *Downing Street Diary: With Harold Wilson in No. 10* (London: Jonathan Cape, 2005), pp 169-70

26.   V. Bogdanor, *Devolution in the United Kingdom*, p. 179

27.   Ibid., p. 178

28.   Quoted in L. Gunn, 'Devolution: A Scottish View'

29.   Quoted in B. Castle, *The Castle Diaries, 1964–76*, p. 546
30.   B. Donoughue, *Downing Street Diary*, pp 284–7
31.   Ibid., pp 491–4
32.   Ibid., p. 540
33.   Ibid., p. 546
34.   *Our Changing Democracy: Devolution to Scotland and Wales*, Cmnd 6348, HMSO, November 1975
35.   Hansard, HC Debs, 13 January 1976, Vol. 903, col. 219
36.   V. Bogdanor, *Devolution in the United Kingdom*, p. 184

14

NORTHERN IRELAND

Catherine McGlynn and Shaun McDaid

THIS CHAPTER EXAMINES the outbreak of the conflict in Northern Ireland and Harold Wilson's attempts to deal with the growing crisis in the region. The chapter focuses on both of Wilson's premierships as well as his key contributions to the debates concerning the region during his stint in opposition. The findings are based on the examination of primary-source evidence such as original and contemporary archival records generated during Wilson's time in office, records of parliamentary debates, as well as the memoirs of some of the key figures from within Labour Party and Whitehall circles during Wilson's tenure. In reviewing Wilson's objectives and impact, the chapter also reflects on the impact of James Callaghan on Northern Ireland, and contrasts the ways in which these key Labour figures approached this thorny issue throughout the entire period. In so doing, the chapter argues that Wilson's approach to Northern Ireland policy has often been misrepresented, and misunderstood, by both his contemporary political opponents and subsequent scholars of the period. Although often caricatured as a devotee of Irish unity, and unwilling to impose a power-sharing settlement over the heads of Northern Ireland unionists, the reality is in fact more complex. Such accounts, this chapter argues, fail to take into account the genuine constraints faced by Wilson and his administrations, and the reality of what was achievable regardless of which party was in power. While critical of many of his policy choices, we argue that Wilson's approach to Northern Ireland policy can, in fact, be characterised as sticking to several core principles: reform of the Northern Ireland state to include power-sharing; an Irish dimension to any proposed settlement; and a determination that unionists would not be forced out of the United Kingdom against their will. Above all, he put personal preference aside to ensure no policy was pursued – namely, British withdrawal – that would worsen the seemingly endemic violence that engulfed the region after 1968.

WILSON'S OBJECTIVES IN NORTHERN IRELAND, 1963–68

It would be easy to assume that, upon election to the Labour leadership, Northern Ireland would not be a priority for Harold Wilson. He had a fractious party to marshal towards an election and a growing awareness of the profound structural frailties of the British economy. Northern Ireland was an issue that had been pushed to the political margins, aided in part by the convention that kept questions about the region out of the proceedings of the House of Commons. The issue had last received significant attention from the Labour Party in the 1949 Ireland Act, which had enshrined the principle that Northern Ireland would remain part of the United Kingdom unless its Parliament voted otherwise, although this was not without protest from several Labour backbenchers. Since then, the region had seemingly ossified not just into a clientelist regime presided over by the Ulster Unionist Party (UUP) but into an economically underperforming region with higher levels of deprivation than the era of post-war consensus was supposed to tolerate. The civil rights activist and journalist Eamonn McCann, for example, remembered the wry amusement in Derry at Conservative Lord Hailsham donning a flat cap and touring the north-east of England to demonstrate his party's concern when the unemployment rate hit what for Northern Ireland would have been a very healthy 5 per cent.[1] In light of this, it could be assumed that, until the violent conflict known colloquially as the Troubles (1968–98) forced the region onto Westminster's agenda, it was not a priority for either Wilson or his party.

However, Northern Ireland *was* actually of concern to many within the Labour Party. As early as 1954, Callaghan led a contingent of MPs to tour Northern Ireland with the specific intention of examining the impact of high unemployment. The discrimination he then found against Catholics in areas such as public and private sector recruitment enraged him. Additionally, individual Labour MPs who would coalesce in 1965 into the Campaign for Democracy in Ulster (which investigated allegations of sectarian discrimination in the region) tried to break the parliamentary convention of silence on Northern Ireland (although it was defended by both the Speaker and ministers regardless of their political party until the events of October 1968). Wilson himself 'was committed to change Labour's Irish policy',[2] evidence of which can be found in a very sympathetic and positive letter of 1964 to the Campaign for Social Justice (CSJ), the forerunner of the Northern Ireland Civil Rights Association (NICRA), formed in 1967, suggestive of active movement towards reform. This gave hope to the CSJ, the formation of which was the first step towards the development of a civil rights movement that would lobby for equality of citizenship through the removal of electoral malapportionment, discrimination in housing and employment, and the draconian security set-up enabled by the Special Powers Act, legislation that troubled both Wilson and Callaghan. Indeed, Wilson was concerned with the possible inconsistency of the UK government's stance on human rights abroad, while they 'were patently denied in Ulster'.[3]

Bernard Donoughue, who headed the No. 10 Policy Unit from 1974 to 1979, later described Wilson as having 'radical instincts on the Irish question', which he contrasted with the conservatism of Callaghan.[4] However, when Callaghan took up the post of Home Secretary in 1967, his approach to reform was in step with what Wilson had already been doing since the 1964 election. This entailed cajoling Captain Terence O'Neill (Northern Ireland Prime Minister from 1963–69) to deliver reform in voting, security, local government and employment practices. In his memoir of the early years of the conflict in Northern Ireland, Callaghan presents himself as joining Wilson in pushing O'Neill, who 'would have made an excellent Prime Minister in the Conservative tradition in easier times', on civil rights, although he laments that he was hemmed in by parliamentary convention (leaving aside the fact that it could have been over-ridden by statute).[5]

On the surface, O'Neill might have seemed like the man to remedy both the iniquities and dustiness of Northern Ireland's political system. He had a similar faith in the 'white heat' view of technology and planning and had seized on the Matthews and Wilson Reports, which offered a blueprint for a Northern Ireland, kick-started by new towns, infrastructure and investment, that would attract new industries such as synthetic fabrics.[6] His openness to reconciliation with the Republic of Ireland, including a meeting with Prime Minister Seán Lemass, echoed Wilson's immediate gestures of rapprochement upon election, such as sending back the Irish tricolour that had flown over a site of the Easter Rising in 1916. And, with visits to Catholic schools along with voluntary initiatives such as civic weeks, O'Neill aimed to offer a friendlier face to the nationalist minority, suggesting the possibility of openness to structural reform.

O'Neill's tenure, however, was plagued by the (re-)emergence in 1966 of the loyalist paramilitary group the Ulster Volunteer Force (UVF) and the rise of the demagogic preacher Ian Paisley, a populist harbinger of doom who would in 1971 form the Democratic Unionist Party (DUP) in his own image. Unionist and loyalist fears were already high in the later 1960s, with many anxious that the fiftieth anniversary of the Easter Rising would act as a catalyst for a republican revival. They need not have worried, since the Irish Republican Army (IRA) was at this time in disarray following a disastrous attempt to end partition by force between 1956 and 1962. Both republicans and loyalists, therefore, contributed to a febrile atmosphere that would come to a head in the autumn of 1968.

However, despite the rising tensions, O'Neill had little interest in reforming the system. Promises such as 'new industries for Newry mean new hope for all its people'[7] demonstrate how he hoped that improvement in the economy, along with gestures of accommodation, would be enough to reconcile nationalists to a polity that was mainly devoted to cementing unionist fraternity. He saw the main threat to his position as the Northern Ireland Labour Party (NILP) and hoped his use of planning would undermine any critiques of his party's domination based on Northern Ireland's significant class inequality. O'Neill was not the man to deliver on the civil rights movement's needs, and neither Wilson nor Callaghan adequately recognised this. It was this inability to see through O'Neill's superficial gesture politics that explains the initial limited impact of a Labour government on Northern Ireland.[8] This was not down to lack of principle on Wilson's part, however, and may be explained by his personal attitude towards O'Neill, whom he regarded as being impeded in his attempts at progress by a 'black reactionary group' within his own Cabinet.[9]

REACTIONS TO CONFLICT, 1968–74

O'Neill's failure to deliver reforms quickly enough inspired further street protest. NICRA raised the profile of their campaign through marches in support of their demands for change. These marches attracted heavy-handed attention from the Royal Ulster Constabulary and their controversial reserve force, the B-Specials. The event that forced the pace of change was the Derry March on 5 October 1968, when protestors were attacked by security forces in the full glare of the world's media. This moved Wilson and Callaghan from talking about the need for action to taking action themselves. As violence spread across the region, Callaghan sent the British Army in to protect nationalists whom he believed were in genuine danger, in areas such as inner-city Belfast, and whom he thought would not accept a security solution led by the existing security forces, even if they had been up to the task.

In addition, Wilson and Callaghan pushed the pace of reform over the heads of the unwilling Northern Ireland government at Stormont. The Representation of the People Act 1969 removed the property qualification that had disproportionately benefited unionists, who were more likely to be the rate-payers and business-owners making up the local electoral rolls. The UDR Act of 1969 paved the way for the disbandment of the B-Specials and the creation of the new Ulster Defence Regiment and the RUC was made more accountable (although the Hunt Report's key recommendation that the force be unarmed was not delivered). Other plans for reform, such as the Housing Executive with responsibility for fair allocation of social housing and the Community Relations Council, were also developed before Labour lost power in 1970.

Out of power, Labour swapped places with the Conservatives in offering bi-partisan support to the government and a large deal of consensus on the need to balance security concerns with continued reform. However, Labour, and Wilson in particular, remained more committed to reform than the Conservative government, which Cunningham argues had taken the view that, as major grievances had been addressed, the violence must now be about something other than issues of injustice.[10] For example, although accepting of the Northern Ireland government's decision to introduce internment of paramilitary suspects without trial, Labour were critical of the disproportionate impact upon nationalists, becoming more vocal after an anti-internment march in Derry in January 1972 resulted in paratroopers killing fourteen unarmed protestors (an event now remembered as Bloody Sunday).

Wilson's contribution in this period, though, is perhaps most associated with his 'fifteen points' speech, made in Parliament in November 1971. While Wilson ultimately envisaged a solution to the Northern Ireland problem in an all-Ireland context, to the chagrin of unionists, this was by no means the kind of state envisaged by hard-line republicans. Indeed, Wilson envisaged such a polity taking a federal form, within the Commonwealth, and with a continuing British military garrison for many years after its establishment. Crucially, he also noted this could only come about by democratic persuasion, not violence.[11] The latter principle was central to Wilson's policy, whether in government or opposition. The creation of the post of Secretary of State for Northern Ireland by the Conservatives necessitated the appointment of a shadow post, which went to Merlyn Rees, but Callaghan maintained his interest in the situation and he, along with Wilson, would be instrumental in the attempts by Labour to sustain moves towards power-sharing when they took office again in 1974.

SUNNINGDALE AND THE ULSTER WORKERS' COUNCIL STRIKE

The Northern Ireland Parliament was prorogued by the Heath government in 1972. This was accepted as an 'interregnum' rather than the first step towards integration, thus a political initiative that could revive devolved government was a priority.[12] This initiative took the form of constitutional proposals, which offered a new power-sharing assembly that would guarantee meaningful representation for nationalists and unionists and which included the recognition of the need for an Irish dimension, rather than a wholly internal agreement.

These proposals became law in May 1973 and elections for a new assembly were held the following month. After a meeting in Sunningdale, Berkshire in the winter involving the British and Irish Prime Ministers and senior politicians from Northern Ireland (subsequently known as the Sunningdale Agreement), a power-sharing executive was drawn from several moderate parties in the assembly and officially took office on New Year's Day 1974. When Wilson was re-elected in February, therefore, the new experiment in Northern Ireland administration was already in motion, but it was also already in trouble.

There was a large degree of vocal opposition to the Sunningdale Agreement among unionists, with the Irish Dimension (which had been realised as a Council of Ireland with cooperation on contentious issues including policing) the main source of both anxiety and anger. The Chief Executive of the new assembly Brian Faulkner (who had been the final Prime Minister of the Stormont Parliament) led an Ulster Unionist Party that was severely divided over the entry into the new arrangements. Constitutional opponents such as Paisley's DUP shared the view of loyalist paramilitaries, such as the UVF and the Ulster Defence Association, that nationalists in the Social Democratic and Labour Party (SDLP) were right to see the Council of Ireland as the embryonic Parliament of a future all-island republic.[13] Politicians opposed to the constitutional proposals of the agreement formed a United Ulster Unionist Council (UUUC) and in the same election that brought Wilson back to No. 10 this grouping won eleven out of twelve seats, suggesting a mandate to rival the pro-agreement majority in the assembly (albeit one distorted by different electoral systems). The assembly carried on despite the general election result. A motion calling for the rejection of the Sunningdale Agreement was defeated by forty-four votes to twenty-eight, a result that served as the backdrop to a public announcement by members of a new organisation called the Ulster Workers' Council (UWC) of a strike that would only end with fresh assembly elections.

The UWC was a mix of trade union activists and loyalist paramilitaries, and this strike was not the first attempt to use industrial stoppages to secure a political goal. A similar grouping, the Ulster Loyalist Council, had called a general strike in 1973 in protest at the internment of loyalists. The strike, which had relied on extensive intimidation, was deemed an alienating failure, especially as a fireman was killed on duty in Belfast. As the UWC strike was also reliant on a fair degree of paramilitary pressure to secure stoppages in the region, it is not surprising that the protests were not immediately regarded at Westminster as a significant problem. However, as the strike wore on, the Labour government did not deal effectively with the situation.

While there is no doubt that intimidation was a feature of the strike, this obscured the fact that it also had genuine support, particularly from key industries. The UWC capitalised on the militancy its forerunners such as the Loyalist Association of Workers had relied on among power station workers, which allowed them to manipulate the supply of electricity. Robert Fisk's immediate work on the strike makes a persuasive argument that the UWC's legitimacy was further aided by the BBC, because it ended up performing the role of information service in broadcasting UWC statements about rationing and distribution.[14]

The UWC's adroit manipulation of antagonism towards the Sunningdale Agreement contrasted with the inability of the Labour government at Westminster to grasp that the strike commanded strong support and therefore a comprehensive strategy to counter its effect and address the roots of grievance was needed. Here we see Callaghan and Wilson taking different paths, reflective of the differences between them, although the end result was the same.

Wilson, sharing the same faith in the power of the media to provide a conduit that connected him to the public, which he displayed in his electioneering, broadcast a stinging condemnation of the strike on 25 May 1974. The speech contrasted 'people who spend their lives sponging on Westminster and British democracy and then systematically assault democratic methods' with 'the people on this side of the water, British parents [who] have seen their sons vilified and spat upon and murdered. British taxpayers have seen the taxes they have poured out, almost without regard to cost.'[15] This speech, which, by implication equated the strikers with the IRA and firmly cast Northern Ireland into the role of unwanted stepchild, only served to solidify the unity of the strike.

Callaghan's approach reflected his faith in the wider labour movement as an agent of change. He 'believed that the British Labour Party should pin its official support to the NILP because of its close links with the trade union movement, which has always been a non-sectarian force in the north'.[16] To this end, while Labour were in opposition, he had tried to encourage trade union members to back a Northern Ireland Council of Labour, which would serve as the backbone of future NILP campaigns. This faith carried over to supporting a back-to-work march involving the TUC leader to try to break the strike from below. However, while trade unions had been instrumental in strengthening the NILP's lobbying of O'Neill for voting reform, many prominent members of the UWC, such as Glen Barr, were well-known shop stewards and union activists. And many within the labour movement had either turned a blind eye to or facilitated events at work places, such as the Harland & Wolff shipyards, which belied Callaghan's faith in a non-sectarian movement.[17] In supporting a back-to-work march, Callaghan had not learned from the events he'd organised to publicise his proposed Council of Labour, which were picketed and heckled by both unionist and nationalist crowds. The march itself met with violent opposition, which Brian Faulkner recorded in his memoirs was no surprise to the politicians it was meant to support: 'In the executive the idea was treated with some levity and regarded as another example of the sad incomprehension with which our well-meaning Secretary of State and his ministers were approaching the whole affair.'[18]

As the protest maintained its momentum, politicians in the UUUC who had previously looked to carve out some distance between themselves and the less respectable forces of the strike put their support openly and firmly behind it and, as the executive finally crumbled on 28 May 1974, the UUUC MPs feted the striking masses. Neither Wilson's approach nor Callaghan's had saved this foray into power-sharing government.

Brendan O'Leary blames Labour's 'abject spinelessness before the strike of the UWC'[19] for Sunningdale's demise and although Bernard Donoughue tried to blame civil servants for doom-mongering ministers into surrender, he too characterised it as 'humiliating capitulation to Protestant violence'.[20] This judgement, however, overlooks what the Wilson government did try to do to hold the new institutional framework together.[21] It also needs to be said that those who followed either UUUC candidates or the strike (and many did both) benefited from a unity of purpose that party-political supporters of the agreement, split between unionism, nationalism and non-affiliated positions, could never achieve. And, in a situation where those committed to the use of extra-constitutional violence maintained optimistic estimations of their strategies, Northern Ireland faced multiple challenges that unsurprisingly encouraged a degree of timidity from those trying to deal with the conflict.

AFTER SUNNINGDALE: 1974-76

Although the collapse of the executive was humiliating for Wilson, and his optimism about being an agent of genuine change was dimmed, he committed his party to continue exploring solutions rather than merely addressing the violence that was spreading in the form of IRA bomb attacks to other parts of the UK. The UWC strike forced Wilson to consider all potential policy options, including, as contemporary archival sources show, the 'doomsday' scenario: an enforced British withdrawal from Northern Ireland, potentially leading to dominion status for the region.[22] Some scholars have posited this as evidence that Wilson abandoned the power-sharing executive and sought to extricate the British state from Northern Ireland.[23] However, the plans were firmly couched in the language of contingency and last resort. Just because Wilson was open to wide-ranging discussion about constitutional change does not mean he was willing to countenance withdrawal. The doomsday document was just one of many produced during Wilson's tenure, and it should not be assumed he was willing to jettison Northern Ireland as a matter of expediency. Indeed, even here, Wilson stated that power-sharing was an objective the government must continue to support.[24] Some within his Cabinet from both left and centre, such as Tony Benn and Roy Jenkins, were later inclined to see the merits of withdrawal: the former on ideological grounds; the latter owing to extreme pessimism that any political solution was possible.[25]

In security policy, some controversial initiatives did proceed, such as the secret discussions between British representatives and the Provisional IRA, as part of a fragile bilateral 'truce' between 1974 and 1975. During these discussions, the British side hinted at the possibility of British 'disengagement' from Northern Ireland.[26] In reality, no such disengagement was either possible or likely. The government actually aimed to diminish the IRA's military capacity while encouraging it towards democratic political action, at the same time recognising that the chances of the latter were slim.[27] With neither side gaining particularly from the exercise, the erratic 'truce' fizzled out by the winter of 1975–76.[28]

The necessarily timid experimentation during this period is demonstrated by the final initiative of the Wilson era. A fresh constitutional White Paper proposed a Northern Ireland convention as the first step towards a political solution. It still talked about the need for power-sharing and cooperation with the Republic

of Ireland, but the meat of the paper was a consultative constitutional convention that would generate proposals of its own for the future. When an election
was held in 1975 for the convention, the majority of both votes and seats went
to the UUUC. As the dominant force, they stuck with the convention's draft
report, rejecting power-sharing even after it was returned for revision following a debate in the House of Commons. In January 1976, Wilson's mind again
turned to radical contingency planning, with further consideration of what
might occur in the event of loyalists staging another UWC-type strike, and
outbreak of full-scale civil war. His 'apocalyptic note', however, is only further
evidence of the range of contingencies discussed during Wilson's tenure, on his
own initiative.[29] In policy terms, the government remained committed to a settlement based on power-sharing between nationalists and unionists. This was
evident when the convention was dissolved in March 1976, with its insistence
on unionist majority rule. When James Callaghan became Prime Minister the
following month, his new Secretary of State for Northern Ireland, Roy Mason,
while not averse to long-term conflict resolution, refocused the government's
energies into security policies designed to normalise the situation in the region.
Like Wilson, Callaghan remained wedded to the principle that devolution could
only return to Northern Ireland in the context of power-sharing.[30]

CONCLUSION: WILSON'S ACHIEVEMENTS AND IMPACT

An assessment of Wilson's impact in Northern Ireland must take into account
the gap between objectives and results. Wilson's sympathy to the nationalist
cause and ultimate certainty that withdrawal was both inevitable and desirable
sits at odds with policies that resulted in military and political commitments
to the region as staunch, if not stauncher, than Clement Attlee's calculated
rebuttal of nationalist aspirations in the Ireland Act of 1949. It is also possible

to find the gap between Wilson's noble estimation of his own position and the less heroic calculations that informed his actions. When Wilson recorded his impressions of the debate on police reform in the House of Commons in 1968, he remembered 'a few grunts from Ulster Unionist members – directed mainly against their hereditary foes in Northern Ireland and to a scarcely lesser extent against Labour backbenchers who had asserted the primacy of human rights in the Ulster situation'.[31] This genuine distaste for the reactionary attitudes of those MPs does not preclude the potential enjoyment he derived from seeing those who 'had acted as a loyal platoon of Conservatives' in his first administration getting their comeuppance.[32]

Reviewing Wilson's two periods of governmental responsibility for Northern Ireland, there are different ways to judge his actions and impact. The Wilson of the '60s joined forces with ministers such as Callaghan to react to the growing conflict with concern for the safety of those living in Northern Ireland and with a determination to deliver equality of citizenship that had been wilfully denied by the Stormont administration. At the same time, Wilson had had the chance to take a lead on this issue and he had made gestures that had reasonably led civil rights activists to believe he would follow through. However, the decision, once in office, to use O'Neill as his conduit for change was undoubtedly an error of judgement.

The Wilson of the '70s seemed one step behind and his 'spongers' speech was a particularly poor decision. However, at the same time, to keep faith with a power-sharing initiative supposedly at odds with his preferred policy in an effort to prevent more alienation and bloodshed, and to keep the search for solutions on the table when an entirely security-based approach could have been forgivably taken, suggests he was not someone without scruple in this complex area of policy-making.

His consideration of radical constitutional options, likewise, was always tempered by a concern not to take action that would increase violence.

Consequently, neither he, nor his ministers or civil servants, actively pursued withdrawal, whatever their personal instincts may have been. In respect of Northern Ireland, Wilson possessed neither the anti-imperialist withdrawal instincts of Benn, nor the unionist sensitivities of Callaghan. And, while prepared to plan for the worst, he never quite resorted to the apparent defeatism of Jenkins.

Throughout, the only realistic option for Wilson was a settlement, broadly similar to the Sunningdale formula, of power-sharing with an Irish dimension, while ensuring unionists should not be forced out of the United Kingdom without their consent. While these principles may not always have been of his own formulation, it seems clear that Wilson felt they were the best and, indeed, only viable option for Northern Ireland's future.

Wilson's dealings with Northern Ireland show a Labour leader, in contrast to Callaghan and his labour movement approach, looking to intervene directly, aided by use of the media and relying on his resources as a shrewd political operator and statesman. Neither approach delivered what either man wanted at the time (moves towards unity in Wilson's case; the removal of the Republic of Ireland's constitutional claim in Callaghan's) but these approaches show an evolution in leadership at Wilson's hands and of a different understanding of the party's relationship with other political and civil society actors. This would emerge again during the leadership of Tony Blair, who, after many more years of conflict, did manage to carve out a more enduring peace settlement.

NOTES AND REFERENCES

1.   E. McCann, *War and an Irish Town* (London: Penguin, 1974)
2.   P. Rose, *How the Troubles Came to Northern Ireland* (Basingstoke: Macmillan, 2000), p. 1
3.   H. Wilson, *The Labour Government, 1964–70*, p. 871
4.   B. Donoughue, *Prime Minister*, p. 128

5.	J. Callaghan, *A House Divided: The Dilemma of Northern Ireland* (London: William Collins, Sons & Co, 1973), p. 5

6.	G. Warner, 'Putting Pressure on O'Neill', *Irish Studies Review*, 13/1, (2005), pp 13–31

7.	T. O'Neill, *Ulster at the Crossroads* (London: Faber & Faber, 1969), p. 130

8.	The commitment to O'Neill as the man for the job is a common theme across literature covering the period. See, for example, P. Arthur, *The People's Democracy* (Belfast: Blackstaff, 1974); P. Bew & H. Patterson, *The British State and the Ulster Crisis: From Wilson to Thatcher* (London: Verso, 1985); M. Cunningham, *British Government Policy in Northern Ireland 1969–2000* (Manchester: Manchester University Press, 2001); and P. Rose, *How the Troubles Came to Northern Ireland*

9.	H. Wilson, *The Labour Government, 1964–70*, p. 349

10.	M. Cunningham, *British Government Policy in Northern Ireland 1969–2000*

11.	Hansard, HC Debs, Vol. 826, cols 1571–678, 25 November 1971

12.	TNA CAB 130/650, Notes of Ministerial Committee on Northern Ireland, 9 February 1972

13.	Hugh Logue of the SDLP famously described the Council of Ireland as the vehicle that 'would trundle unionists into a united Ireland'

14.	R. Fisk, *The Point of No Return: The Strike That Broke the British in Ulster* (London: André Deutsch, 1975)

15.	For text of speech, see the *Irish Times*, 27 May 1974, p. 8

16.	J. Callaghan, *A House Divided*, p. 152

17.	For example, on 28 June 1970, approximately 500 Catholic workers were expelled from the shipyard. A walkout was also staged from the yard in March 1971 in protest at the murder of three off-duty Scottish soldiers

18.	B. Faulkner, *Memoirs of a Statesman* (London: Weidenfeld & Nicolson, 1978), p. 267

19.	B. O'Leary, 'Northern Ireland', in A. Seldon & K. Hickson (eds), *New Labour, Old Labour: The Wilson and Callaghan Governments of 1974–79*, (London: Routledge, 2004), p. 241

20.	B. Donoughue, *Prime Minister*, p. 132

21.	S. McDaid, *Template for Peace: Northern Ireland, 1972–75* (Manchester: Manchester University Press, 2013), pp 126–53

22.	TNA PREM16/148, Wilson to Robert Armstrong, 30 May 1974

23.	M. Kerr, *The Destructors: The Story of Northern Ireland's Lost Peace Process* (Dublin: Irish Academic Press, 2011), p. 13; T. Craig, *Crisis of Confidence: Anglo-Irish Relations During the Early Troubles, 1966–74* (Dublin: Irish Academic Press, 2010), p. 182

24.	TNA PREM16/148, Wilson to Robert Armstrong, 30 May 1974

25.	TNA PREM 16/152, Northern Ireland: Future Trends of Policy, 22 November 1974; T. Benn, *The Benn Diaries* (London: Hutchinson, 1995), pp 305, 335

26.	E. Moloney, *A Secret History of the IRA* (London: Penguin, 2002), p. 148

27.	See F. Cowper-Coles, '"Anxious for peace": The Provisional IRA in Dialogue with the British Government, 1972–75', *Irish Studies Review*, 20/3, (2012), pp 223–42; S. Aveyard, *No Solution: The Labour Government and the Northern Ireland Conflict 1974–79* (Manchester: Manchester University Press, 2016)

28.	McDaid, *Template for Peace: Northern Ireland, 1972–75*, p. 176

29.	TNA PREM 16/959, Apocalyptic note for the record, 10 January 1976

30.	Hansard, HC Debs, Vol. 921, col. 35, 24 November 1976

31.	H. Wilson, *The Labour Government, 1964–70*, p. 719

32.	B. O'Leary, 'Northern Ireland', p. 241

15

FOREIGN AND DEFENCE POLICY

Rhiannon Vickers

THE FOREIGN AND defence policy of the Wilson governments was marked by the ongoing debate about Britain's role in the world. Wilson, despite coming from the centre-left of the party, was committed to maintaining Britain as a great power at the heart of international events. However, his ability to deliver on this was undermined by the gradual and unwilling realisation that Britain's relative economic decline, and in particular the need to devalue sterling, meant that it would have to cut defence expenditure and commitments, and withdraw from east of Suez. In addition, Labour had expectations of a new, radical, political dawn upon winning the general election on 15 October 1964, not least in foreign policy, and so Wilson's governments were marked by a divergence between the expectations of Labour supporters and backbenchers, and the viewpoint of those of the inner Cabinet. Wilson tended to appoint colleagues from the right of the party to the key posts of Foreign Minister and Defence Minister. His Foreign

Secretaries were Patrick Gordon Walker, Michael Stewart, George Brown and James Callaghan, and his Ministers of State for Defence were Denis Healey and Roy Mason. Wilson worked closely with his Foreign and Defence Secretaries, but whereas he took a very hands-on approach to foreign affairs during his first period in office, by the 1970s he had lost much of his energy and desire to be in control of external affairs, and allowed his ministers more leeway and independence in their actions.

It is difficult to identify Wilson with a particular foreign policy approach. He did not appear to have an underlying ideological vision shaping his foreign policy. Like all British Prime Ministers, he had an enduring attachment to Britain's world role and power, but was constantly faced with the problem of how to pay for the commitments that these entailed. His initial solution was to maintain Britain's defence commitments, but with a reduced budget, which then became unfeasible. Like all Labour Prime Ministers, he felt that Britain had a position of moral leadership in the world, especially when it came to Commonwealth countries, and was baffled when they did not behave in the way he expected. He had a very strong commitment to the Anglo-American relationship, but this caused him unpopularity within the party, especially over the Vietnam War.

This chapter will focus on these three key issues as a way of demonstrating the direction of Wilson's foreign and defence policy. If anything, his approach could best be described as an attempt to make the best of a difficult situation, without quite revealing the extent to which Britain had lost influence, or making any new commitments, and without undermining his own position as party leader. Thus, to a large extent, he was a pragmatist. In the 1960s, '70s and '80s, much of the Labour Party was vociferously critical of Wilson's foreign and defence policy, precisely because of this pragmatism. However, looking back from a greater distance, it is possible to reassess Wilson and give him greater credit for his approach and his judgement, not least in his handling of the Anglo-American relationship. It is to this issue that the chapter will now turn.

THE ANGLO-AMERICAN RELATIONSHIP

Labour had regained power at a time of change, when questions were being asked about the role that Britain could, or should, play in the world. Britain still had a vast military commitment across the globe, with troops in Europe, the Middle East and Far East, including Germany, the Mediterranean, Aden, the Persian Gulf and Malaysia. However, it was becoming increasingly apparent that Britain's relative economic decline meant that it could no longer project itself as a major force in the world in the way that it had in the first half of the twentieth century. It was also clear that Britain had become increasingly dependent upon the US in terms of security policy. Wilson's response to discovering upon gaining power that there was a £800 million balance of payments deficit was to shore up sterling by turning to the US for financial support, while introducing a series of severe financial restraints domestically. Both these measures alienated the government from the wider Labour Party and shaped the way that Wilson's foreign and defence policy developed over the next few years.

Wilson was firmly committed to the Anglo-American relationship and made much of what he felt was his personal rapport with Lyndon Johnson to his Cabinet colleagues. However, the relationship did appear to be somewhat one-sided. The 'special relationship' has always been more special to the British than the Americans, and a Labour government was viewed with some alarm in Washington. Nevertheless, the US administration did need Britain's support. An American review of Anglo-American policy relations noted that 'the simple, hardly debatable answer' to questions of the future of the special relationship is that we need the support and sympathy of the British. If they are unable

to go it alone, in their relative weakness, neither can we everywhere. We

touch one another at too many points and are still affected by what the

other does in too many situations to be able to dispense with mutual sup-

port of some kind.[1]

There were three main issues. First, in economic terms, the US administration needed Britain to keep sterling at $2.80, and not to devalue, in order to protect the dollar at a time when the US was suffering its own balance of payments problems. It was feared in the US that it might be forced to devalue if the pound devalued, which would cause instability in the international financial system. Second, in terms of defence, the US wanted Britain to continue to provide military support, and in particular to retain its bases in the Persian Gulf, Aden, Singapore and the Indian Ocean. It was feared that if Britain reduced its defence commitments east of Suez then the region might fall prey to Soviet influence or control at a time when the US was devoting increasing defence resources to Vietnam. Third, the US administration wanted British support over Vietnam, preferably by providing troops, but if not troops, then at least strong public diplomatic backing. This was so that the US could present its actions in Vietnam as multilateral rather than unilateral, in order to allay any domestic sense of guilt over American actions in Vietnam and to demonstrate to the world that a 'socialist'-governed country agreed with American policy.

To a large extent, Wilson agreed with the first two of these three US objectives. It is not necessary to go into detail about Britain's economic and balance of payments problems here as they have been dealt with in other chapters. Suffice to say that Chancellor of the Exchequer Callaghan had been concerned before the election that a Labour victory would be followed by an attack on sterling. When a sterling crisis followed the Budget of 11 November 1964, he was able to turn to the Americans for help, and the British government received large-scale support for sterling from the US Federal Reserve Bank. Then, in the summer of 1965, when the pound came under increasing pressure at a time of dwindling exchange reserves, Wilson agreed to a rescue package from the US to support sterling and prevent devaluation.

Debate has subsequently raged over whether Wilson agreed privately to maintain British world-wide defence commitments in return for the rescue package, and the degree to which the US was able to use its financial aid as leverage over Wilson. To a large extent, however, Wilson's goals coincided with those of the Americans, namely, to avoid devaluation at any price and to maintain defence commitments east of Suez. Wilson, while aware of the need to cut defence expenditure, did not want a dramatic decline in Britain's defence commitments internationally. While paying lip service to the need to rationalise Britain's commitments to reflect its loss of its imperial role, at the same time Wilson emphasised Britain's continuing world role. He implied to Cabinet members that his hands were tied in that he could not withdraw from the Far East without damaging the Anglo-American relationship, which could endanger further financial support. It seems likely that this was a useful political tactic on Wilson's behalf, rather than the result of an actual agreement with the Americans, for, despite strong pressure from the US administration, Wilson did not provide what Lyndon Johnson really wanted, namely, British troops in Vietnam.

Less than two months after gaining power, Wilson visited Washington with Healey and Gordon Walker, where Vietnam had been one of the key issues discussed. The US Congress had authorised Johnson to undertake direct military action in Vietnam in August 1964 following the Gulf of Tonkin incident, and hostilities, and the US commitment to Vietnam, were set to rapidly escalate. During the talks, Dean Rusk, the US Secretary of State, asked for a British commitment to Vietnam, stressing that 'it was important to have a significant number of people in the country in order to create the necessary

international effect, both in Saigon and Hanoi, and on public opinion in the
United States'. Wilson, Gordon Walker and Healy emphatically refused the
request to provide British troops, and offered to provide training in jungle
warfare and policy advisers instead.[2] The US administration and President
Johnson repeatedly demanded that Wilson commit British troops to the Vietnam War, but he steadfastly refused to do so.

It is difficult to know exactly what Wilson's views on Vietnam were. He
tended to argue that he could not send troops because his hands were tied,
that Britain did not have the troops, or that his MPs would not support such a
move and his government would fall given that it only had a tiny majority. He
did not tell the US administration that he was opposed to the idea in principle, and he worked hard to avoid criticising US policy in Vietnam. Wilson's
policy of giving the US moral support for its war in Vietnam, while resisting
the pressure to send troops, satisfied neither the anti-Vietnam lobby within
Britain nor the Americans, who wanted a more concrete form of support.
However, it was, perhaps, the most realistic policy option at the time, given
the conflicting pressures on the government. Ben Pimlott, Wilson's biographer, says that 'Wilson, courageously, persistently and despite the strongest
inducements, declined to provide [troops]. Words of support were one thing,
British lives another.'[3] The Vietnam War was of course a hugely emotive issue
for the Labour Party, and one that caused vociferous criticism of the government. There were multiple resolutions forwarded to the party that criticised
Britain's support for the war, and the left wing of the party felt that the government was not only being weak by not condemning the US, but also immoral.

It was not just the rank and file of the party who were critical of the US
military intervention in Vietnam. During Wilson's visit to Washington in
December 1965, he had read out a telegram from Labour MPs demanding
an end to the bombing, and explained that if US aircraft bombed North
Vietnamese cities, the British government would have to remonstrate.

This situation occurred six months later when the conflict intensified and the US started bombing oil installations in Hanoi and Haiphong in the north. On 29 June 1966, Wilson announced that the government had decided to 'dissociate itself from the bombing of oil installations in the Hanoi and Haiphong areas' and made a statement in the House of Commons to this effect following repeated requests from his own back benches on 7 July. This was a polite way of criticising that particular US action while not being seen to actually criticise the war.

It was not just the Labour Party that wanted the government to condemn American actions in Vietnam. In 1967 and 1968, an anti-war movement grew in strength and presence. Wilson was plagued by vociferous anti-Vietnam War demonstrators when visiting towns around the country. Two enormous demonstrations took place in London in March and in October 1968, which included people from across the political spectrum. One way that Wilson did seek to reassure public opinion, and to deal with the massive pressure coming from within the Labour Party for the government to reverse its policy and to publicly condemn the US, was to act as a go-between for the US and the Soviet Union in an attempt to broker a deal on the cessation of hostilities. If Wilson had managed to broker a peace deal, this would have legitimised his stance on Vietnam and pleased the party, as well as raising his profile as a world statesman who could succeed where so many others had failed. However, these attempts were not always welcomed by the US; the Soviet Union did not actually have authority to negotiate a deal on behalf of the Vietnamese, and none of Wilson's diplomatic efforts resulted in an agreement, which possibly undermined Wilson's international standing while distracting him from other foreign policy issues. The Labour Party continued to complain vociferously over Vietnam, and Wilson's refusal to condemn the US undoubtedly hurt the party in terms of alienating many liberals as well as those on the left. Wilson was seen by many not only as a pragmatist, but also as having sacrificed his socialist principles for the sake of keeping 'in' with the Americans. As soon as Labour lost the 1970 election, the party line changed to one of outright condemnation of US intervention in Vietnam and criticism of the Conservative government for not doing more to put pressure on the US to withdraw its troops.

DEFENCE AND BRITAIN'S ROLE IN THE WORLD

There were a number of security issues facing the Labour government in the 1960s. The two most immediate and far-reaching issues to be dealt with were the future of Britain's independent nuclear deterrent and Britain's overall defence commitments given the financial problems and over-stretch of Britain's conventional forces. Labour's 1964 manifesto had pledged a review of weapons expenditure, a greater emphasis on conventional forces, and had promised to end the 'Tory nuclear pretence' of an independent British deterrent. It had said that Labour was against the development of national nuclear deterrents and so would either cancel the purchase of Polaris from the Americans or the Polaris submarines would be handed over to NATO. However, once in power, Wilson, Defence Minister Healey and Foreign Secretary Gordon Walker decided not to cancel the purchase of the Polaris missile system on the grounds that it was too far advanced to be cancelled except at an inordinate cost. This, in effect, meant the rejection of the manifesto commitment to ending Britain's independent nuclear deterrent. As Dean Rusk noted, while other defence commitments were being cut, 'the British nuclear deterrent has so far escaped the economy axe. The reason is simple. The nuclear deterrent is the most important of the great power symbols still in British possession. Although Wilson is committed to give it up, he has so far shown no disposition to do so.'[4]

The other main security issue that the Wilson governments faced was over the future of Britain's overall defence commitments, given the twin problems of over-stretch of existing defence resources, in particular troops, combined with the need to cut defence spending in light of Britain's economic problems. When Labour came to power in 1964, Britain still retained the bulk of its global network of military bases that it had assembled during the heyday of the empire to protect Britain's colonies and trade and supply routes. Given Britain's financial problems, especially the massive balance of payments deficit, much of which could accounted for by defence expenditure, it was clear that existing defence commitments could not be maintained. Nor was it clear why certain bases had been retained for so long, given that Britain no longer had to protect the trade routes to India, and rising nationalism meant that retaining such bases was increasingly problematic.

On 16 December 1964, Wilson told the House of Commons that he would initiate a comprehensive review of Britain's defence needs and commitments. The 1964 defence estimates were for £2 billion, representing 7.1 per cent of gross national product, and were expected to rise to £2.4 billion within five years. He said: 'We have to relate our decisions in the field of defence to the broader objectives of our foreign policy and we have to relate both to the realities of the economic position which Britain faces and has, indeed, been facing for the past few years.' Indeed, 'the plain fact is that we have been trying to do too much. The result has been gravely to weaken our economic strength and independence without producing viable defences.' However, Wilson, like all of his predecessors, did not want to appear to be downgrading Britain as a world power. He therefore continued that 'we cannot afford to relinquish our world role – our role which, for shorthand purposes, is sometimes called our "east of Suez" role'. Our world role, he added, was 'one which no one in this House, or indeed in the country, will wish us to give up or call in question'.[5]

Healey presented the long-awaited Defence Review on 22 February 1966, calling it 'essentially an exercise in political and military realism'. He outlined how Labour would cut the previous Conservative government's planned expenditure by 16 per cent through savings gained by getting better value for money; by reducing substantially the deployment of Britain forces in the Mediterranean; by cutting the level of forces in the Far East once the confrontation with Indonesia was over; and, from 1968, Britain would give up its Aden base. Britain would maintain its 'east of Suez' role, but with a reduced number of troops.[6] This plan was condemned by many within the Labour Party, who had hoped for a more far-reaching review that got rid of Britain's residual imperial role, and by some from within the defence establishment, who wanted Britain to focus on its defence role within Europe. It appeared that Labour's new defence policy amounted to keeping the same roles as before, but just reducing the means allocated to doing so.

Shortly after the Defence Review, Wilson called a general election for 31 March. The 1966 election manifesto argued that the Defence Review had achieved its objectives, and under Labour there was a new realism in Britain's defence policy. Labour was returned with a larger majority, but, somewhat ironically, the improved majority marked the deterioration in Wilson's fortunes. People's expectations of what the government could achieve increased with the increased majority, but Wilson's ability to deliver solutions to the multitude of problems that Britain faced appeared to diminish. His colleagues and the electorate were no longer willing to give him the benefit of the doubt. The balance of payments crisis continued, which impacted on all areas of policy, including foreign policy and defence. While Wilson had been committed to maintaining Britain's east of Suez role, it rapidly became clear that it was in no position to do so. The tide of opinion shifted during the economic crisis of 1966, which coincided with the cessation of the Indonesian policy of 'confrontation' towards Malaysia in August 1966. The issue became not *whether* Britain should withdraw from east of Suez, but *when*. In addition to Britain's economic constraints, the British Army was suffering from over-stretch, with 54,000 men stationed in the Far East and 27,000 in the Middle East.[7] There was also increasing nationalist discontent to deal with, as British bases in Aden, Cyprus and the Suez Canal became targets of nationalist agitation and symbols of continued British imperial repression, and thus increasingly expensive to maintain in return for a decreasing amount of security.

On 27 July 1967, Healey outlined the Supplementary White Paper on Defence in the House of Commons, which marked the culmination of the Wilson government's defence review and laid out Britain's defence strategy for a projected ten years ahead. It included major cuts in the armed forces in the Far East and South East Asia, the removal of forces from Borneo and a reduction in the forces in Malaysia and Singapore, with the intention of total withdrawal (i.e., the withdrawal of troops from east of Suez) by the mid-1970s.

The US administration did not approve of Wilson's plans and continued to strongly urge Britain to keep its military presence in the Far East. Despite this, Wilson went ahead. The reasons for the withdrawal of troops were financial, military and political: financially, Britain could not afford to maintain its defence commitments; militarily, British forces were over-stretched and could not meet their commitments; and, politically, Wilson wanted a statement to appease the left of the Labour Party, which was growing increasingly restless over defence issues. Wilson further annoyed the US in November 1967 by stating that sterling would be devalued. In January 1968, it was announced that Britain's withdrawal from east of Suez would be accelerated to the end of 1971. Thus, the three main issues that the US had wanted British cooperation on, and to which Wilson had agreed in the first few years of his government – no to devaluation; retention of military commitments east of Suez; and, of course, support in Vietnam – had been rejected by the end of 1967.

Once Labour lost power at the 1970 general election, the party moved to the left on issues of defence and nuclear policy. Party divisions over whether Britain should join the European Community (EC) re-emerged, but the biggest shift was over defence policy and nuclear weapons. Whereas the party had been fairly acquiescent over Britain's nuclear policy during the 1964–70 Wilson government, once Labour lost power, its attitude changed. Resolutions passed at the 1972 and 1973 annual conferences advocated the dissolution of NATO, the closure of nuclear bases and the rejection of a British defence policy based on the threat of the use of nuclear weapons. The growth of the peace movement in Britain, combined with a period of *détente* in East–West relations, led to optimism in the possibility of arms control, disarmament and defence cuts. The Labour Party's manifesto for the February 1974 general election promised that Labour's foreign policy would be 'dedicated to the strengthening of international institutions and global co-operation', that Labour would reduce defence costs to bring them in line with Britain's European allies while supporting *détente* and multilateral disarmament. Most controversially, a Labour government would seek the removal of American Polaris bases from Britain while it worked towards the objective of the mutual and concurrent phasing out of NATO and the Warsaw Pact.

Wilson's return to power in 1974 was problematic. He had a strong team to support him, with Callaghan as Foreign Secretary, Healey as Chancellor of the Exchequer, Roy Jenkins as Home Secretary and Roy Mason as Defence Secretary. However, Labour's electoral victories in 1974 were very different from those of the 1960s and, in particular, having Wilson as party leader was no longer seen as an electoral advantage by many in his party. In terms of foreign policy, Wilson took far less of a direct interest than he had in the 1960s. According to Callaghan, when he became Foreign Secretary, Wilson told him that 'he would not want a meticulous account of my handling of foreign policy with the exception of two areas – Israel and South Africa',[8] countries in which he took a particular interest. Callaghan became Wilson's closest adviser on both government policy and the Labour Party and, following the surprising announcement of his intention to resign the premiership in March 1976, Wilson unofficially endorsed Callaghan as his successor. He had come to rely greatly on Callaghan and treated him almost as Prime-Minister-in-waiting, as well as his Foreign Secretary. Wilson, Callaghan and their senior ministers did not agree with the sentiment of the party on security issues; or, rather, they might have agreed with the sentiment, but they did not agree with the policies promised by the 1974 election manifestos. Both Wilson and Callaghan were concerned that the Anglo-American relationship had deteriorated during Heath's premiership. They supported *détente*, but not a shift in defence policy. Consequently, both Wilson and Callaghan largely ignored Labour's defence manifesto pledges, or at least chose to interpret them extremely broadly.

THE COMMONWEALTH

Wilson placed considerable significance on the Commonwealth, de-colonisation, and what would now be called international development. Upon gaining power in 1964, Wilson established a new ministry, that of Overseas Development. His first appointment to the post was left-winger Barbara Castle, but she was only in the post for a little over a year. Interest-free loans were introduced to developing nations for the first time and expenditure on development initially increased substantially. The vast majority of the devel-opment aid went to Commonwealth countries, with India being the biggest single recipient of aid during most of the 1960s and '70s. Wilson had an endur-ing emotional attachment to the Commonwealth and one of the key reasons that he was initially opposed to joining the European Community was that this might look like Britain was turning its back on it. Wilson continued the process of decolonisation, granting independence to Botswana, Gambia, Guyana, Lesotho, Barbados, the Leeward Islands, the Windward Islands, Mauritius and Swaziland, and Labour promised independence to all territories that wanted it and could sustain it. As part of the retreat from Britain's east of Suez commitments, troops were withdrawn from the British base at Aden and, on 30 November 1967, the new Democratic People's Republic of South Yemen came into being. However, Wilson's support for national self-determination, the continuation of decolonisation and maintaining a united Commonwealth clashed with his strong anti-apartheid views over the case of Southern Rhodesia, and this issue became somewhat emblematic of Britain's weakened world role and influence.

Southern Rhodesia was a self-governing British dependency, a member of the Commonwealth and, like many countries in Africa, was seeking independence from the UK. The problem that Wilson faced was that it was run on the basis of apartheid and white-minority rule. Britain had been urging Southern Rhodesia to widen the franchise to include the black population, while the Rhodesian regime wanted to continue its existing system of white rule. The Rhodesian Front had been elected to power in Southern Rhodesia at the end of 1963, and had asked Britain for independence, which the Conservative government had refused. In April 1964, Ian Smith ousted the existing Prime Minister, Winston Field, and immediately threatened a unilateral declaration of independence or UDI. This threatened Britain's credibility in the Commonwealth and the international arena as the Rhodesian Front regime was seen as completely unacceptable to the rest of the Commonwealth. Wilson refused to grant independence unless the Smith government promised unimpeded progress to majority rule and progress towards ending racial discrimination, but Smith was not prepared to offer any concessions and embarked on a clampdown of opposition groups. The black Zimbabwe African National Union

(ZANU) and Zimbabwe African People's Union (ZAPU) were banned, their leaders imprisoned without trial and the press tightly controlled.

While some of the Commonwealth members proposed that Britain consider taking military action to overthrow the Smith regime, it was not really seen as a serious option within British political circles. Wilson attempted instead to negotiate privately and publicly with Smith in order to find a solution. Negotiations ended in deadlock when, on 11 November 1965, the Rhodesian Prime Minister Ian Smith issued a unilateral declaration of independence. Britain refused to acknowledge the legal independence of Rhodesia before satisfactory constitutional arrangements could be made for African majority rule, and so declared the Smith government to be illegal. However, Wilson, while saying that it was the duty of the people of Rhodesia to refrain from doing anything that would assist the illegal Smith regime in its rebellion against the British crown, also said that it was the duty of public servants in Rhodesia to carry on with their jobs in order to help to maintain law and order.[9] The result was that public servants continued to function as before, and this enabled the new regime to function.

Southern Rhodesia was an unwelcome remnant of a colonial era, and the problem of what to do about it was one that the previous Conservative government had also grappled with. Indeed, the Conservative Party was even split over whether to impose sanctions and an oil embargo in response to UDI. However, given Labour's anti-colonial and anti-racist stance, it had more to lose if it failed to take retaliatory action and force Smith to backtrack. Simply turning the matter over to the UN, which was what some in the Labour Party urged, would have made Britain look weak at best, and would itself have achieved little. Wilson's response to the announcement of UDI was to impose sanctions on imports from Rhodesia, an embargo against oil exports to Rhodesia, and to freeze financial assets in London. Wilson thought sanctions would be enough to force the Smith regime to back down, and reassured the Commonwealth states at the Commonwealth Prime Ministers' Conference on Rhodesia in Lagos in January 1966 that the collapse of the Rhodesian economy would occur in 'weeks rather than months'. In this, he was mistaken. Wilson over-estimated the effect of sanctions – which were ignored by Rhodesia's main trading partner, South Africa – and underestimated the amount of time it would take for the Smith regime to fall. Over time, 'the survival of the Smith regime became a testament to British impotence, and fallen status'.[10] The Rhodesia problem continued to haunt the Labour government throughout the 1960s and was not resolved until the late 1970s, after Wilson's resignation from power.

CONCLUSION

The foreign and defence policy of the Wilson governments was marked by the ongoing debate about Britain's role in the world. Like all British Prime Ministers, he was keen to present himself as a key player on the world stage, and his romantic attachment to Britain's world role and its imperial legacy prevented him from accepting sooner what many in his party argued, namely, that Britain should retreat from its old imperial commitments east of Suez, not merely for economic reasons, but for ideological ones as well. Whereas Wilson's foreign and defence policy caused a great deal of disillusionment within the party at the time, the more long-term view, in light of events of the early twenty-first century, was that Wilson did well to keep Britain out of costly military entanglements and that his pragmatic approach to foreign affairs was the least-bad option at the time. Wilson demonstrated his political tactical skill in avoiding engagement in the Vietnam War despite pressure from the US, and, in fairness to him, it is difficult to see what other action he could have taken over Rhodesia. Thus, while at the time Wilson was criticised for his pragmatism in foreign affairs, and for not having a grand vision that saw Britain reordering the world, from the lens of the twenty-first century, his approach had much to recommend it.

NOTES AND REFERENCES

1. US National Archives II, RG59 1964–66, POL 1 UK–US, Box 2786, airgram A-2843 from US Embassy in London to State Department, Washington, A View of US–UK Policy Relations, 23 May 1966

2. TNA PREM 13/104, The Prime Minister's Visit to the United States and Canada, 6–10 December 1964, p. 31

3. B. Pimlott, *Harold Wilson*, p. 388

4. US National Archives II, RG59 1964–66, POL 7, Box 2779, memo from Dean Rusk to the President, visit of Prime Minister Wilson July 19, 1966, 27 July 1966

5. Hansard, HC Debs, Vol. 704, cols 418–21, 423–6, 16 December 1965

6. Hansard, HC Debs, Vol. 725, col. 240, 22 February 1966

7. H. Hanning, 'Britain East of Suez: Facts and Figures', *Review of International Studies*, 42/2, (April 1966), p. 253

8. J. Callaghan, *Time and Chance*, p. 290

9. Hansard, HC Debs, Vol. 720, cols 349–62, 11 November 1965

10. B. Pimlott, *Harold Wilson*, p. 381

16

EUROPEAN INTEGRATION

Gillian Peele

MORE THAN FORTY years separates David Cameron's referendum on the United Kingdom's membership of the European Union and that held by Harold Wilson on the same issue in 1975. Much has, of course, changed between the two referendums. A national referendum was a constitutional novelty in 1975, its use itself provoking extensive controversy. By 2016, the United Kingdom had acquired substantial experience of these devices, including two highly significant ones (on the electoral system and the union with Scotland) under the 2010–15 coalition government. Both major parties have experienced a series of serious internal ruptures and the party system itself has fragmented as a result of the emergence of third parties. And the European project has gone through transformations and crises so that its future looks much less certain than it did it in 1975.

In revisiting Harold Wilson's approach to Europe, the parallels and similarities between Cameron's contemporary dilemma and Wilson's are striking, although there are evident and stark dissimilarities. Wilson's handling of European policy, from his first administration in 1964 until his successful delivery of a 'yes' vote in 1975, was shaped by a tension between maintaining party unity and his perception of the wider national interest of the United Kingdom. At the stage at which Wilson began to address the European issue, the Common Market was a relatively recent item on the country's political agenda. David Cameron, by contrast, has lived through a period in which division over Europe has plagued the Conservative Party and created a body of internal opposition to his leadership as well as fuelling support for a potentially influential third party in the form of UKIP. And, just as the outcome of the referendum vote in the early twenty-first century will be likely to have a powerful impact on Cameron's historical reputation, so too Wilson's handling of the United Kingdom's relationship with Europe is an important factor in any reassessment of his overall legacy and historical achievement.

WILSON'S EUROPEAN ODYSSEY

Bernard Donoughue, writing in a 2007 volume about the experience of the 1975 referendum, noted that for over a decade Wilson had coolly taken many positions on the EEC.[1] Certainly, Wilson's attitude towards the European Union has puzzled observers and many, especially ardent pro-Europeans such as Roy Jenkins, would see his twists and turns over European policy as opportunistic and tactical, reflecting a political style that was wily and cunning rather than ideological or principled. This focus on short-term political tactics rather than any overriding vision became a familiar criticism of Wilson's political style, generating distrust on all sides of the Labour Party. Philip Ziegler, Wilson's authorised biographer, quotes interviews with Peter Shore and Gerald Kaufman that underline the extent to which Wilson, even in the early years of his first government, was neglectful of strategic planning and unwilling to focus on long-term issues.[2]

Initially, Wilson, like his predecessor Hugh Gaitskell, was hostile to the Common Market that Harold Macmillan had applied to join in 1961. Gaitskell and Wilson disliked and distrusted each other but on this they seemed in agreement. Gaitskell's speech to Labour conference in 1962 famously argued that membership of the Common Market would mean 'the end of Britain as an independent European state' and the end of 'a thousand years of history'. It would also mean the end of the Commonwealth. The emphasis on the Commonwealth was one important factor shaping the attitudes of many in the Labour Party about Europe; but so too was the suspicion that the Common Market was not only a threat to British economic autonomy but also inherently at odds with the socialist vision. It was, in short, a capitalist club. Wilson himself, unlike the Europhile Ted Heath, had little natural sympathy for the European vision. Wilson had been taken as a child for a six-month stay in Australia, which Ziegler notes was the foundation for his future enthusiasm for the Commonwealth.[3] At the stage of Wilson's childhood visit, the Commonwealth was a very different entity from what it was to become later and romantic attachment was, by the 1964–70 period, tempered by a series of problems within it, especially Rhodesia. Wilson's background, values and personal tastes inclined him towards the Commonwealth and the United States rather than continental Europe. As Anthony King noted in his authoritative study *Britain Says Yes*, Wilson embodied a range of provincial British values. These values, as caricatured in *Private Eye*, were hardly cosmopolitan or sophisticated and ranged from football and golf to Worcestershire sauce. Wilson's natural holiday preference was the Isles of Scilly, not the Continent. Although there were some strong pro-Europeans inside the Labour Party, including George Brown, one of Wilson's rivals for the leadership, Wilson was certainly not one of them. Brown's erratic behaviour perhaps made his championing of the European cause less effective but, from 1966 onwards, the pro-Europeans had increasingly influential spokesmen in a younger generation of political heavyweights, especially Roy Jenkins and Shirley Williams. The Labour Party generally, including the National Executive Committee, was negative about the Common Market and wanted to see a series of prior conditions imposed before membership could be agreed. These prior conditions included, importantly, the protection of Commonwealth interests and British agriculture and the maintenance of sovereignty – Britain's right to control its own economy and foreign policy. The Labour manifesto of 1964, while emphasising the desirability of closer links with Europe, stressed that the United Kingdom's primary responsibility was to the Commonwealth.[4] Ziegler notes that, while in 1964 Wilson's concern was to 'take up a position which almost everyone could accept, if not actually share, on Europe he came closest to taking up an identifiable position'.[5] It was a position that was sufficiently opposed to membership of the European Community that Arthur Bryant wrote to congratulate him on saving the country.

Wilson's attitude to Europe changed markedly, however, as a result of being in government. Between 1964 and 1970, he moved from being an opponent of entry (at least on the terms suggested by Macmillan in 1961–62) to being a convert to the British membership. It is difficult to chart the cause of that conversion. There was pressure from the United States to bring the United Kingdom into Europe. There was pressure from the Foreign Office, reflecting a changing vision of the United Kingdom's role in the world. Powerful individuals also exercised influence on Wilson. These individuals included strong pro-Europeanists such as Sir Michael Palliser, who served as Wilson's private secretary between 1966 and 1969, and Michael Stewart, a committed pro-Europeanist who took over as Foreign Secretary in 1965 and again in 1968–70. The *Daily Mirror* magnate Cecil King may also have been an influential voice, although King was to launch a bizarre attack on Wilson in 1968.

More generally, Wilson in government was increasingly sensitive to the rapidly changing nature of Britain's position in the world and the changing nature of its relationship both with the Commonwealth and with the United States. Wilson's position as Prime Minister afforded him greater authority over colleagues in Cabinet (which he was skilled at manipulating) and more confidence in relation to party management, although he was still very aware of the constraints imposed by the party. Wilson's government made Britain's second application to join the Common Market in 1967. Although the aging de Gaulle vetoed it, the stage was set for Wilson to commit to British membership of the EEC and a radical restructuring of the United Kingdom's trading and diplomatic orientation. The second application perhaps created less internal opposition than might have been expected because strong Cabinet opponents, such as the left-of-centre Barbara Castle and Richard Crossman, were content to accept the initiative because they, correctly, anticipated a French veto. Wilson himself had also grown subtle and confident in his handling of the issue in government. His conversion to the European cause may have been of the 'head not the heart', in Sir Michael Palliser's words, and it underlined his inherent pragmatism. But his willingness to evaluate the arguments for and against entry dispassionately and his strategic handling of Cabinet provided increasingly firm direction for a pro-entry policy. Equally importantly – as recent scholarship has underlined – Wilson's government did not retreat from its application after the de Gaulle veto. Rather, it maintained its commitment to eventual membership anticipating that, once de Gaulle had passed from the scene, the major impediments to British membership would be overcome. The government took advantage of the opportunity afforded by de Gaulle's '*non*' to build foundations for eventual entry, using diplomatic means to build alliances within Europe and to reorient the priorities of British foreign policy.[6] How important this period of consolidation was for securing Britain's eventual participation in Europe is a contested issue. As Melissa Pine suggested, Heath would have found his task in 1970 much harder had Britain withdrawn its application after de Gaulle's veto, although

Edward Heath was hardly swift to acknowledge his debt to his predecessor.
And she quotes Uwe Kitzinger's judgment that, without Wilson, the United
Kingdom could not have entered the European Union.[7] Pine is one of the
few to acknowledge Wilson's role through a range of domestic and overseas
strategies, including the placement and support of key pro-Europeans in the
Foreign Office (at various stages George Brown, Michael Stewart and Alun
Chalfont), the promotion of figures such as George Thomson and the mar-
ginalisation of fierce critics of the European enterprise such as Peter Shore.[8]
Pine notes that Wilson's use of Cabinet committees and sub-committees
to obtain authority for a British initiative in 1968 was masterly, echoing the
judgment of Peter Hennessy that Wilson's tactic was to remove key strategic
decisions from the purview of full Cabinet.[9]

The saga of Wilson's management of European policy did not end with
the loss of the general election in 1970. With the surprise Conservative victory it was Edward Heath who was able to conclude successful negotiations
for British entry to the Common Market. As John Campbell has commented,
had Wilson been re-elected in 1970, a Labour government with Roy Jenkins
as Foreign Secretary and George Thomson as chief negotiator would have
represented its application and 'Wilson as Prime Minister would have remained
committed to its success'.[10] Indeed, Campbell quotes Wilson's assurance to
Jenkins that he was not just committed but 'dedicated' to European membership. And there is also evidence cited by Campbell that both Jenkins and
Wilson wanted to move towards a single currency.[11]

It was not to be, however. The application that had been so carefully prepared by Labour was swiftly picked up by Heath and Tony Barber, the Minister
for Europe, 'within days' and, almost as quickly, Labour began to backtrack.
As Campbell writes, all of Labour's 'old suspicion of Europe was fanned back
to life by the election and by its loathing of Heath; and in the interest of party
unity and the doctrine that the opposition's job is to oppose, Wilson began to

equivocate about what terms of entry Labour would find acceptable'.[12] The internal politics of the party became increasingly bitter as the debate over Europe reopened the old fault lines between right and left in the party but also foreshadowed new ones about the character of the Labour Party, especially the role of the unions and its commitment to socialism. Despite public endorsement of the terms of entry secured by Heath by Labour's chief negotiators, the debate had taken on a life of its own. During 1971, the Labour Party moved to the left and in opposition to European membership. Following a special NEC conference in July 1971, the annual conference voted overwhelmingly to reject the terms of entry, thereby increasingly isolating the pro-Europeans. As the divisions became deeper, the position of the pro-Europeans in the party became more difficult. Wilson, although urged by Jenkins and others to allow a free vote when the issue of the principle of European membership came before Parliament, imposed a three-line whip on the vote in October 1971. The tactic was an effort to maintain party unity but it failed. Sixty-eight Labour MPs, led by Roy Jenkins, voted against their own party and a further twenty abstained. This vote was ultimately to lead to the resignation of Jenkins as deputy leader of the party in the wake of its increasingly anti-European stance and its decision to pledge itself to renegotiation of the terms of membership and submit them to a referendum. Ultimately, of course, Jenkins, following a period as president of the European Commission, was to lead a formal breakaway from Labour in the form of the SDP.

Party considerations usually play a greater role in opposition than in government and the decision to hold a referendum of renegotiated terms of entry reflected Wilson's sense of the direction of Labour opinion and his determination, despite his own somewhat demoralised state after 1970, that the party must be held together at all costs. The referendum idea had initially been opposed by Wilson but, by 1973, he saw it as a mechanism for maintaining unity. Wilson's fragile majorities in the two elections of 1974 changed the context again, but he saw quickly how he could secure acceptable terms from Europe without antagonising opinion at home. By March 1975, the Cabinet had been persuaded to accept the terms of entry, which included concession to the Commonwealth. For those opponents who wished to oppose membership, there was an agreement to differ for the duration of the campaign. Keeping the campaign in the referendum low key was an important part of his strategy, but with the government effectively backing a 'yes' vote there was little doubt about the outcome, though perhaps about the level of victory. Throughout, Wilson seemed less than totally enthusiastic about the campaign. As Bernard Donoughue wrote, Wilson saw the issue not as one of principle as both the Jenkinsites and the left did but as a question of party management. His twin goal was to prevent Labour inescapably committing itself to withdrawal and to maintain Labour unity.[13] But, and this is the important point, Wilson had almost certainly made up his mind by 1974 that the United Kingdom needed to retain its membership. This was not a ringing endorsement, for Wilson's own political position was agnostic, accepting the arguments that it was, on balance, better to stay in. Donoughue shows how Wilson's skill at Cabinet management endorsed a 'yes' vote and he underlines the role of the referendum unit in the Foreign Office in energising the campaign. Tellingly, he paints Wilson as unenthusiastic in the campaign itself and notes that he did not seem to enjoy the victory he had secured.

CONCLUSIONS

So how should we rate Wilson's handling of European issues? Donoughue's view is that Wilson never warmed to Europe and, as noted earlier, that he would 'probably have preferred that the EEC did not exist'.[14] On the other hand, Donoughue, like most commentators, acknowledged Wilson's ability to grasp political reality and to adapt to it. Given that it did exist, Wilson accepted the need to be in and to stay in once the United Kingdom's bid for membership had succeeded. Overwhelmingly, however, his priority was to keep the Labour Party together. This goal had guided his handling of the Gaitskellite/left split through the period of opposition in 1963–64 and in government from 1964–70. But the task had become increasingly challenging as a result of changing dynamics within the Labour Party, inside the unions and the constituency parties, as well as in the parliamentary party, rendering the kind of compromises over doctrine and policy at which Wilson excelled, redundant. After 1970, Wilson's long period as leader and premier meant that he was at the very least weary and losing some of his technique, and that a series of short-term tactical gambits would be increasingly inadequate to heal Labour's divisions. As it happened, the formal breach in Labour's ranks did not occur until the 1980s, although when it came the split was bitter and the fissures within the movement have remained.

What Wilson did achieve, however, was the promotion of the entry of the United Kingdom into Europe and, more surprisingly, sustaining membership against the odds given the volatile politics of the 1960s and '70s. Wilson's achievement in preparing the ground for the eventual success of the negotiations and by keeping the application on the table in his second administration, despite the disappointment of the veto, have been acknowledged. His achievement in keeping Britain in Europe after the intense urge to reject Heath and all his works in Labour ranks should also be recognised. Wilson's style was perhaps inherently obfuscatory, but it usually achieved its ends – at least in the short term. Whether the circumstances of the current referendum or the skills of David Cameron and his team will allow a similar outcome for a second referendum on the issue of Britain's role in Europe remains to be seen. Politicians have to live with their party constraints and Cameron would probably be delighted to achieve the kind of result Wilson secured in 1975, unheroic though it may have seemed then. The referendum of 1975 did not close the issue of British membership and it is unlikely also that a referendum called on the issue in 2017 or before will end debate. The interesting, key question facing David Cameron is whether and when that debate will further split his party.

NOTES AND REFERENCES

1. B. Donoughue, 'The Inside View from No. 10', in M. Baimbridge (ed.), *The 1975 Referendum on Europe: Vol. 1, Reflections of the Participants* (London: Imprint Academic, 2007), p. 131
2. P. Ziegler, *Wilson*, p. 183
3. Ibid., p. 9
4. M. Pine, *Harold Wilson and Europe: Pursuing Britain's Membership of the European Community* (London: Tauris Academic, 2007), p. 16
5. P. Ziegler, *Wilson*, pp 140–41
6. M. Pine, *Harold Wilson and Europe*
7. Quoted in ibid., p. 175
8. Ibid., pp 175–6
9. P. Hennessy, *The Prime Minister: Office and Powers* (London: Penguin, 2000); M. Pine, *Harold Wilson and Europe*, p. 176
10. J. Campbell, *Roy Jenkins*, p. 370
11. Ibid., p. 370
12. Ibid., p. 371
13. B. Donoughue, 'The Inside View from No. 10', p. 28
14. Ibid., p. 132

PART THREE

PERSPECTIVES

17

A VIEW FROM THE LEFT

David Coates

A VIEW OF HAROLD Wilson's premierships taken from the left necessarily varies depending on which left is being considered and when the view is being taken. The nearer in political sympathy to the Labour Party the particular left happens to be, the less critical will be the judgement; but the nearer to Wilson's own time the exercise is placed, the more critical is likely to be the outcome, regardless of the particular left involved.

For, when Harold Wilson was in power, the level of class struggle in the United Kingdom was both far higher than it is today and appeared to be on an upward trajectory. Accordingly, the options facing left-wing activists were significantly wider then than now. The number of days 'lost' in industrial disputes in 1968, for example, was over 4.6 million – 2 million higher than when Labour was first re-elected in 1964 – and 1968, of course, was also the year of the May riots in Paris, of the Prague Spring and of growing student and African-American militancy in the United States. Labour under Wilson's leadership was a target, not an ally, of much of that domestic class action; and though the target changed after 1970 – when miners, electricians and railway workers all struck against the Tory government's attempt to limit trade union power – Labour under Wilson remained, at best, only an agnostic bystander. With the political options looking wider, therefore, and membership of revolutionary socialist groupings beginning to grow, the critique of the Labour Party as a barrier to the achievement of socialism became fashionable in many radical quarters during Wilson's tenure as party leader.

It was never dominant there, of course, because in both the 1960s and '70s many socialists still looked to the Labour Party as the key route through which to achieve radical political and economic change; and for those left-wingers too, Harold Wilson remained at most an enigmatic and ultimately a resistant figure. He had come to the leadership of the Labour Party, after Hugh Gaitskell's untimely death, with a faint aura of left-wingness about him because of his brief association in the early 1950s with the Bevanite wing of the party. But to be a parliamentary socialist in the early 1960s was to favour unilateral disarmament and, by the end of the decade, to oppose the Vietnam War, and Wilson would do neither. To be a parliamentary socialist by the 1970s was to favour withdrawal from the European Economic Community, and Harold Wilson was by then a committed European. And, to be a socialist in either decade was to favour an extensive return to public ownership, and Harold Wilson was at best pragmatic on nationalisation, using public ownership only when private sector failure was unavoidably obvious. Indeed, one of the last significant acts of his premiership was the removal of Tony Benn from control of the Industry Department after the defeat of the left in the referendum on EEC membership in 1975. The Labour Party had tacked to the left in the interregnum between his two stints in power; but Wilson used the first period to consolidate only a centrist political agenda and the second to pull government policy back towards the centre after Labour's brief flirtation with a more egalitarian resetting of class power. With Wilson in office, therefore, there were plenty of reasons for left-wing activists to be critical of him – and they were.

Time, however, and the subsequent trajectory of Labour Party policy, now allows a slightly more nuanced judgement. For, with the wisdom of hindsight, it is clear that the Wilson years were more than a lost opportunity for a radical resetting of class power in Britain. They also marked the high point of power-sharing in the UK between the representatives of private capital and the leaders of the British labour movement. They also marked the high point of the UK state's willingness to use public policy, and public funds, to steer the private sector into areas of new investment. For, though Harold Wilson was never a socialist in either a parliamentary or a revolutionary sense, he did prove to be a committed *corporatist*. Even his ill-fated 1969 trade union reforms (*In Place of Strife*) were designed not so much to weaken trade union power as to strengthen the position of elected trade union leaders relative to their factory-based challengers; and, certainly, after returning to office in 1974, Wilson was entirely comfortable with a form of government that involved direct, regular and public negotiations between those same union leaders and their business equivalents.

We should never forget that the iron spine of economic policy during both Wilson periods in office was the agreement and implementation of a series of incomes policies, and that at least during his second period of government his industry ministry gained real policy teeth. It was a Wilson government that, by 1975, was directly responsible for over 40 per cent of gross domestic capital formation. It was a Wilson government whose National Enterprise Board took both whole industries and key companies into public ownership; and it was a Wilson government that sought both to extend industrial democracy and to create a system of working parties and planning agreements linking government and labour to corporate decision-makers across the entire private sector. When Tony Blair wanted to put clear water between his understanding of Labour politics and the tax-and-spend Labour politics of the past, his target was not just the Alternative Economic Strategy of 1983. It was also the full-blooded corporatism of the Wilson years. Wilson was too left-wing for New Labour, not too conservative: which is why – with the benefit of hindsight – it is the modernising radicalism of Harold Wilson that needs to be recognised by left-wing critics of New Labour just as much as by New Labour stalwarts themselves.

In fact, the contrast between Tony Blair and Harold Wilson is a salutary one to make, particularly when it also stretches out to foreign policy: where it points to another Wilson achievement that Blair failed to replicate. Politicians need sometimes to be judged by what they avoid, as well as by the things that they actually put in place. Harold Wilson was just as keen as his illustrious successor to see the UK punch above its weight on the global stage; but, even so, it was his government that eventually pulled UK troops back 'east of Suez', and it was his government that kept UK troops out of Vietnam. Harold Wilson took a lot of heat from Washington on both these issues, but restricted his support for the US mission in South-East Asia to statements alone. For, whatever else Harold Wilson was or was not, he was certainly not America's poodle. And the fact that he was not points to a more general truth: namely, just how quickly any examination of the weaknesses of New Labour necessarily triggers in the open-minded a re-evaluation of the strengths and weaknesses of its Old Labour predecessors. For all the limitations of the Wilson governments, there were residual and radical strengths there that the current Labour Party leadership might do well to re-examine, and perhaps even attempt to replicate.

18
A VIEW FROM THE CENTRE

David Steel

HAROLD WILSON BECAME Prime Minister in the 1964 general election with a tiny majority that ensured a second election two years later. I had stood, unsuccessfully, in 1964 and won one of the first by-elections during his tenure, when I became 'baby of the House' in March 1965. My victory took the Liberal Party to over ten MPs and being in what was still a small group meant that I became a party spokesman.

As a Liberal I believed that Britain should be a more civilised country and that there was scope to further extend personal liberty. In that, there was cross-party support but also opposition.

I was fortunate enough to be one of the MPs who was pulled out in the ballot to introduce a Private Member's Bill in 1966. I thought about the cause I wished to promote and settled on abortion law reform. This was eventually passed in 1967 after a difficult parliamentary process. Private Members' Bills could only really survive in the face of parliamentary opposition with the help of the government. I was ably assisted by the likes of Roy Jenkins as Home Secretary, Dick Crossman as Leader of the House of Commons and

John Silkin as the Chief Whip, even though the official position of the government was that this was a matter of conscience and that each MP could therefore choose whether to support the Bill.

I always envied those who believed in unconditional moral principles on both sides of the debate – either the woman's right to choose or the absolute sanctity of the unborn child. My main concern was to find a way in which these two conflicting rights could be balanced in the medical decision of whether or not to allow an abortion to take place. The horror of illegal abortions weighed heavy on my mind. I believe that the passing of the Bill was a progressive measure that saved women from such illegal abortions, while I have subsequently accepted that the legal limit for abortions should be reduced given advances in scientific knowledge. The issue generated considerable feeling inside and outside of Parliament and I received a good deal of press attention and correspondence from the public, including some hate mail.

This was my major personal achievement in Parliament in these years, although it was just one way in which Britain became a more civilised country. The Wilson governments of the 1960s saw the abolition of the death penalty, and relaxed laws on divorce, homosexuality and censorship. As a Liberal, I supported all of them.

Harold believed that education was the key to universal advancement and greater social equality, and certainly the creation of the Open University was one achievement of his premiership that can never be taken away.

One major blot on this record, though, was the measure to restrict immigration with the 1968 act. This measure was implemented in immediate response to the worsening situation in Kenya, although the racialist statements of the likes of Enoch Powell and Duncan Sandys had a direct impact on the Labour government. The effect of the immigration controls was to create a panic among the Asians wanting to leave Kenya, believing correctly that their rights to enter the UK would be taken away. Had the measure not been introduced, it would not have led to such a significant level of immigration from Kenya at the time. The act was uncivilised and opportunistic and we opposed it in the Commons and the Lords. I was proud to be a Liberal at that point. It was one of the worst legislative measures in my lifetime.

Except for the 1968 act, I often found myself seeking to advance the cause of liberalism though cooperation with other parties. We explored the possibility of forming a pact with Labour before the 1966 general election. Although the scale of Wilson's victory in that election effectively excluded the possibility of a pact, it was to come about in the 1970s under his successor Jim Callaghan in 1977–78 – by which time I was leader of my party – and then with the electoral pact with the Social Democratic Party in the 1980s, before the two parties merged in 1988, when I decided to stand down as leader. My concern throughout was to find a way of creating a progressive alliance in British politics. We also managed to help secure that the Wilson government established a review into the workings of the British constitution.

For some reason, though I did not know him well as Prime Minister, we always got on well, possibly because I reminded him of his student days at Oxford as a Lloyd George Liberal, when he acted as research assistant to that great Liberal William Beveridge, one of the principal architects of the welfare state.

I really only came to know him after his retirement in 1976, just before I became leader of the Liberal Party. The organisers of many grand lunches and dinners seemed to decide that the Liberal leader and the ex-Prime Minister ranked about equal, and so we found ourselves sitting next to each other on several occasions and I greatly enjoyed his conversations, laced as they were with free advice.

The overall impact of the Wilson premierships was positive. His achievements were humane. Britain was generally a more free and civilised country by the time he left office in 1976, although some of these achievements at least were rowed back on under Margaret Thatcher.

My abiding memory is of a man of innate decency and ability.

19

A VIEW FROM THE RIGHT

Theodore Dalrymple

THE GENERAL ELECTION in 1964 that brought Harold Wilson to power was the first that I remember in any detail. The main slogan of the Labour campaign was 'Thirteen years of Tory misrule'. At an election meeting of my local MP, a Tory, I shouted out, 'What about Profumo?', which I thought then was the acme of wit, though the assembled faithful did not agree, to put it mildly. Actually, the wittiest remark of the period was that of Alec Douglas-Home, when Mr Wilson appealed to raw prejudice by suggesting that Douglas-Home could know nothing of ordinary people's lives because he was the 14th Earl of Home. 'I suppose Mr Wilson, when you come to think of it,' retorted Home, 'is the fourteenth Mr Wilson.' These days, of course, the nuclear family having disintegrated, such an assumption would be much less justified.

From the standpoint of today, Harold Wilson was in many ways a reassuringly traditional figure. He dressed conservatively, lacked flamboyance or apparent egotism (though, like any politician, he could be devious), usually spoke with moderation and, despite his cleverness, exuded the moral steadiness of his Nonconformist background. His pipe was a symbol of a calmness under pressure, and if at the end of his career his reputation for probity was somewhat sullied by his close association with and ennoblement of the inventor of Gannex, Joseph Kagan (a most remarkable man, incidentally), this was the result of an error of judgement rather than the far deeper level of corruption associated with at least one of his successors.

His first prime ministership had some achievements to its name that few people would now deny. The establishment of the Open University was imaginative and generous, giving many people another chance who, for whatever reason, had missed a tertiary education the first time round – while maintaining high academic standards.

Mr Wilson may have been personally less enthusiastic about other social reforms that took place under his leadership, such as the decriminalisation of homosexual relations between consenting males and the legalisation of abortion under certain conditions, but few people would now wish to undo them, or not concede that they were overdue. The death penalty was also abolished in the face of public disapproval, which took a certain political integrity. (I am against the death penalty not because it is unjust or ineffective as a deterrent to murder – I have found evidence that it was partially effective – but because, however scrupulous the judicial system, heinous errors are inevitable, and I cannot, moreover, depute to others what, on ethical grounds, I would not do myself.)

Perhaps, unsuspectedly, these reforms ushered in a new era in which social reform became for many almost a substitute religion, a transcendent meaning of life. Harold Wilson was, at least by the time he achieved prime ministerial office, an old-fashioned Labour politician who was more corporatist than socialist, and who wanted to extend a share of the good things of life to a larger proportion of the population rather than change the general notion of what the good things of life actually were. In actual effect, he was a transitional figure in the change from Old to New Labour, and I preferred the Old: not because I thought its economic prescriptions were likely to work – quite the contrary – but because it was far less culturally radical and its leaders were better men.

Contrary to the stated intentions of the Abortion Bill, abortion on demand was its almost immediate *de facto* consequence and then became, again in practice, an inalienable right. Subsequently and increasingly, moral questions were debated almost exclusively in the vocabulary of such rights, which led both to a coarsening of discourse about complex matters of human existence and to a new shrillness and querulousness in which disputes required ever greater bureaucratic, state and legal interventions to settle. Thus the reforms, necessary in themselves, had the effect of opening a Pandora's Box, an effect that Mr Wilson might not personally have liked.

His government's destruction of the grammar-school system – a process that continued, or even accelerated, under the Heath government – was in my view a cultural disaster, which seemed to me to have precisely the opposite effect to that of the establishment of the Open University, though it was very much more important. It represented a levelling all right, but a levelling down, the consequences of which (including economic) are apparent today. No one who arrives in Britain from any other country in Western Europe can fail to be struck immediately by the almost militant vulgarity and lack of refinement in its general culture, in small things as in large, and this in part may be traced to the abolition of the grammar schools, which symbolised a loss of confidence that there is a hierarchy of cultural achievement and attainment. Nominally an egalitarian measure, its effect on social mobility was probably negative. Except in endeavours such as professional football, elitism became elided with social exclusivity. Our predominant celebrity culture might almost be defined as sub-mediocrity worshipping itself.

I doubt that Harold Wilson would personally have approved of these developments, but in politics above all the law of unintentional consequences applies. The abolition of the grammar schools was the beginning of a slippery slope that led to the present situation, in which much tertiary education is essentially a fraud practised on the young and a means to make them pay for their own unemployment, giving them little of value either vocationally or intellectually in return.

For me, Harold Wilson is almost a tragic figure, decent by the low standards of contemporary politicians, a man who wrestled with indifferent success with intractable economic problems and who may, contrary to his wishes, have exacerbated social ones. The fate of most politicians, except for the truly wicked, which Harold Wilson certainly was not, is to be swiftly forgotten once they have strutted and fretted their hour. Of his personal tragedy borne with dignity – descent into dementia – I do not speak.

20

WILSON IN HISTORY

Kenneth O. Morgan

ABOUR'S LEADERS, FROM Hardie to Corbyn, have been a miscellaneous lot – planners and prophets, pragmatists and plotters. Harold Wilson, who could be placed in all of these categories, was perhaps the most enigmatic of them all. His reputation upon retirement in 1976, after winning four general elections and spending eight years as premier, was less than complimentary. Yet, his years in office witnessed profound changes in our history at home and overseas, in which he himself played a crucial, and sometimes highly imaginative, part. He was always hard to classify ideologically. A young Liberal as an undergraduate at Oxford, he was a product of wartime technocracy. He emerged as a Whitehall planner under Beveridge. As a youthful president of the Board of Trade under Attlee, he was best-known for the post-war 'bonfire of controls', even if his contacts with the Soviet Union attracted the interest of MI5. But then, unexpectedly, he gained a reputation as a left-winger by resigning with Nye Bevan over Gaitskell's 1951 Budget with its cuts in the Health Service. He steered a careful course, however, in the party conflicts of the '50s, and joined the shadow

Cabinet in 1954 in succession to Bevan. But he was elected leader of the party in 1963 as the left's candidate over the right-wing George Brown and Jim Callaghan. He took Crossman, Foot and Barbara Castle of the old Bevanites over with him to look at a portrait of the dead Nye and drink a toast to him. As Prime Minister, he was wont to see himself as a latter-day Bolshevik heading a Tsarist Cabinet.[1]

He was an outstanding Leader of the Opposition in 1963–64; his style a blend of the Nonconformist pulpit and the Edwardian music hall – John Wesley and Max Miller rolled into one. He showed qualities of passion and personal sparkle not detected before. He reinvented himself as Huddersfield Town's Harold, a folksy populist posed against the grouse-moor's 14th Earl of Home. In Labour's ranks, he appealed cunningly both to the radical left and the technocratic right; the old Bevanites and the newer Gaitskellites. He uttered leftish noises on race relations, South Africa, Vietnam and the bomb. But the keynote of his speeches was to bypass old ideological conflicts, what he called 'theology', with an apolitical appeal. In a remarkable party conference speech at Scarborough (1 October 1963), he linked socialism with science, technological modernisation and automation, instead of class war and Clause 4. It got him into No. 10 in October 1964, but with a tiny majority of just four.

In some ways, though, his new government seemed unprepared. In particular, economic planning, supposedly Wilson's strength, was never properly worked out. There was a crisis over possible devaluation right at the very start. The impact lasted for the rest of Labour's six years in power, with endless balance of payments difficulties and constant threats to sterling as a reserve currency. Nor was the modernising of the economy, including the promotion of science and technology, a success; Professor Blackett, its scientific mastermind, resigned from the government. The government tied itself down from the start by dividing economic policy, most uneasily, between the Treasury and a new Department of Economic Affairs; the first supposedly to deal with the short term and the latter with the long.[2] It was alleged to be a scheme for dealing with the rival ambitions of Jim Callaghan and George Brown: had these two combustible characters been plaster saints, it is difficult to see such a system ever working. After being 'blown off course' with a serious run on sterling in July 1966, the government limped along until devaluation eventually came in November 1967. Not until Roy Jenkins built on the aftermath of devaluation in 1969–70 did the balance of payments recover. Economic growth, planned for 4 per cent annually, reached only half that total. Ben Pimlott has written that the failure of '60s planning left an ideological void at the heart of Labour's socialist message henceforth.[3] Wilson, telling unbelieving viewers that 'the pound in your pocket is not being devalued', took most of the blame.

In other areas, however, the Wilson government did bring refreshing change. This was the era of the allegedly 'Swinging Sixties', with which Wilson eagerly identified himself by giving all four Beatles MBEs and by parading in public alongside the victorious England football team in 1966 when they won the World Cup. He encouraged the spectacle of working-class young people embracing the pop music and fashion of the supposedly 'permissive' consumer society, and middle-class students flocking to universities (including several impressive new ones) on full grants. In policy terms, the values of the young were endorsed in government policy. Roy Jenkins at the Home office launched a remarkable programme of cultural and moral libertarianism in which the old censorship of stage and screen, the persecution of private homosexuals dating from Oscar Wilde's time, and illegal abortions of unwanted pregnancies all came to an end in a new era of tolerance and civilised liberalism. The grisly spectacle of capital punishment disappeared; the British no longer hanged or flogged. New experimental arts policies were subsidised by the government, notably by the Minister of Arts (a new creation), Jennie Lee, the widow of Wilson's old comrade-in-arms Nye Bevan. Implementing the Robbins Report plans for greatly expanding higher education went on apace.

An outstanding innovation was the Open University, the so-called 'University of the Air', for home-based distance learning, offering a second chance for advanced education through modular courses and the use of television, for which Harold Wilson deserves immense credit. Benn said that Wilson's was the 'real political drive' behind it and was 'unstoppable'.[4] It was, in its way, a social landmark from a Labour government as profound as Bevan's National Health Service.

The government also responded, with varying degrees of success, to several other profound changes in the later '60s. Race relations became increasingly tense in many cities. The government responded positively through a new Race Relations Board. Its decision, however, to exclude many black Kenyan Asians, holder of British passports, was severely attacked by liberal-minded critics. Celtic nationalism was another new phenomenon that challenged the old political order. In Scotland and in Wales, the hitherto small nationalist parties, the SNP and Plaid Cymru respectively, posed a new threat to the union of the United Kingdom, not to mention a threat to the ascendancy of Labour in the Celtic nations from by-election defeats in Carmarthen and Hamilton. By the 1970 general election, with the help of, among others, Prince Charles, installed as Prince of Wales in a highly unionist ceremony at Caernarvon Castle, the nationalist challenge seemed to have receded. But the appointment of the Crowther/Kilbrandon Commission looking at the constitution of Britain as a whole was an ominous portent for the future. More serious still, the civil rights movement among the long-persecuted Catholic minority in Northern Ireland brought much violence, including some loss of life, between the Protestants of the unionist cause and the Orange Order, and Provisional Sinn Féin. Callaghan, as Home Secretary, handled the crisis with much skill. The hated B Specials, a paramilitary Protestant force, were abolished, and some of the grievances in jobs, housing and political manipulation received long-needed attention. For the first time in modern history, a government left Ulster better run than when it took office.[5] However, the fact of the British Army patrolling Belfast streets, and a new threat of terrorist violence spreading to the British mainland, were alarming signs. It was all part of the Wilson years witnessing a new sense of dissolution – ethnic, social and especially cultural – all of which posed fundamental questions about the long-term future of the country.

Wilson's later phase, from 1969 onwards, was a slow *diminuendo*. In 1969, his government was buffeted not only by Ireland and the balance of payments, but also by a huge internal party argument over Barbara Castle's attempt to reform the trade unions and the conduct of industrial relations. There had been a growing threat of strikes, official and increasingly unofficial, through the '60s by the unions, now larger than ever and approaching a record total of 13 million members. But it raised a fundamental challenge to traditional industrial relations by interposing the force of the law into a hitherto voluntary system. Callaghan, the Home Secretary, most of the Parliamentary Labour Party and all the unions rose up in rebellion and Barbara Castle and Wilson had to climb down humiliatingly. The following summer, June 1970, the Wilson government was defeated in the general election by the Conservatives under Edward Heath, to the surprise of the journalists but not, perhaps, to the historians. Labour had been hollowed out by the challenges of government. Its vote fell by over 1 million from 1964 and many derelict constituency parties were ripe for takeover by Marxist militants on the pattern of the young Jeremy Corbyn. Wilson returned to office in March 1974, rather unexpectedly, with just four seats more than the Tories. He was now a man diminished by illness and the onset of Alzheimer's. He had, however, one great service still to provide for his party, when he cleverly held them together over joining the European Common Market by having a referendum, the first ever, in 1975. When he retired through ill-health in March 1976, his party, battered and somewhat discouraged, was still nevertheless a party of government.

The Wilson years in the '60s witnessed enormous changes and challenges in our history. Merely to list them indicates their huge significance. The devaluation of 1967 marked a major step towards the end of the post-war financial order, the Bretton Woods system of fixed exchange rates. It was strongly resisted by the Americans who feared for the devaluation of the dollar. 'It is now Britain first.'[6] Again, under Wilson, Britain took giant steps towards becoming a full member of a united Europe. Even if rebuffed by President de Gaulle in a bid for Common Market membership in 1967, Europe was henceforth firmly on the national agenda, and Wilson's second term in office was to see British membership confirmed. Conversely, the old Commonwealth, almost all of it independent in status by 1970, with the ambiguous exception of rebellious Rhodesia, was manifestly in decline. The Wilson government, through Denis Healey, confirmed this by taking the fateful decision to withdraw British military and naval personnel from east of Suez, with profound (and controversial) implications for the base at Singapore in particular.[7] Wilson thus presided over the end of empire, a programme begun by the Labour government in India and Pakistan in 1947. Joining Europe, and winding up the empire, also posed implications for the structure of the United Kingdom itself. The Wilson government again implemented change by its measured response to Celtic nationalism in Scotland and Wales, and by launching, with some ominous implications for the future, a new policy of trying to improve the age-old communal balance between Protestants and Catholics in Northern Ireland, and thereby redressing the civil and social injustices of three centuries.

Harold Wilson left office amid much public condemnation. He seemed morally diminished by his conspiratorial style of government, his paranoid fears of 'moles' and 'leaks'. Like Lloyd George, he was discredited by a fatal honours list (on lavender-blue note-paper this time), which surrounded his administration with an air of sleaze. But, over the passage of time, his reputation has surely risen. A decent, kindly man of much ability, unlike

Mrs Thatcher he always identified with ordinary people and respected their civil liberties and personal freedoms. His government retained a sense of humanity and a commitment to social justice. It looks almost noble compared with the monetarism, privatisation and dogmatic inequality imposed by the Thatcher regime that followed it. If Wilson's children were the young people of campus 'sit-ins', Thatcher's children were the hungry, homeless residents of cardboard boxes on cold nights on the Strand. Wilson's administration looked towards a more modern role for his country, freed from the burdens of empire, close to, if not at the heart of, Europe, looking afresh at the composition of the United Kingdom. Harold Wilson also deserves gratitude for something he did not do. Despite intense American pressure and threats of financial and defence blackmail from the Johnson administration, he kept Britain out of a brutal and unwinnable war in Vietnam. Tony Blair's reputation has never recovered from Western aggression in Iraq. Fifteen years on, the implications for policy in Syria still tears his party apart. Harold Wilson, a humane pragmatist who, like Lyndon Johnson, 'flew by the seat of his pants', surely left a far better and more honourable legacy.

NOTES AND REFERENCES

1.   J. Morgan (ed.), *The Backbench Diaries of Richard Crossman* (London: Hamish Hamilton and Jonathan Cape, 1981), p. 987; diary entry for 12 March 1963

2.   TNA CAB 129/19, Note by Cabinet Secretary, 'Co-operation between the Department of Economic Affairs and the Treasury', 16 December 1964

3.   B. Pimlott, *Harold Wilson*, p. 567

4.   P. Hollis, *Jennie Lee* (Oxford: Oxford University Press, 1997), p. 302ff.

5.   K. O. Morgan, *Callaghan*, pp 354–5

6.   President Johnson Papers, Cabinet papers, box 11, US Cabinet meeting, 20 November 1967, Lyndon Baines Johnson Library, Austin, Texas

7.   Interview with Lee Kuan Yew, 21 September 1993, Istana Negara, Singapore

RETROSPECT

Tom Watson MP

T HE METRIC BY which the British establishment grades the contribution to public life made by former party leaders is as nuanced
as it is brutal. There are the biographies and the authors who write
them, the artworks dedicated to the subject, the organisations affiliated with
legacy ideas; they all form history's tableau to the great and the not so great.

In death, as in life, Harold Wilson has suffered at the hands of a disdainful
establishment. Poor Harold, born into the 'lower middle classes', was never
fully trusted by the artisans of the working classes and actively distrusted by
their public-school rivals in the upper classes.

A century after his birth, the historians give him a mixed review. In Chapter 20 of
this book, one of the country's greatest political biographers, Kenneth O. Morgan
describes Wilson's tenure as leader as a 'slow *diminuendo*' from 1969 onwards.

Despite a small but vociferous lobby who try to persuade the parliamentary
art committee to commission a full-sized statue to stand alongside Churchill,
Thatcher and Lloyd George, poor Harold is relegated to a head-and-shoulders
bust, placing him in the company of Ted Heath, John Major and perhaps,
before too long, David Cameron and Tony Blair.

There is no 'Wilson Institute' to further the ideas he championed about technological advance, no Wilsonian think tank dedicated to the cause of social mobility or higher education reform. His ideas do not permeate the thinking of a new generation of political leaders. Though a leader who was the architect of the Open University, created the post of Arts Minister and presided over a period when homosexuality and abortion were legalised surely deserves such recognition.

Yet, in these troubled times, with the Labour Party at a crossroads in history, we should all pause to recognise the remarkable achievements of a masterful leader who, through the power of his intellect, charisma and cunning, channelled powerful forces into four general election victories and a 'yes' vote in a European referendum.

The achievements of a man who could accommodate Tony Benn, Roy Jenkins, Shirley Williams, Anthony Crosland, Denis Healey, Frank Cousins and George Brown on his front bench deserve to be considered afresh by history, and any new assessment must acknowledge the gene pool from which he was selecting his team.

In 2015, Liverpool granted a full-sized statue to the Beatles fifty years after they were given an MBE by Prime Minister Wilson. Harold, who, like Churchill and Thatcher, captured the spirit of the age, deserves a full-sized statue in Westminster. And Labour MPs can admire the man who pragmatically steered his party to general election success in the most testing of times.

INDEX